THE TRUTH ABOUT ENGLISH

Robert C. Pinckert

PRENTICE-HALL, INC., Englewood Cliffs, New Jersey

The Truth About English
by Robert C. Pinckert
Copyright © 1981 by Robert C. Pinckert
and Millicent E. Pinckert
Address inquiries to Prentice-Hall, Inc., Englewood
Cliffs, N.J. 07632
Printed in the United States of America
Prentice-Hall International, Inc., London
Prentice-Hall of Australia, Pty. Ltd., Sydney
Prentice-Hall of Canada, Ltd., Toronto
Prentice-Hall of India Private Ltd., New Delhi
Prentice-Hall of Japan, Inc., Tokyo
Prentice-Hall of Southeast Asia Pte. Ltd., Singapore
Whitehall Books Limited, Wellington, New Zealand

10   9   8   7   6   5   4   3   2   1

Library of Congress Cataloging in Publication Data

Pinckert, Robert C
    The truth about English.

    1. English language—Rhetoric.   2. English language
—Grammar—1950–   I. Title.
PE1408.P535   808'.042   80-26938
ISBN-0-13-932012-1
ISBN-0-13-932004-0 pbk.   AUG 6   1981

Contents

Popular books on English really aren't about English but about words. And textbooks with their endless pages of Do This, Don't Do That are depressing. Here is the first readable, adult book on English. Everything you never wanted to know about English and were always being told is supplied here in brief, entertaining essays. The puzzles and exercises are fun and there are no maxims to memorize.

Lesson One

Levels of the Game

The Game of English

Language is so clearly a blessing and a curse we hardly know what to think of it. Is it better to be glib or silent? Why wrestle with these shifty words, why be at their mercy, why not just grunt now and then and recite koans and mantras and make movies? The question whether humans aren't a mistake makes us wonder about their language too. Never has it been so distrusted.

Too much depends on it. Communicating well with others is essential to our happiness, but we can't seem to get it right. Disagreements and misunderstandings arise from badly used words, causing broken homes, injustices, violence. The political order depends on open, truthful communications, and where are they? A heavy sense of how difficult language is causes shyness, stammering, stage fright, page fright (the inability to read), and pen fright (the inability to write). Why should we be judged by the way we wag our tongues?

People are competitive, to put it mildly, and play many games to see where they stand. Among people the pecking order is not established by pecking but by talking, by using words that assert, probe, silence. As a teacher I have often seen students flinch from my words. All of us have to play this tough game, and whoever cannot express himself, as an old saying has it, gets to be a slave. We compete to say things better than others, and resort to special language to distinguish ourselves. We tell others what we know and they don't.

Not everything that is said is merely a self assertive move. Sometimes there's a message, as well as a medium for it and a motive behind it. But the presence of content should not obscure the fact that we speak primarily for the same reasons that dogs bark and birds sing.

Everywhere people can be heard barking—talking *down* to others, teaching them, enjoying being *up*. Let's imagine you get into a taxi, you say Good morning, and the driver says What's good about it? He begins grumbling to you about the traffic and then about the price of groceries. You find this boring and start telling him about food preservatives, especially sodium nitrite. He doesn't know sodium nitrite and shuts up.

He jabbed you first, you took the round. Neither of you realizes just what you were up to. An opponent can be done in by a single word or by a sound, yet we pretend that our use of language has nothing to do with us. Either the language is being used correctly or it isn't. A master strategy in the Game is to make our opponent doubt his equipment. We find mistakes in his language and avoid them in our own. That's why mistakes are important and that's why we go to school to learn them.

We take the Game too seriously, correcting our children for every mistake, laughing when someone says *He do,* pretending to be annoyed by accents. Sadistic Englishmen sneer at Yank words, masochistic Yanks kneel in awe of English intonations. Bernard Shaw said the two peoples were separated by the same language. Everyone is separated from everyone by language. Language may well have been invented for lying. What was the caveman up to when he said *mammoth* and the mammoth wasn't even there? Doubletalk may be worth more than talk. Jargon and slang are developed as secret languages. Class accents are cultivated to keep up class distinctions. Advertisers are those who master Blurbese, professors master Bookish. A reason there are so many languages in the world—tens of thousands—is that people work to thwart communication and to limit the number of those who can speak their language.

Instead of thinking about language in the old way—you against English—you should try to see it in a new light—you and English against the others. If you think you're fighting the language, you're going to lose. The language belongs to you, and you shouldn't let anyone claim a bigger share in it than your own or try in any way to muzzle you.

Winning Attitude

The first step in becoming a winner is to realize you're in a Game, a tough one. No matter how sharp your Game gets, you will always have tougher competition to face. You must play all the time, and have suffered many defeats already. You may have been put off your Game by a late start or by teachers who loved to tell you when you were wrong. Some of the rules they hit you with from their motheaten rulebooks were pretty silly. Many of your supposed mistakes weren't mistakes at all, but attempts to use perfect Informal English. Why must you use Formal? Why can't you say *ain't*? No one seems to know. Who teaches Formal? They do.

You shouldn't assume that any teacher wants you to win. I don't want your English to be better than mine. I became a professor to prevent that. We others want you to lose. Those in charge of spelling, the publishers, have not reformed spelling because it's such a wonderful test for players. The point of the Spelling Bee, which exists only in America, is not to produce a better speller than the teacher, but to produce a classroom of losers.

If you're ever going to do well in this Game, see it as a Game, see that you need the will to win, and then play to win, play in your style. You don't look like George Washington; why did your teachers want you to write like him? The secret of winning is not taking the Game so seriously. While your grim faced opponents continue to believe that the Game is serious, you can run circles around them if you're relaxed.

They think that Good English exists and that they have mastered it, but they can always be done in by players who know more English than they do. Wilson Follett, for example, has twenty two pages on the distinction between *shall* and *will* in his

Modern American Usage. That's a world record. But somewhere, deep in the hills, is growing up a young challenger who will break that record.

Since no player can ever feel confident of his skill, there's no reason to remain in awe of your opponents. They may be more afraid of errors than you are. You can't play well if you're afraid. Shakespeare wasn't afraid. He never took English, he gave it. The best writers are the bravest.

Children see things clearly and are delighted by language, before the teachers take it away and chop it into ABCs. Think of jump rope rhymes, pig Latin, word puzzles, riddles, puns, wisecracks. How did we get this wonderful toy, our favorite toy? The mystery of the gift is not likely to be solved. Any human being can learn any language, but a machine can't, and an ape won't, maybe because it doesn't want to be mistaken for one of us.

Language is handled best by those who aren't afraid to play with it. Be curious and sassy, find out what's really going on. Nonchalance helps your game and throws your opponents off theirs. Are you afraid of the paragraph? Why? No one knows what a paragraph is. Having trouble with transitions? A bag of tricks. Upset because your footnote numbers are a hair off the right spot? You deserve to be.

Loosen up. Practice. Read aloud. To talk well, talk a lot. To write well, write a lot and do it fast. Let the pen flow. Don't agonize and rewrite and rewrite. In times past, writers wrote well by writing naturally and fast, by writing the way they wanted to, and seldom rewrote.

However expert the pros, no one's game is perfect. Everyone errs, frequently in speaking, occasionally in writing. When you make a mistake, pooh pooh it and tell yourself everyone does it. If you want, join in happily when the fogies start talking about how the Game has gone downhill, how the language is being debased. But don't take such talk seriously. When they talk about keeping English up, they don't mean it's sinking, they mean keeping it out of the reach of the wrong people. Those who know a lot about the history of the Game do not get upset over changes. They do not have fits over clever ungrammatical ads, they are not scornful when people can't bring themselves to speak plainly and directly. (Few things are more difficult.) They do not foam at the mouth when someone says *due to* instead of *because of* or uses the word *quote* as a noun.

Don't think about rules, think about you. Golfers work on their swing and try to ignore the water, trees, and sandtraps. Success in the Game depends on attitude and practice rather than on knowledge and analysis. The Game can't be fully known. There are different sets of rules for different levels of play and the rules are always changing. Calculations do not help. For example, if the people you talk to say *I ain't* and *I seen him* that doesn't mean they want you to talk like that or that you should do what they want. If you think only of what has been done or what you're *supposed* to do you're not thinking of what *you* want to do.

Formal and Informal English

We have two kinds of clothes—ordinary and dress up—and these correspond in language to Informal and Formal. Ordinary or Informal gets the heavy use, dress up or Formal gets our special attention. (I'm using *Formal* rather loosely to mean dressy, not Black Tie.) I could refer to the two kinds of language as Normal and Improved, or Illiterate and Literate, or Slob and Snob. Informal and Formal have the right neutral tone.

Here are samples of the two kinds of English.

Informal	Formal
She got mad.	She became angry.
This is different than that.	This is different from that.
Easier said than done.	More easily said than done.
He made a big bet.	He made a large bet.

Now put your hand or a piece of paper over the column of Formal expressions and see if you can guess what they are.

Can I use the car?	May I use the car?
How bad do you need it?	How badly do you need it?
I've got to have it.	I have to have it.
Loan me your keys.	Lend me your keys.
I can't find them anyplace.	I can't find them anywhere.

They're laying on the table.	They're lying on the table.
This one key is kind of bent.	This key is a little bent.
Drive careful.	Drive carefully.
You almost ran over the cat.	You nearly ran over the cat.
Let's throw a party.	Let's give a party.
Carol's anxious to be invited.	Carol's eager to be invited.
Nobody cares about dressing up.	No one cares about dressing up.
I'm thinking about wearing red.	I'm thinking of wearing red.
That dress looks well on me.	That dress looks good on me.
You think so too?	Do you think so?
I think so myself.	I think so.
Have you got any matches?	Do you have a match?
This drink has less calories.	This drink has fewer calories.
I want to always call you up.	I always want to call you.
Most everyone says that.	Almost everyone says that.
I heard that one before.	I've heard that before.
I guess so.	I suppose so.
If I was her, I'd ask him.	If I were she, I'd ask him.
Maybe she will.	Perhaps she will.
She asked if he wanted to.	She asked whether he wanted to.
I haven't ever done that.	I have never done that.
They're liable to leave.	They're likely to leave.
My philosophy is live and let live.	I believe in live and let live.
I didn't eat yet.	I haven't eaten.
That tasted real good.	That tasted good.
Have another drink.	Would you like a drink?
Take care. Have a nice day.	Goodby.

There are thousands of subtle distinctions like these that separate Formal and Informal language. The word *whom,* for a prize example, is almost dead in Informal but gets around fast in Formal. How many secretaries say Who did you want to talk to? and how many say To whom did you wish to speak? The many distinctions between Formal and Informal were not invented by teachers in order to torment you, but by the English speaking people who want the distinction preserved between the two kinds of language. How you and I feel about this does not affect anything. Anyone is free to think that *whom* is pompous, or free to think that if you can't use *whom* you shouldn't graduate from college. Opinions of this sort are like noses—everyone has one.

It's silly to argue that Formal is better than Informal, or vice versa. The differences between the two are matters of convention: each can be effective, each can be precise. Formal has advantages in that it avoids wordiness and clichés. It's succinct and limits its vocabulary. Informal, on the other hand, has a huge vocabulary and is talkative, friendly, and easy. Informal: *She's a pain in the neck.* Formal: *She's annoying.* Although Informal is often wordier than Formal, it makes up for it by being spirited. Informal: *You asked for it.* Formal: *You started it.* Informal: *My car's acting up.* Formal: *My car's not running right.* You can think of many more examples like these. Some ideas call for Formal (*I love you*) and some for Informal *(cough it up, what's the catch? knock it off)* but most ideas can be handled well in either. By being lively and colorful, Informal is more poetic than Formal. Formal is quieter, less emphatic. Formal suggests that you know good manners and are trying to express yourself carefully and considerately. Formal does not mean stuffy or affected, it does not mean sounding like a book and using words like *shall, moreover, indeed.*

Some people learn Formal by hearing it at home, but others acquire it more slowly and laboriously in school and thru reading. They associate Formal with being correct and with writing. This is not a useful way of looking at the matter, since speech can be very Formal and writing very Informal. The fear that writing is terribly Formal holds people back in learning to write. The hope that spoken language can be relaxed and loose, that no one cares what you say, leads people to make a bad impression when they talk.

Speech should not babble, and writing should not be puffy and artificial; it needs ballast, the sound of a person talking. You need to know and love Informal to keep from soaring into excessive Formality, and you need to master Formal so people won't assume you're lacking in manners or that you've never read anything. The pitfalls in expression lie in Very Formal and Very Informal. Compare: *Man, I was cracked up to hear your aunt died. I'm sorry that your aunt died. I was grieved to hear of the passing over of your aunt.* The safest way to express an idea is the way that would not be characterized as Formal or Informal. The most common style in writing today could be called a natural Formal or literate Informal. This comfortable level avoids slang but uses colloquialisms, uses some Formalities but avoids stuffiness. Studies show that Informal instruction is much better remembered than Formal, so I'll instruct you in Formal Informally.

Why Learn Formal?

You have to. Just as you have to eat with a fork and wear shoes. Formal is much harder to learn than Informal. It has innumerable rules and many of them are finicky. But before you get too angry about Formality in language, think about when and how it's used. A few people, such as professors, speak and write almost nothing but Formal. A garage mechanic may never have to use it. But most people have to use it from time to time, and if you hope to rise in society, your language will have to become more Formal. Since Formal is learned by most people thru reading, skill in Formal is a mark of literacy and hence a mark of status. If you've grown up among those who speak Formally, you have a head start, and other players have to catch up to you.

When we want to make a good impression, our language becomes more Formal. In talking to an attractive member of the opposite sex, we lower the tone of our voice and raise the level of our pronunciation and grammar. A man speaking to a pretty girl will not drop his final *g*s (talkin n listnin) as he normally does, and will not say *ain't.* He will try to elevate his language without even being aware he is doing so. When we talk to our superiors, to older people, to attractive people, our language becomes more cautious and Formal. Business letters are Formal; so are speeches, job resumés, term papers, reports, answers to exam questions, etc. People require Formality, and are not so open and chummy as is often pretended. For a stranger on the telephone to call you by your first name—it happens—is bound to raise your hackles. Being too Formal is a mistake, but not so bad a mistake as being Informal—or what's worse, being tongue tied—on a Formal occasion.

Our society is said to be getting more casual and Informal all the time. Unfortunately this is not so. For every slob that appears, a stuffed shirt rises up to oppose him. There is more concern than ever with indicators of status, and one's language is the most important indicator. The steady increase in years of education has led more people to expect to rise socially, but at the same time there has been a steady decline in the mastery of Formal. Increasing education has strangely been accompanied by increasing illiteracy—the deleterious effect of TV on the left hemisphere of the brain. Standard tests for students show worse performances every year. In an increasingly illiterate society, the literate person is bound to move ahead.

If you believed that you could leave your language alone, you wouldn't be taking these easy lessons. You worry about Formal, and you should. You should be a little nervous in order to avoid mistakes. When professors of linguistics, who are supposed to take a scientific, value free view of language, advise you to leave your language alone, they are not helping you to face the world. They argue that the distinctions between Formal and Informal are disappearing. Some are, but those that remain take on more significance than ever. You have to know them. You have to use *whom* correctly, and to do it, you have to be able to take a sentence apart, with the tool of traditional grammar.

Surprise Quiz

Let's have a little quiz to see if you know Formal. I'll give you a Formal and an Informal version of the same sentence and you tell me which is which. Ready?

> Everyone at the party had a smile on their face.
> Everyone at the party had a smile on his face.

Which is Formal? *Everyone had a smile on his face.* In Formal, everyone is followed by *he, his, him,* and in Informal by *they, their, them.* Formal *man* still embraces Formal *woman,* so you never say *he or she,* and you never write *he/she,* you just use *he.* Or you refuse to be Formal. Next question.

> She is taller than me.
> She is taller than I.

Which is Formal? *She is taller than I.* Few people still say this, so it is very Formal and close to stuffy. Next.

She is one of the doctors who work in the clinic.
She is one of the doctors who works in the clinic.

Which is formal? *She is one of the* doctors *who* work *in the clinic.*

For you and me to say ain't would be wrong.
For you and I to say ain't would be wrong.

For you and me to say ain't is Formal. This choice of the *objective pronoun (me, us, him, them)* is explained in Lesson Four.

Those sort of people always win.
That sort of person always wins.

That sort of person always wins is Formal. You couldn't say *Those sort;* Formally, you'd say *Those sorts.*

Bob and Carol each has a bike.
Bob and Carol each have a bike.

Each has a bike is Formal. The rule now is that the subject closer to the verb (*each*) decides the verb form.

None of the characters in the movie are likeable.
None of the characters in the movie is likeable.

You can say *None is* or *None are* as you like. *None* means *no one* (singular) or *not any* (plural). Here's a rare situation where you can choose without making a mistake. And now our last question.

Let's you and me dance.
Let's you and I dance.

That was a trick. Neither of them is or are Formal. *Let's you and I* is ungrammatical. *Let us* would have to be followed by *me,* not *I. Let's you and me* is grammatically correct but sounds wrong, sounds Informal. A Formal person would avoid a problem and say *Let's dance* or *Shall we dance?*

If you got half right on this quiz you show lots of promise.

You see how hard some apparently simple questions of usage can be. But most questions of usage aren't hard, and they seldom present themselves. When we have something to say, we generally say it right. When we worry about *how* to say it, we're probably worried about *what* we're saying.

Language Levels

Life would be simpler if we didn't have to know different kinds of English and could rely on what the Authorities told us to do. But there are no Authorities, and what is correct always *depends*. An audience decides what's correct, not a set of rules, and whenever we express ourselves it's to a *particular* audience in both senses of the word. They expect language at a certain level of usage. This level can be generally Formal or Informal or, more specifically, technical, elegant, breezy, obscene—anything. What teachers and books tell us about Correct and Incorrect English may actually hamper us as we try to adjust to the many different audiences we face. We talk to people to get something, and seldom do we just want them to acknowledge that our language is correct. To make them give us what we want, we avoid language that upsets, distracts, or annoys—unless of course that's what we want. We don't always aim to please. If a friend phones you and says *Hi* and you say *Hello* you've probably made a mistake in English. If someone says *I'm pleased to meet you* and you say *How do you do* you've made a mistake in English. If you say *It is I* you've made a mistake, if you write *It is me* you've made a mistake. If you correct your mom when she says *I laid on the couch* you've both made mistakes and you've hurt her feelings.

Mistakes are only mistakes if they produce unintended results. They are of two kinds: the careless mistake, the slip of the tongue or pen that you didn't mean, and the misunderstanding or miscalculation of what the audience expects. A mistake is saying something you did not want to say or something the audience does not want to hear. The audience never makes mistakes. If you're doing the talking or writing you're making the mistakes. It may not matter how many in the audience catch a mistake, because if you make a few people very upset that's as bad as making many people a little upset. The Game is much trickier and more interesting than the one Miss Thistlebottom tried to teach you in the seventh grade.

Can you get a list of mistakes? Yes, in any drugstore. But if you look up a supposed mistake in a guide to usage and find it there, that means lots of people make the mistake. Maybe it's no longer a mistake. How old is this guide or handbook? You can only rely on a few mistakes that have stood the test of time, like *ain't*.

The choice of correct language is like the choice of clothes. Clothes and speech have a lot in common—they distinguish us from animals, and we hide behind both. It's good to have a large wardrobe; no one should want to wear jeans all the time or have one way of talking. In Formal we have to wear a uniform of some kind. Though people devote much time and effort to improve their looks, spend a bundle on clothes—they're even alert to crude means of expression called *clothes language* and *body language*—they tend to neglect their language, and fail to study it and practice it as they should. The time they spend in front of a mirror would be better spent in reading aloud. Some people give up too soon in the effort to improve their English, believing that they can't do it unless they suddenly become more intelligent. That's not so. The ability to talk and write is connected with native intelligence, but big improvements come thru instruction and effort.

Arbitrary Rules

Using the language would be easier if we could rely on what was logical to say. But language isn't always logical. Logically, we would say *this friend of him,* not *this friend of his. Idioms* are illogical in that they can't be translated. *Sleep over* does not mean *oversleep.* Spelling and punctuation swarm with illogicalities. A word should logically have only one meaning, but many words have a number of established meanings. Grammarians always concede that language isn't logical, and then go on to tell us what we shouldn't say.

English is alive and wriggling. New words and expressions—some good, some destined for short lives—enter the language, and old words and expressions die. Even simple words die: *son* and *sea*, for example, are dying. New ways of using the language, whatever their merits, are liked by Informal people for a bad reason (they are fashionable) and disliked by Formal people for a bad reason (they are fashionable).

Some new ways do seem unreasonable. Reason or logic tells us to say *between you and me. Between you and I* is a mistake as old as the language itself, and is now what most Americans say. Should you try to correct most Americans? Go ahead, that's part of the Game. What would you say? If you want to be logical, say *between you and me,* and if you want to be normal (do you?) say *between you and I.* You should have a choice. It's boring to always be the same.

Because language is not logical, it's hard to decide on what is correct, hard to learn it, and hard to use it. Most Americans say *I seen him, leave go the handle, I didn't do nothing,* and *I laid down.* If you question them about these usages, some will admit they knew all along the usages were wrong. Then why did they say them?

Take some supposed mistakes from Black English. Many blacks use old features of the language now referred to as Black English. *She close the door on him and she complain, but take him back because he been good.* To white ears these verb forms are so unusual as to seem foreign or perverted. They are only unconscious attempts to remove useless inflections and streamline the language in the way that, say, Chinese is streamlined. *He do* conveys its meaning and (to me) sounds more forceful and less buzzing than *he does.* Old Man River, he keep on rolling along, and so do English. Formal don't.

He do can't be objected to because most Americans say *he does,* because that would mean that most Americans were right. *He do* can't be objected to as a novelty—it's been used for centuries. The only objection to *he do* is irrational: white people don't like it because it's not the way they say it. That's why blacks shouldn't use it among whites. If one doesn't care what the audience likes, why talk, why not just hit them? Should blacks say *he does* among whites? Sure. Should whites say *he do* among blacks? Sure, unless blacks want it for themselves.

Be Your Own Professor

Before you went to school, you loved language, loved to learn new words, and maybe laughed when you misused one. Let me try to rekindle your former interest in language with some questions. How do you know when you're misusing a word? Your supposed misuse may now be the common use. Does *status quo* mean the way things are? It used to mean the way things *were*. *Verbal* now means *oral*, as in *verbal agreement*, and it also means *talkative*. Formal people insist it can only mean *having to do with words*. Is *data* singular now or plural? If you say *the data are in* you may feel you're correct, but those who hear you may feel you're peculiar.

Many questions of usage can be settled by consulting a dictionary. But dictionaries are seldom consulted. And not all questions of usage can be settled by them, since they differ in their advice, some being strict and others tolerant. Your problems may be solved by relying on a dictionary, but what about the poor souls who write the dictionary—do they rely on you? They mainly rely on the printed word and on the usage of educated people. But linguists say that uneducated speakers are closer to the spirit of the language and are more willing to invent. In our society, celebrities are considered important, and they are often polled about their use of the language.

You can argue that the educated should decide matters of usage. That is the conservative approach—an understandable one, though it leads to irritability, and tries to stop the language from changing even when the changes would be beneficial. Too much conservatism is responsible for the international scandal of our English spelling and punctuation. You can take the position that the majority should decide. The majority ultimately does decide of course. In the meantime the educated have strong veto powers. They have kept *ain't* in the Siberia of illiteracies for hundreds of years.

If the dictionary doesn't decide usage, if the majority doesn't, if the educated do not, if famous writers do not, who does? English teachers? They'd be the last to decide. No one is in charge. You must decide questions of usage yourself, on the basis of who you are, the situation you are in, and what your audience expects. The question whether a usage is good or bad should be, good or bad for what? Whether you like it or not, you have much more freedom in these matters than you perhaps know.

Although no one is in charge of the language, someone may be in charge of you—a boss, an editor, a teacher. But don't let her push you around: you can always find someone to help you. If you're jumped on for using *escalate* in the sense of *increase,* find a new dictionary that recognizes this usage.

Here are some puzzles about usage. When others are slanging or swearing should you join in? If you're a professional, should you use the jargon of your profession or plain English? If you have an accent, should you soften it, stress it, or forget about it? In England, should you ask for a tomāto or a tomăto? Obviously, only you can answer such questions. I can't tell you how to live. You must ask Ann Landers.

Slob and Snob Meanings

To be Formal is to be safe, to prefer three inch wide neckties and four inch wide lapels. When a word has two meanings, the Formal person chooses the older meaning. And you should too, when you're with him. The older meaning is usually stricter or narrower than the newer meaning. But there's no cause to get serious about your Game and insist that any word has a correct meaning. Words don't have meanings, people have meanings for them. The meaning of a word is whatever the audience thinks it is. (Sometimes they confuse us by thinking different things, but we must never let on that we're confused.)

Take the word *etymology*: it means the study of the original meanings of words. This word is itself *misused,* since according to its roots it means the *true* meaning of words. The true meaning cannot be the original meaning, it can only be the present meaning. If words didn't change meaning, there would be no etymology. No one can argue that the true meaning of a word is its original or older meaning.

Words struggle for survival. The fittest survive, not the best. Good words get old and die, their meanings decay. That's sad, but nothing can be done about it. One must look on the bright side—the new words being born. Formal people get upset when old words are given new meanings, because these new meanings tend to be looser and vaguer than the old ones. But sometimes they only pretend to be upset, and are hoping to catch the other players making *mistakes.*

Many words have an older Formal meaning and a younger Informal meaning. Well known examples are *smart* and *dumb. His clothes look smart but he is dumb with fatigue.* Words like this with double meanings are closely watched by mean players. I'll warn you about some of these words so you don't get caught misusing them, that is, using their Informal meaning in a Formal situation.

Aggravate does not mean annoy, it means worsen.

Answer does not mean reply. It means a reply that gives satisfaction. *The witness will answer the question.* Never tell people to answer you.

Cohort does not mean crony or buddy, it means a company of soldiers.

Continual does not mean continuous, it means repeated. *The Army lost battles continually, the war went on continuously.*

Didactic does not mean preachy, it means instructive.

Dilemma does not mean problem, it means a choice between evils.

Disinterested does not mean uninterested, it means impartial.

Fabulous does not mean excellent, it means doubtful, like a fable.

Fulsome does not mean full or generous, it means annoying.

Incredulous does not mean incredible, it means disbelieving. Events are incredible, people are incredulous.

Infer does not mean imply or suggest, it means deduce.

Microcosm does not mean sample or miniature, it means a little world.

Optimistic does not mean hopeful, it means believing that *all* is for the best.

Personable does not mean affable or amiable, it means good looking.

Protagonist does not mean enemy, it does not mean proponent, it means the hero in a play. There is only one protagonist in any group.

Reaction does not mean response, it means a passive and automatic action following upon an action. Don't ask anyone for his reaction, ask him for his response.

Technical does not mean specific, it means having to do with a science or technique.

Viable does not mean practicable, it means able to live.

Many more words than these are misused, and I've only listed some that have caused a lot of protest. These words are dangerous. If you use their Informal meanings in Formal expression you'll be in trouble, and vice versa. In ordinary circumstances if you use *smart cohort protagonist disinterested* and so on in their earlier meanings you will not be understood. If there's some problem about the meaning of a word, don't use it. There are plenty of words. Nobody is twisting your arm and making you use a word that could cause trouble.

Whenever you express yourself you open yourself to attack from both the right and the left, so stay in the middle of the herd. Unless you're a leader. To be Formal is to keep a low silhouette. To be Superformal, to insist on using a word in a meaning no longer current, is to be pedantic and maybe even nasty. To be personally concerned about changes in the language is grandiose: you can oppose changes, welcome them, discriminate among them, but whatever you do, it won't matter. Those who lament the language falling apart are only projecting.

Slob and Snob Sounds

You'll be happy to know you're not likely to be defeated in the Game merely because you don't make the right noises. No special effort is required to make the noises of Formal. Ordinary effort gets you thru. There are class accents in the US, but they don't mean much.

Let's begin by seeing if you know what correct pronunciation is. How do you pronounce *want to*? As *want to, won teh, wuh neh,* or *wuhnuh*? The answer is, all are correct. Just as there are levels of usage, there are levels of pronunciation. What is correct depends on the situation. In an unstressed position *want to* would be incorrect, would be *over*pronounced. He said he *didn't* want *to* come. In a stressed position *wuhnuh* would be incorrect, would be *under*pronounced. Do you really *wuhnuh*?

How do you pronounce the suffix -*ing*? Do you say *ing, in, en,* or just *n*? Here again, correctness depends on the situation. I'd like *something* to eat. I'd like a little somethi*n*. You have *some*then for me? *Sumpn* wrong? Another: Please stop *pushing*. You're *push*in too hard. I spent the *day* pushen *papers.* Mom, *he's* pushn me. Dropping your final *g*s is supposed to get you into trouble, but not dropping them can be as bad, by sounding like you're putt*ing* on airs. The rain may keep fall*ing* on *your* head, but it keeps fall*in* on everyone else's.

We overstress our consonants to show we're angry and understress them to show we're relaxed. But ordinarily, the care we take in pronunciation depends on what the words mean and also on what the audience expects. On Formal occasions they want us to at least seem to be careful. All audiences insist that we be intelligible. Spoken and written words have to be clear.

Questions about pronunciation are like other questions of usage. When choosing words, it's not helpful to think of ok words and taboo words, and in saying words it's not helpful to think of win or lose pronunciations. In such complicated matters, being rigid will hurt us. Correctness never depends on the word considered by itself. Since dictionaries tell how a word is pronounced by itself, they offer limited help in pronunciation. Words appear in sentences, and in a sentence few words are separated from each other by pauses. Pronunciation involves strings of words, or phrases; proper *phrasing* is needed for intelligible speech.

The dictionary often gives two or more pronunciations for words, and these variations are multiplied by the effect the context has on pronunciation and by accents too. Take the following sentence: *The chocolate sundae was invented in St Louis, Missouri.* You could pronounce *chocolate* as *choclit, choclut, chalklit, chalklut, chocuhlit, chocuhlut, chalkuhlit, chalkuhlut.* You could say *sunday* or *sunduh.* You could say *St Louis* or *St Louie.* You could say *Missouri, Missourah, Mizzourah, Mizzouri.* In view of this wide choice, one does well to avoid ever saying This is the *Right* pronunciation. Most people are well advised not to worry about a particular pronunciation. Say it the way you want and be proud of it. No party or parties decide the meaning of a word, and no one decides the pronunciation. Only in dead languages are things decided. You have a piece of the action in English.

Though you shouldn't worry about a particular pronunciation you should be alert to the need for the right *level* of pronunciation. Listen to this: I wa*nt to* remin*d* all of you *to* bri*ng* a pen*cil to thee* mee*ting*. And listen to this: Ah wuhnuh rmine ulluhyuh tuh bring uh pensl tuh thuh meetn. The first version is overpronounced, the second version, underpronounced. Safety lies in the middle. In Formal situations, we do pronounce our words more carefully, without being aware of it, and if we're not aware of it, let's leave it that way. Being too cautious in pronouncing draws attention to itself. Formal must never be artificial.

Fortunately, almost everyone, in speaking naturally, avoids these two extremes, of staccato and mumbling speech. Few people nowadays botch pronunciation. Americans are perfectly sensible in not caring a hoot about it. Inarticulateness, not mispronunciation, is what sends people to defeat in the Game. It used to be thought that a distinct and careful pronunciation was most desirable, but no one believes that anymore except a few speech teachers. In the days of radio, actors and announcers had to make an impression by means of their voice alone, and exact enunciation became a shibboleth. In these days of television, announcers charm the audience through the eyes and not the ears, and their pronunciation moves between relaxed and sloppy. They say *wuhnuh, guhnuh,* and *awduh* even in stressed positions, and some are guilty of *genuwine, durring, childern, hunderd, offten, kep, perty,* and *sparkeling. Fur* is often used fur *for. Butter* and *letter* are *budder* and *ledder.*

These new relaxations need not be deplored. The only justification for an older and stricter pronunciation is that it prevents confusion. If a new pronunciation, like *genuwine, hunderd,* and *fur,* causes no confusion, it's mean to object to it. Seldom does a mispronunciation cause confusion. The only confusing pronunciations I can think of are negative contractions that sound positive: *can't* as *can,* *doesn't* as *does* (n), and *didn't* as *di*(n)*t.*

A while ago I said that when you choose your words you should not rely on what you think the word ought to mean. In pronouncing words you should not rely on how you think the word ought to be pronounced: pronounce the words as you hear them. Don't worry about how they're spelled. Spellings lead you into overcorrect pronunciations such as *offten, calm, Jehovah,* and *Xmas.*

You should drop unstressed consonants and vowels. Say *boundry,* not *boundary, cabnet,* not *cabinet,* and also *canidate, comfterble, factry, Febuary, jography, goverment, intresting, histry, labratory, pome, pliceman, probly, supprise, valueble,* and so on. Seriously consider not working so hard on all the *-ally* words. Say *accidently,* not *accidentally,* and *finely, genrally, naturly,* and *useuly.* I'm not kidding. Go over these streamlined pronunciations and I think you'll agree they are what you hear all around you. Dropping feeble syllables and letters is a classy thing to do. Upper class people do it. Middle class people think their teachers wouldn't approve. To think that sounds should follow *spellings* is arsey versy!

It's ok to drop useless sounds, but it's not ok to stick in new sounds that don't belong: *arthuritis, disasterous, drownded, electorial, evening, fartherest, fillum, grievious, hinderance, incidentally, mischievious,* and *rememberance.* A flock of words with *l* bring forth an extra syllable: *athalete, bubbeling, burgalar, grizzally, handeling, sparkeling,* and *translate.* People are annoyed when you add extra sounds: that's the underlying reason for the strong objection to the intrusive *r—idear, lawr,* and *umbreller.*

A few words are mispronounced because sounds are transposed: *bronical* for *bronchial, calvary* for *cavalry, modren* for *modern, perscribe* for *prescribe, revelant* for *relevant,* and *tradegy* for *tragedy.* Maybe I shouldn't have mentioned these mistakes, since they have a way of sticking in the mind. But if they stick in many minds they'll no longer be mistakes, and you won't have to worry about them.

Occasionally we stress the wrong syllable: *abdómen, anchóvy, compárable, éntire, evidéntly, exquisite, secrétive, úmbrella.* But we seldom misplace the stress, since it's so important in the word.

We misplace it in words we've read, like learned and foreign words, rather than in words we've heard. As less reading is done, fewer words are mispronounced.

In the old days, experts in the Game separated sheep from goats by failure to pronounce *oo* as *eeoo*. It was forbidden to say *nood, redooce,* and *stoopid.* One had to say *niude, rediuce,* and *stiupid.* Fancy people even said *siuit, siuper,* and *reciuperate.* This distinction has disappeared and we get along with each other better now. A few of us still say *niews* and *diew,* but no one lives forever.

A word now about accents. Everyone is said to bear the burdens of a class accent and a regional accent, and some people have a whole flock of them. Because of travel, relocation, and the influence of the media, accents all over the country are being leveled, though it's unlikely they'll entirely disappear. Our society does have social classes, but luckily they are not separated from one another by pronounciation, which happens in less fortunate countries. Our ears are not attuned to subtle distinctions of class accents. Some people believe that membership in the upper class can be established by pronouncing the magic words *vahse, ahnt,* and *lahff.* The only accent that is widely (and unfairly) considered low is the one from New York. (The general New York accent has upper and lower divisions, the lower being referred to as a Brooklyn or Jersey accent.)

Throughout the country people will be assigned to slob status not by peculiar pronunciations but by *lazy* speech: *something* and *nothing* become *sumn* and *nuhn,* consonants disappear, and vowels are neutralized to the mumbling *uh* sound or else drawled out. But careless speech, like careless diction, can be found anywhere. In the land of the free, even the upper classes can be slobs.

If you have a regional accent, should you soften it? People do soften their accents unconsciously when they're among those using another. Should you consciously soften your accent? Don't bother. Regional accents are not so offensive as is supposed. They're now heard on national television, they attract attention, and are a source of good clean fun. What has to be guarded against is the odd, glaring regionalism that suggests that the speaker is quite mistaken about a word. President Kennedy could say *Havvid* and *Bahston* as much as he wanted, but could not say *Havaner, Cuber. Cuba* is not *Cuber*. President Johnson could say *Amurricuns,* and *lot* and *tom* for *light* and *time* as much as he wanted, but could not say *nucular* and *inviduous*. He said that every time he opened his mouth he lost money. If so, it wasn't because he came from Texas. When we don't like a speaker, his voice, manner, or matter, we pick on him for regionalisms. If he's otherwise likeable he can almost get away with *moider*. Mispronunciations are often suspected but hard to prove, and usually we give the speaker the benefit of the doubt. But if he's annoying us by being inarticulate, we'll find something wrong with him. As Proust so delicately put it: We are always less at our ease in the company of one who is not of our station.

Learning to Listen

For people without a speech problem, pronunciation is only a minor aspect of speaking. More important are volume, pitch, tone, pace, and quality of the voice. But what always counts most is having something to say. When we have something, we generally manage to put it across, whether speaking or writing. Only a few people gifted with eloquence manage to speak and write acceptably while saying nothing.

Having something important to say makes expression easy. But it's not always easy to find something important, so be content with finding something important for *you* to say. You can only discover what's important to you by being in touch with yourself. Ideas worth expressing are generated thru talking and listening to yourself. No one becomes articulate without getting in the habit of listening to the voice of the self. Looking and not listening, reading and not listening, will leave a person dumb.

In the beginning was the Word—some say—and others say the Big Bang. *Sound* is the first perception. For nine months in the womb before we ever *look* we *hear* iambic heartbeats and the sound of the ocean. First we listen. Then much later we talk and read and write. No one learns to write without mastering the three preparatory skills. The three later skills all depend on listening. So valuable is listening that all you have to do is *look* as if you're listening and others will think you are a wonderful person.

A good way to improve skill in listening is to do a lot of reading aloud. And there's no charge for this lesson. One has to get used to hearing oneself instead of constant noise from the outside world. My poorer students have never been able to read aloud what they wrote. And many educated writers prefer not to do this with their own prose.

The notion that writing doesn't have to be heard is quite a mistake, though a common one since so much that is written today has no sound—no believable person could say it. Writing meant for the eye alone is never as lively and persuasive as writing that sounds like talking. Before the time of print no reader thought of reading silently, everyone read aloud. The great works of literature are meant to be heard, not read silently.

I have never met anyone who could talk well and could not write well. Some fine talkers have much preferred talking to writing, but that's understandable, since talking is so much more important. The more writing there is, after all, and the more books there are, the more they are like each other and the less important they are. Homer, Buddha, Socrates, and Jesus never wrote a word. Shakespeare never published one. They did not listen to tapes discs tweeters woofers voiceovers, they did not watch a box, and they read little if anything. They listened to themselves making sentences. When you write, listen.

Many young writers are so unused to listening to themselves, they do a better job of writing when they pretend to be someone else. Just as children improve their speech by constantly playing roles, beginning writers learn a lot about writing by pretending to be moonwalkers, fashion models, frozen millionaires, fetuses about to be aborted, tropical fish, hot water bottles. *Person* comes from Latin *persona,* a mask. Oscar Wilde said, Given a mask, we'll tell the truth. Try it, you'll like it. If you become expert at it you could even pretend to be an English teacher.

There shouldn't be anything odd about writing. It's only a way of pretending, and we're used to that. Whether we're apes pretending to be angels or angels pretending to be apes, we know pretending. So never fear that when you write you're supposed to drop your mask and be yourself. To write you never have to be yourself, but you have to be able to hear yourself speaking in someone's voice.

Spelling

That people are playing language games is clearly shown by their refusal to reform English spelling. The English language has the worst system of spelling of any major language. It could easily be simplified, but the publishers refuse to do it. What do they care? They'd just as soon everyone toed the mark. The silly apostrophe could be removed from the language, if typewriter manufacturers stopped making apostrophe keys. They'd never be missed. Think of the billions of woman hours wasted in erasing apostrophes from *it's*.

A wholesale reform of spelling is probably impossible, but little reforms could be made every year. While the publishers are stalling and having a big laff, and while students are suffering, you can do your bit by refusing to put in apostrophes and hyphens and by using spellings like *lite, thru, ment, frend*—whatever you feel strongly about. You could also spell all the *-ant* and *-ance* word endings with an *e* instead of an *a*, and all the *-ible* word endings as *-able*. Do it, and use me as your authority. Of course, if you misspell, you may only do it on purpose. If you misspell unintentionally and get caught, say you did it intentionally.

There's no easy way to become a good speller. You're lucky if you're born with a good visual memory for how words look. Most words can be figured out from the way they sound, but there are still hundreds of important words whose spelling has to be memorized, such as those with double consonants—*recommend, transferred, committee*—those where the *y* and the *i* keep changing on you—*mercy, merciful, pay, paid*—and the great army of words that end with *-ent* or *-ant*, and *-ence* or *-ance,* such as *dependent, significance, prominent*. Some brilliant people go thru their whole lives without ever figuring out how a word like *ocurrance* is spelled.

Punctuation is important and involves the mind, spelling is unimportant and involves the mind's eye. Many famous writers were poor spellers. But they probably could spell correctly if they had to take it seriously. Today, until things change, we have to take it seriously, since it has a crazy symbolic importance for the public. Since English spelling is so hard, it is used as a test, a rather unfair test, of a person's carefulness and literacy. If one can hardly spell anything, chances are he is illiterate—that's what the word means, unlettered. Most spelling mistakes do come from being unfamiliar with the *written* words. *I could of died.*

An occasional misspelling should not be a terrible offense, but it is. Misspellings have to be caught by careful proofreading. Too many people do not proofread, being afraid of what they might find. No matter how much you trust your own spelling, there will still be words you ought to check in a dictionary. This dictionary for spelling should be small and handy, and should be kept open at your fingertips, reminding you of the importance of spelling and comforting you in your hour of need. The ability to catch your own misspellings is seen by others as a sample of your accuracy in all other matters. Check every word that looks phunny.

If you read a lot and are still a poor speller, you have a fate worse than you deserve. Maybe there's a vision problem. If you transpose letters, experts in eye training can help you. If that's not your problem, do this: keep a list of the words you misspell and see what kind of mistakes you make. Do you compulsively misspell the same few words? Do you confuse homonyms like *to* and *too, than* and *then, accept* and *except?* These confusions count for most of the mistakes in spelling. The three most frequently misspelled words are *to, their, its,* and their soundalikes. Are you misspelling words because you speak a minority dialect? Are you leaving final *s* or final *d* off the verb? Do you write down pro-nunciations like *alot, enviorment, hunderd, perfer,* and *athalete?* If you misspell common words, you tell the world you don't read. Since verbs are so important, any misspelled verb equals ten ordinary misspellings. The reader assumes you're an illegal alien with his own verbs, like *drownded murderd layed hitted hurted choosed chosed meaned knowed lead* (led) and *use* (used).

Looking at the kind of mistakes you make helps you get

to the root of the problem. Maybe you didn't learn phonics in school and need practice in spelling the sounds in the word, syllable by syllable. Maybe you go too fast when writing the word, not proceeding syllable by syllable. Don't try to visualize the word. Sound it out. Maybe you don't proofread. Proofreading must be laborious, letter by letter, syllable by syllable, until you get faster at it. When you proofread, do it slowly *out loud.* Poor spellers get help from proofreading backwards, since there are many more misspellings near the end of words than near the front. With long words, the speller focuses on the outline of the word and botches the middle.

Whenever you hear a *mnemonic* (memory device) for spelling a word, learn it. Remember that your princi*pal* was a *pal,* there is a *rat* in sep*arate,* defend*ants* have *ants,* there are three *e*s in d*e*p*e*nd*e*nt, *al*ready is *not all* right, *we* are *we*ird. When *full* is added to another word, it has to spill one of its *l*s: grate*ful,* hope*ful, spoonful.* Exaggerate the pronunciation in learning to spell the word: pro *nun* ciation   cal *en dar*   con ver *ti* ble   def *i nite* exis *tence*   prom *i* nent. When you have a hunch a letter should be doubled, follow your hunch: co*mm*i*tt*ee   impe*ll*ed   o*pp*ressed. Conceive of prefixes and suffixes separately: open ness   com- plete ly   love ly   lone ly   dis appoint   re commend.

In the past, dictionaries offered a page or two of spelling rules. They don't anymore. There are no useful rules except the famous Write *I* before *E* except after *C* or when sounded as *A* as in n*ei*ghbor and w*ei*gh. Here is a typical spelling rule from a popular handbook.

> Double a final single consonant before a suffix beginning with a vowel (a) if the consonant ends an accented syllable or a word of one syllable and (b) if the consonant is preceded by a single vowel. Otherwise, do not double the consonant.

If you can remember that you can probably spell any word. This rule explains why you write *permitted* with two *t*s and *blooming* with one *m.* That's not much help, since you're not tempted to write *permited* and *bloomming,* or are you?

So good luck in spelling, and try to remember it's all a Game, and this time, they really are trying to get you.

Is Formal Dying?

In this First Lesson you may have been surprised at my sassy attitude towards Formal, and may have wondered why, if I'm teaching Formal, I didn't treat it with more respect and tell you do this, do that. I did so because I believe you have to think about questions of usage for yourself. You will handle Formal better if you are not looking up to it or looking it up. And finally, you should be confused, as most people are who have not yet decided to attack or defend Formal language.

The movement towards Informality is accelerating. Formal is opening up and relaxing. Contractions, colloquialisms, and slang are showing up in surprising places. A few simplified spellings are gaining acceptance. Pronunciations based on spellings are losing their hold. Ancient battles, between *who* and *whom, like* and *as, lie* and *lay, loan* and *lend,* are being fought by fewer zealots every year. The *New York Times* encourages its writers to use slang, though not in the sacred news items. There, hotdogs are still called *frankfurters,* but who knows how long they can keep that up? Silly rules, like don't use contractions in Formal and use contractions in Informal, are losing support.

These are good developments. Whatever brings the two languages closer improves them. Pointless Formalities should be removed from the path of those struggling to become articulate. Struggling, I might add, against strong cultural pressures on them to remain silent and docile. The gulf between the inexpressive citizen and the expert, like the gulf between the poor and the rich, ought to be narrowed, not widened. We must love one another or die. Language should be used in a loving way, not in a special or putdown way.

Linguists, lexicographers, and the savvier English teachers have long deplored the excessive Formality of English as it is taught by the schools, and some of us have wondered whether it should be taught at all. Composition courses never seem to work—they're always being removed, restored, renamed, and revised. Everyone believes in them—except the students and the teachers. Much of my time as a teacher is spent trying to convince students that writing is not artificial, confining, and punishing. In correcting papers I have to correct more defects caused by fear than mistakes caused by ignorance. That's why I'm interested in making the language teachable, not just in teaching the students the language.

I don't believe they have a right to their own language—theirs is mine too—but I believe they need more encouragement in having their say. If they balk at writing professorese and plagiarize instead, they may only be trying to protect themselves. If they refuse to learn certain distinctions (*its* and *it's*) maybe they're saying life is more serious than that, or it isn't *that* serious.

It's hard to know what they're saying, they're so unused to saying anything. They're used to looking, used to being told, and not listening when they are told. Schools blame the TV monster for the literacy crisis. TV blames the schools. Others blame the culture of capitalism for the TV and the schools. Who blames himself?

The new illiteracy is confused in the public mind with the welcome new relaxations of Formal language. That written English is becoming suppler and more personal, more like the spoken language, is a great blessing—though it still has far to go. That many people today do not read or write is a great curse, and the language should be made easier for them. But they should also be told they are accursed, that Circe's drugs turn people into swine.

Those who have an investment in Formal language—editors, professors, lawyers, anyone who has painfully mastered it—are for the most part upset by the movement toward Informality. They shouldn't worry. Formal is not about to disappear. The defenders of Formal remain powerful, and send to defeat any player in the Game who is ignorant or defiant of the rules. But the player who knows Informal as well as Formal will be better at Formal. Besides, it's plain unAmerican to be Formal. The glory of our English has been its Informality.

In the next lesson, Choosing Words, we'll look at the vocabulary appropriate to Formal.

Lesson Two

Choosing Words

Finding the Tone

This lesson is on *diction*, the choice of words. Diction also means pronunciation, but I'm using the word in its older, Formal meaning. To build good sentences you need proper raw materials—well chosen words. Most complaints about how badly people express themselves and most books on expression focus on questions of diction: Don't use that word! That word gives me fits! Use short words! Use clear words! Omit unnecessary words!

Of course words are important. Gerald Ford probably lost the presidency when he said that Eastern Europe was not *dominated* by the Soviet Union. But if you concentrate on diction, that distracts you from the main problems in expression. Words are badly chosen and misused when one has little or nothing to say. With something to say, the right words come, and come in sentences. To speak well you want something to say. You can know all the words in the dictionary and not know what to do with them. This lesson is about words, but the other lessons are about putting words together.

When finding something to say you first work on the problem of tone. Tone involves three things: you, your subject, and your audience. What do *you* want to tell *them* about *it*? In expression you always have a you, an it, and a them, so you might as well admit it, and begin negotiations. If you concentrate on *you* (what do I think? what do I want? what can I say?) you get nowhere. If you concentrate on your *subject* (what is it? why is it?) you won't get very far, because our knowledge is strictly limited, and much of what we know is useless or boring. If you concentrate on your audience (how can I please them? will they like this?) you won't come up with anything *you* want to say.

Let's imagine you're asked to say something on littering.

The subject is dear to you because you're fed up with having cans and bottles thrown into your front yard. You think how much you hate litterbugs and plan to write a piece heaping abuse on them. This approach goes nowhere: no one cares if you hate litterbugs.

You should think about the subject too: What is litter? Garbage. Do I want to talk about different kinds of garbage? Not much. What is littering? Not easy to say. Is it conscious or unconscious? Is it carelessness or defiance or both? How much of each? How can I find out? Can a litterbug tell me why he does it? Maybe I'll ask a few, but it's not likely they'll know. So I'll do a heavy think piece on the reasons for litter. Is that what's needed?

You should also think about the audience: What are they willing to listen to? Do they hate litterbugs too? As much as me? Less than me? Some of them might be litterbugs. Can I reform them? Fat chance. Do they want a pop psychology treatment of why people litter? Maybe some of that. How to solve the litter problem, is that what they'd like? Probably. Work on that. I like that. How to prevent litter. How to clean it up. There's a lot to say. How to say it—serious, witty, angry, cautiously hopeful? Maybe I better see first what I have to work with, then decide how to say it.

You see from this example how you get well into your work by thinking of what *you* want to tell *them* about *it*. Each of the three has its rights and must not be slighted. Finding the tone of the piece may sound to you like a new and difficult business, but it's not. It's not artificial, since the mind works on it automatically whenever you express yourself. I'm only urging you to think about the tone. You communicate well when you have some notion of what you're up to, some grasp of the subject, and some sense of what the audience wants.

A keynote in music determines the scale to be used. In writing, the tone determines the vocabulary to use. If your subject is abstract you can't call on vivid, concrete language. If you're writing swift narrative you can't use fancy words. If you're reporting, you use transparent language and stay out of the picture yourself. Choosing the right words has nothing to do with avoiding those few words said to be taboo, has nothing to do with knowing a huge vocabulary. The right words are right for the job and have the right tone. An audience decides which words are acceptable, as it decides which statements are acceptable. You wouldn't say *hung up* during a job interview or tell a convention of gays that boys like girls. You need passwords, not just words.

Finding the tone limits your choices, but you want that. With half a million words in English to choose from and an infinite number of sentences to make, if you don't start with a tone, as a musician does, you're lost.

Your Vocabulary

Most words are technical and of no importance. Four out of five are nouns. You should know as many words as you'd like. You don't need to know many. A study showed that 96% of the conversations on the telephone confined themselves to a vocabulary of about 700 words! (which can lead you to think that people are twice as smart as gorillas who know 350 words, or else they should stop talking over the phone). Most people use only a few thousand words, though they recognize five to ten times that number when they read.

The Bible has only several thousand words. The Basic English vocabulary of 850 words allows you to express yourself very well. As a matter of fact, trying to limit your vocabulary is a way to purify your style. You should aim at the simplest, most common vocabulary that gets the job done. Aristotle said that the writer should use the language of common men (though he should try to think like a wise man). You're better off knowing and using a small number of words well than knowing a great number and using them badly. The vocabulary that is available to writers today, if jargon is excluded, is smaller than it has been in the past four hundred years. We live in serious times and are not supposed to use words that are made up, old, learned, or foreign.

Why then would you want to increase your vocabulary? Because that helps you in reading, makes it easier and more enjoyable. The more words you know, the easier you read and the more fun you have when you find a new word. A new word tells us what other people are interested in. Also, enlarging your reading vocabulary increases your ready vocabulary.

New words are acquired not from lists in magazines but by seeing them in contexts that make you want to figure out their meaning. Words that are heard are much more easily acquired, so prick up your ears when you hear a new one. Make a habit of referring to the dictionary, which should be handy as you read. No book, not even the Bible, contains more surprises.

People buy vocabulary building books thinking them to be shortcuts to literacy, but there are no shortcuts. There's no substitute for the years of reading that lead to mastery of Formal. Formal takes practice. People who are tired won't practice: they'll turn on the TV rather than read a book, telephone rather than write. Often they're not so much tired as bored, and mistakenly avoid making an effort that would release them from boredom. It's not boring to read and write, it's a challenge. Two out of three people in the world can't do either one. Twenty five million Americans can't read, and countless millions don't. TV has made reading unnecessary, as motors have made walking unnecessary and intravenous feeding has made eating unnecessary. Think about the word Tube.

What should we read? Books that engage the mind and require a personal and thoughtful response. Any book that can be read in less than a week is an entertainment. The longer you spend on a book the better it is. What reads fast is not worth the eyestrain. You learn about language by reading slowly and critically. Reading fast is a modern disease. We got into Viet Nam because President Kennedy took a speed reading course. That slow you down? Good.

Fluency

Some people avoid reading in the belief they read too slow, some remain silent in the belief they speak too slow, some avoid writing in the belief they write too slow. Even Moses thought he was a poor, slow speaker. But speed is not important. Reading talking and writing are often done too fast, much more often than too slow. If one is convinced that she is too slow and can't be persuaded otherwise, then there's only one thing for her to do— it's not give up—it's practice. Like piano keys, words get easier to use thru practice. No one learns to play a piano by looking at it. And the point in playing is not to hit the keys fast, but make them sing. If you make one sentence that sings, that's worth a shelf of books that mumble and drone.

There are two problems in diction—choosing the right words, and choosing them without taking all day to do it. People are more concerned about the latter, and seek to increase their vocabulary in order to seem more fluent and articulate, not because they want to go around sounding like a dictionary. Whatever one's concern, both problems of diction are solved the same way—thru practice, thru reading writing talking and listening.

So stop looking at books, magazines, and TV and start listening to them. (You'll find that the sound of the TV doesn't matter, and you'll decide to leave the set turned off.) There are plenty of things to look at, if you just want to look, but there's not a lot worth listening to. You have to go out and find it. You may even have to say it yourself. When you look you want to look more, but when you listen, you think.

Read out loud. If that turns out to be boring, what you're reading is not worth listening to. Throw away what reads fast or easy. Talk to yourself: get better at this by keeping a journal. Or talk to anyone by writing a letter: write to editors, politicians, dead people. Hang around the library until you hear a book talking to you. Recite your creed: I believe that nothing can be more important than a book. Someday the book I am looking for will be written. Maybe I will write it. Deliver speeches to the mirror. Say to it: My best feature is not my smile, my eyes, my hair, it's this, my tongue. You, tongue, are my instrument. I wag you, you don't wag me.

If you practice in this way for years you'll become fast and fluent. But no matter how fast you get, you must not break the Formal speed limit. Whether speaking or writing, Formal requires you to walk, *andante*. You don't want to dally (chatting, dithering, wool gathering) and you don't want to rush (gushing, babbling). Joe Louis said When a man's got someth'ng to say he don't need all week to say it. Experience also tells us that when someone has something to say, she takes her time to say it r'ght.

A reader always assumes that when you write you have time. Therefore you can't be hasty or doubtful in your choice of words. You can't offer alternatives and corrections, you can't hold out a handful of synonyms. You can't submit *notes* or *remarks*, for what you submit is assumed to be in final form. Any slip of the pen is a more serious matter than a slip of the tongue.

Audiences are lenient with the speaker, because they know she's under pressure of time. Even serious slips are forgiven, so happy is the audience that someone is talking to them. Good speakers know this and derive their confidence from it. (They also know that few people are listening: the audience is looking, and is catching words and phrases rather than sentences.)

In view of the audience's tolerance, there's no excuse for being tongue tied. The secret of speaking well is the air of confidence. People sense that this is so, and in their eagerness to seem to have the situation under control, they get anxious. Because of this pressure to sound articulate—some even think they should sound glib—they're tempted to speak fast, and then they stumble. Upset by any pause, they fill the pause with *um uh ah er* and other noises.

These little horrors are called *audible pauses* and are the most annoying fault in speech—annoying because easy to remedy. If trying to speak fast causes the problem, don't try. Refuse to be rushed. The audible pause only appears in Formal, where one is not supposed to rush. Fast speech is not impressive and has the opposite effect to the one intended. Fast speech shows insecurity, the need to please, to sell. Only in comedians is it acceptable. Slow careful speech is effective speech, and marks the quick mind. You must show your listeners you care about what you're saying, that you're weighing the words, and some weigh more than others. Pauses convey meaning. There are pauses at the ends of sentences and pauses before verbs and direct objects that bring out these words in the sentence. Canceling these pauses by blurting *uh uh uh* wrecks your speech.

The audible pause sometimes pops in when we find ourselves embarked on a sentence with no idea where it's going. Since we use the *uh* when we're in trouble, using it frequently suggests we're having lots of trouble. As we become more articulate, we find ourselves less frequently caught in sentences we have to fight our way out of. We gradually acquire the skill of framing the whole sentence in the mind before saying it. At this level of skill the audible pause disappears once and for all.

Wordiness

What's wrong with these? *I'll see you at 10 AM in the morning. It's over and done with. My tardiness was due to the fact that I was late.* The fault is obviously wordiness, because that's what the heading says. But wordiness is not obvious. In Informal it's used all the time for emphasis and clarity, and then it ceases to be wordiness. Make sense? Multiple negatives are common examples, and are found in all languages: *I didn't ask for nothing, no, no, I don't want none.* These are no more objectionable than reflexive pronouns: *He cooks himself.* But in Formal they are wordy. Formal tries to be brief and achieves emphasis not by repetition but by omitting the unemphatic.

The sin of wordiness takes two forms. When expression is dull and long winded, the sin is mortal and called verbosity. When some apparently useless words creep in, we have the lesser sin of redundancy. Redundancy is seldom detected, but when it is, the audience resents having their priceless possession, their time, taken from them. An audience can be killed with a joke or a redundancy.

Deliberate repetition for heavy emphasis is sometimes allowed. The device grabs attention because it is annoying—a fact to which advertisers seem oblivious. Though an effective speech has often been described as one in which the speaker tells you what she's going to say, says it, and then tells you what she said, she shouldn't get caught. Amplifying the message, or saying it in different ways, hides the repetition. To amplify, you need lots of material. That's Lesson Six.

Redundancy is hard to detect because we allow it in Informal. Simple English sentences teem with unnecessary letters and words. Words could be abbreviated, and many modifiers and most inflections could be left out, but this isn't done, since people don't want language to be too dense and streamlined. Curt messages, though complete and logical, are often misunderstood. Much that seems redundant helps make the meaning clear and allows the audience to get away with being inattentive, which is their normal state.

Before swearing never to repeat ourselves, let's know a little more about why we do it. Why do we say *At this point in time my answer is affirmative, and in the month of June you'll have my promise for the future* instead of saying *Now my answer is yes and in June you'll have my promise?* Maybe we love to hear the sound of our own voice. (Did you catch my wordiness—*hear the sound?*) Sometimes we use a lot of words when stalling for time. (*Stalling for time?*) Sometimes we use a lot to appear to be helpful or humble. (*Appear to be?*) But usually, we're just careless and say things twice over again because we don't recall the less familiar shorter expressions.

The following is a bore of phrases not to be used in Formal. Boiling them down makes for instant elegance.

Normal	Elegant
appear on the scene	appear
bring to a conclusion	conclude
bring with you	bring
enclosed herewith	enclosed
explicitly state	state
make a motion	move
sent under separate cover	sent
substitute in their place	substitute
will leave tomorrow	leave tomorrow
whether or not	whether
more preferable	preferable
well off financially	well off
inside of, outside of, off of	inside, outside, off
where to, where at	where
one and the same	the same
each and every, each one	each

any and all	any
and etcetera	et cetera
as compared to	compared to
in this day and age	today
satisfactory enough	satisfactory
round in form, square in shape,	round, square
many in number, blue in color,	many, blue
two acres in area, small sized	two acres, small
in spite of the fact that	although
due to the fact that	because

For practice, why don't you remove these Laurel helpers from these Hardy nouns? *early beginnings end result existing problem free gift general consensus of opinion hard question to answer important essentials mutual cooperation other alternative overall length pair of twins past history potential danger reason why self will separate groups tangible sales widow woman.*

And then cut the tails off these verbs: *explain about follow after include in mix together penetrate into proceed onward protrude out recall back repeat again rock back and forth.*

In English, you have to watch for little adverbs—*off, in, with, together*—drawn to the verb like a magnet. In Formal, don't say *rest up, rise up, burn up, eat up, drink up, start up, settle up, hurry up, write up, open up.* Listen up now: the *up* is seldom needed (it is in *put up, hold up,* and *let up*).

However natural the redundancies, they are not allowed in Formal. You are to be as brief as possible without being obscure. You shouldn't be *terse,* though, moving so fast the message has no time to sink in. Tight lipped laconic style is for New Hampshire farmers and tombstones.

What Are the Right Words?

The first requirement of a right word is that it not be *used* wrong. The user understands what the word means among her audience, not what it means in Heaven. The right word conveys its meaning and does the job you want it to do. If you want a flowery word, it will be flowery, if you want a vague word, it will be vague, if you want a shocking word, it will shock. Should you be flowery, vague, or shocking? Informally, be what you want. Formally, behave or get spanked.

A right word can be right *on*, not just suited, but delightfully suited to the purpose. No better word could be imagined. The word is suited not just in its denotation, or dictionary meaning, but in its connotations, its flavor, its tone. Knowledge of denotations and sensitivity to connotations—neither is easy to acquire. Neither can be taught to you, because there are far too many words. Word meanings soak in thru hearing and reading the words over a long period of time. You discover the more mysterious *qualities* of words by falling in love with them. Reading poetry and learning new languages will make you fall in love.

A dictionary can tell you that *children* is Standard and *kids* is slang, it can tell you that the experts frown at *downplay* and *input,* but it can never tell you what word *you* should choose. The choice of words is never an impersonal matter, nor an indifferent one. Even when words seem to have the same meaning, they have different sound and rhythm. In a business letter, should you *ask, beg,* or *request*? Do you drink *cheap* or *inexpensive* wine? Should a hiway sign read *Watch out for falling rock* or *fallen rock*? Is your neighbor an *officer, policeman, cop,* or *fuzz*? He may *have* his faults but he *possesses* his good qualities. *Did* he *leave* or *has* he *left*? If he *has left* maybe you can catch him.

The right word looks right, feels right, sounds right. If it doesn't, it draws attention to itself, and draws attention to the user. Sometimes you want that, usually you don't. Good expression swallows up its words. A word here and there may sparkle, but when many do, the style is flashy.

The right word often appeals to the senses. Vivid words stir the senses—*shiny, heavy, square, lifts, pushes.* Diction is dull when it's too abstract and no longer refers to what is seen, heard, and felt. As a rule you should avoid abstract words and choose vivid ones, avoid general words and choose specific ones. Be as precise, as specific as you can without being distracting. Instead of saying that something is *pretty,* say why it's pretty—it's well made, smooth, colorful, bright, balanced.

Abstract words are usually longer than concrete ones: that's why it's a good idea to look for shorter words. You use short words not because people are busy but because short words are more forceful. Instead of saying *This is antagonistic to our interests* say *This hurts us.* Instead of *There are differences between the two* say *They differ.* English is basically a language of one syllable words, and these words, being more common and natural, are more forceful than the longer ones. *He departed, He left. I'm secure, I'm safe. She telephoned, She called. He accepted the bribe in this manner, He took the bribe this way. We located the vehicle, We found the car. Our society is male dominated, Men run things.* English is a snappy, forceful language of little words that are the devil to put together right.

Suppose you're thinking of choosing the word *overweight.* Should you use that word or say *plump, stout, well fed, gross, enormous, like a hippo?* What would a doctor say? *Obese.* What would a retailer say? *Portly.* A teenager? *Chubby.* A journalist? *Gargantuan.* An aristocrat? *Fat.* You might well want to stick with the neutral word *overweight.* Usually the right words come to you when you first form the thought. The more practice you get in writing, the more you trust the words that come right away without your hunting for them. If you agonize over diction you get bogged down.

It's easy to go too far in hunting for specific and vivid language. Journalese, written by those who are paid by the word, has the words jumping off the page. People never *eat,* they *nibble* or *gobble;* they never wear *clothes,* they wear *Guccis* and *Puccis.* Much advertising copy and magazine writing is overstimulated, and the hysterical words wipe each other out. When everyone is using the language of the blurb, the cool understatement stands out. Classy language is cold language. Snappy diction is sloppy diction—*a rash of delays on the subways, an explosion in higher education, desperate for some coffee, heavenly mousse, Macy's sofa riot.*

Language doesn't have to be precise; in fact, it can't be, but if it's too hyped, it doesn't say anything. The exactly right word need not be an exact or narrow word at all. Amateur writers root around in the thesaurus and come up with unnatural words. Words are not ornaments to hang on the writing. Concentrate on the idea, and the right words come. Effort is better spent in studying the problem of tone and in strengthening the sentences.

In Formal diction you try to be natural and avoid the extremes of too abstract or too vivid. You don't make your language picturesque; you shouldn't seem to be painting, you're revealing. You don't make your language musical either, because that would mean you weren't serious about what you're saying. These are serious times. Haven't you heard that the Russians have 40,000 tanks?

Wrong Words

There aren't any. There are wrong uses of words. Every word accepted into the language has lovable features. I've never met a word I didn't like. Words can be wrongly used in two ways: when they're chosen from an inappropriate level—slang in a graduation speech or naughty words at a teaparty—and when they're given meanings that don't belong to them. When a word is badly misused it's funny, and called a malapropism: *the crutch of the matter, penny larceny, you misconscrew me to the upmost, your multi fauceted talents wet my appetite, my mother is psychosomatic, my wife runs the househole.* Malapropisms are words used in ignorance of their meanings. When words are used without remembering their meanings, we have *fuzziness.* Though fuzziness is a more common and less glaring fault, it can be as amusing to the connoisseur; as when a Harvard professor say *This fills a much needed gap,* or when Professor Chomsky talks about the *concrete steps the Israeli government has taken,* or when the weather forecaster says it will be *clearly cloudy* and *fairly rainy.*

Among the delights of misused words are mixed metaphors. *With one foot planted firmly in the Middle Ages, with the other Dante salutes the dawn of the Renaissance. There's something fishy here that has to be stamped out. She was putty in his hands and he got his fingers burned.*

We've all been guilty of such mistakes. Misused words are much commoner than people suppose, since language is by its nature incorrect and funny. All language is figurative; all words are metaphors, inadequate signs and sounds trying to represent what's in the real world. Language cannot mean exactly what it says. Nothing ever *is* another thing. Mathematical language is more precise and reassuring. But if one gets too worried about the shortcomings of words, he may wind up like the professors whom Gulliver visits, who reject words and hold up in their hands the objects they want to talk about. The thought should not be upsetting, but comforting, that no one chooses words perfectly.

Smart people try to avoid using words whose meaning they're unsure of. But even they err in choosing words that *sound* like the right ones. (These misuses are as often misspellings as mistakes in meaning.) Examples: *accept except, affect effect, allusion illusion, born borne, complementary complimentary, council counsel, eminent imminent, ever so often every so often, felicitous fortuitous, flaunt flout, flounder founder, past passed, prophecy prophesy, raise rise, respectfully respectively.*

A common and well intentioned mistake occurs when people stretch a word out. Feeling that big words are better than small, that the air should be filled with syllables, they are guilty of stretching the following words:

definite becomes definitive
determine becomes determinate
full, fulsome
history, historiography
life, lifespan
mingle, intermingle
method, methodology
oblige, obligate
often, oftentimes
plural, pluralist
practical, practicable
regardless, irregardless
readers, readership
simple, simplistic
standard, standardized
use, utilize
view, viewpoint, overview
visit, visitation

If you love short words, you won't want to stretch them.

Vagueness

When the exact word is found, a better cannot be imagined. When a poor word is used, a better is easily imagined. A word can be faulted on a number of grounds: it's vague, ambiguous, fancy, phony, old or new. Vagueness is the worst and most common fault in diction. For every word used wrongly, dozens are used vaguely. As pride is the underlying sin of sins, so vagueness is the underlying fault in poor words.

Vague words are useful, certainly. If they weren't they wouldn't be called on so often. They let us talk without thinking. In Formal we have to appear to be thinking. It takes effort to choose among words that have clear meanings, and we have to show we're making the effort. Laziness is resented even more than vagueness. What happens when you hear someone talk like this? *I got bored so I got my coat on and I got into my car and when I got to the bowling alley I got there too late so I got drunk instead.* The words convey their meaning, but the lazy reliance on *got* and *and* suggests that the speaker is not trying to sharpen her diction and please her listeners. It also suggests that maybe she couldn't sharpen her diction if she tried. The words haven't been chosen, they emerged.

In Formal each word must look like it has been chosen. Words that come easy are resented. Frequent colloquialisms, no matter how natural they are, are resented. Overused words like *got, case, thing, very,* and *great* are resented. Audible pauses—*er, like, you know, man, I mean*—are resented. The speaker is telling her audience she's not about to knock herself out for the likes of them.

Vague and Wordy are the inseparable Laziness twins. We say *in the case of a layoff* instead of *in a layoff, in the line of retailing* instead of *in retailing, in the field of economics, in economics, from the point of view of safety, for safety.* Vagueness leads us into annoying novelties. Though it's clear English to say *clockwise* and *crosswise,* it's not to say *methodwise* or *legalwise. Filmwise* is vague, *taxwise* is ok. Lacking energy to search for the precise language we want, we fall back on cloudy words like *relationship tendency climate situation atmosphere area data phenomenon.*

Vagueness allows us to hold on to vague ideas that we like. We know from experience that when we try to make an idea clear it often disappears, leaving us speechless. But we owe it to others, if they owe it to us, to try to be clear and to stick our neck out and say something. It can generally be said in our defense that we're vague from laziness and not from intent, but sometimes we do intend to be vague. We would want to say *deal with* if we didn't know how a thing should be dealt with, or say *contact the mayor's office* if we didn't care whether the contact was by phone, letter, or in person, or say *we are processing your application* if we were stalling the applicant.

Sometimes the vagueness is just downright cowardly, and we may not be able to get away with it. What's being said here?

> I want a meaningful job and an employer I can relate to.
> We want an aggressive manager who can grow with the organization.
> With quick and certain punishment I will bring back law and order in the streets.
> I pledge allegiance.
> She's a ballbreaker.

Vagueness allows us to say one thing and mean another. Doing this on purpose is called equivocating, and despite the fancy name, it's common as dirt.

When trying to be vague we need to avoid slipping into ambiguity. Vagueness is soothing but ambiguity is upsetting— unless it's in poetry, where some people say they like it. Vagueness suggests a cloudy meaning, ambiguity presents a puzzle of meanings to choose from: *I have nothing on. Your figure is wrong. I am the furrier. My, you've grown another foot. Let me back into the bed. You've taken the part for the whole. Do you hate homos like me? No more than small farmers, frozen food managers, or photos of photographers.*

Can you open the door? is objected to because it means *Will you?* and *Are you able to open the door? Would you pass the sugar?* means *Please pass me* and *Are you willing to* pass me the sugar? A common ambiguous construction that should be avoided is the negative statement followed by *because*. *He's not angry because he knows the truth. She couldn't leave him because he's rich.* Turn these sentences around another way. *With* phrases cause many ambiguities: *I am not going with her.* Are you going at all?

Many words have different meanings, but with most of them the context clears up the meaning. Some words though have different meanings that are close to each other, and when these words fail to make their meaning clear, they flunk the ambiguity test. *Brainwash* means persuade, train, torture. Are brains washable? *Finalize* means end, prepare to end, officially end. *Verbalize* means talk, talk for relief, talk too much. *Togetherness* means being together or liking to be together. Such words, doomed to be ambiguous all their lives, will have short lives.

So never pick an ambiguous word when you're only groping for a vague one. Whatever you think you're doing, Formal audiences will get mad at you if they catch you being ambiguous or too vague. They'll think you're tricky, or what's worse, that you have a loose grip on the words and are not able to manipulate them properly. When people object to your words, they're objecting to you. A helpless little word cannot be offensive—it's only a noise a person makes. You really have to be clumsy to offend with your diction, since people are so uncritical of words. They love words, and love is blind. They believe that the only bad words are bad words, but deep inside, they love these best.

Old Words

Nobody knows why a good old word dies. The words *kin* and *gotten* are dead now in England, though alive and well in the US. Only a few oldtimers in the Middle West still say *bidden* and *dassn't,* which are fine words. Sometimes a new word kicks an old one out, often a good word dies without being replaced. I cry over the loss of *weep* and *lest* and the adjective *cross.* Once a word starts to slow down, more people stop using it, and then it goes fast. Words are now slipping from the language at an unbelievable rate, owing to the triumph of TV over print.

Dead words are called *archaic* or *antique*. Many people have the notion that antiques, such as *yon, tarry, thence, whence, deem,* and *amidst,* can be used in Formal. The opposite is the case: you can use antiques all you want Informally—to show off or have fun—but you cannot use them in Formal. Though there are hundreds of antiques, I'll only warn you about the following, which still show up and are tempting: *alas, albeit, amidst, aught* and *naught, aye* and *yea, beauteous, behoove, betwixt, deem, delve, ere, erstwhile, fraught, goodly, hither, impudent, joyous, morn, nether, nigh, oft, save* (meaning *except*), *swoon, tarry, wax* (meaning *to grow*), *whereon,* and *wondrous.* You can't even use the handy words *whence* and *thence. Hence, henceforth, drunken,* and *sunken* are going fast. It's now chancy to start a sentence with *yet.* The IRS has killed the word *spouse* on its tax forms.

In the past, poets enjoyed use of the grand vocabulary of antiques; today we're serious and can't use antiques even in light verse. Not long ago Kipling could say *East is East, and West is West, and never the twain shall meet.* Try using *twain* today and see how far you get. Try using *shall.* The mass media have brought about a standardization and shrinking of the usable vocabulary. On the whole, this has benefited the language, by helping to protect it from jargon and by removing distinctions among the language levels. But many lovable old words have been lost forever. Today, only bold or important writers dare try oddities in their diction. Much as I want to, I can't recommend that you try using them. Formal expression, remember, requires a certain squelching of personality.

We'll now turn to the huge category of words and expressions that are so feeble they'd be better off dead. Familiar phrases are called shopworn, threadbare, flyblown, readymade, second-hand, hackneyed, trite, clichés, stereotypes, catchphrases, stock phrases, and commonplaces. From all these bad names you can see how much they're disliked. Do these annoy you?

Jack, the picture of health and the spitting image of his old man, was as honest as the day is long, but he swore like a trooper. Far be it from me to criticize his way with words, but it goes without saying and it's plain as the nose on your face his use of the King's

English made him stick out like a sore thumb and got him into a lot of hot water.

Clichés look lively, but are vague and wordy: *heave a sigh, sleep like a top, sustain an injury, mount a massive assault, token of our esteem, water over the dam.* There are so many clichés, certain people use them for a language. Dictionaries of clichés have been compiled, but you don't have to look up phrases in a dictionary to see if they're clichés. All readymade phrases except ones like *How do you do* should be avoided in Formal. You must choose the words one by one and they must be yours. Whenever you compare, using *like* or *as,* watch out for a cliché. Instead of saying that someone is happy as a lark or happy as a clam at high tide, say happy as a bride, as a poodle, as a chicken with an egg, or payday happy, Friday night happy, or just say happy. What's wrong with *happy*? Trust the words. In a fruit store you don't have to squeeze all the fruits, and in writing you don't have to squeeze all the words.

Informally, you can use all the clichés you want. In fact they're needed for the relaxed tone. Some clichés manage to preserve a charge of meaning. When they work, they're no longer called clichés, but proverbs or idioms. Here are oldies but goodies: *Keep your shirt on. Out of the frying pan. On the warpath. Up to his ears. Barking up the wrong tree. Best thing since popcorn. Drink him under the table. After my scalp. Crying over spilt milk. Butter side down.* You can think of many others. It's hard to avoid such common expressions, but in Formal you must.

There's a special category of clichés known as rubber stamps, that let us know what is Very Good and what is No Good. VG is expressed by *nice, natural, terrific, dynamic, fantastic, amazing, phenomenal, exciting, significant, creative.* Some bizarre new terms of approval are: *operative, relevant, sensual, luxe, executive, organic, meaningful, fulfilling, aggressive, hard nosed, hard driving, vibrant, staggering,* and *mind blowing.*

NG is expressed by *insecure, negative, bureaucratic, liberal, reactionary, imperialist, populist. Ists* and *isms* are bad news. *Scientists* and *capitalism* are ok, though.

Smart people try to avoid rubber stamps, especially in

Formal. These words shed no light on the subject but only signal that the user, who has the right ideas, is purring or snarling. To avoid vague adjectives kick the adjective habit. Instead of using a linking verb and a VG or NG adjective, tell what the subject *does,* make clear why it's good or bad. If someone is *uptight* is he worried, priggish, or inhibited? If something is a *ripoff* is it a gyp, clever profit taking, or theft? If a society is *permissive* what does it permit?

Our emotions are vague, and any word that calls for an emotional response has to be vague too. *Sexist, democracy, rights, free enterprise, exploitation*—grand words, vague words. The more powerful the word—take *love* and *death* for examples—the vaguer it is. Vague suggestive words are the meat and potatoes of politics and advertising. One can get somewhere by clever use of these words, but maybe it's not a place she would like once she's there.

Fancy Words

A former authority, H W Fowler, said: There is nothing to be ashamed of in *buy* or *see* that they should need translating into *purchase* and *observe.* He might have added that there's nothing to be ashamed of in *purchase* or *observe* either. If *buy* is as good as *purchase* and saves five letters every time you use it, why not stamp out *purchase* altogether? I'll answer that one. Variety is the spice of life. *Purchase* may offer no improvement over *buy* but offers a change. If you choose *purchase* you're saying For one reason or another I like *purchase*. In expressing yourself you're allowed to express yourself, if only a little. Even in Formal you can kick up your heels now and then and show off your diction without having to be questioned about every word , just as musicians are allowed their *rubato.* Don't know rubato? Get smart, play the Game.

Unless you're aiming at an unusually simple style, you do well to slip in a fancy word from time to time, to wake people up and show how confident you are. You add sparkle to what you're saying and you may flatter the audience. A two dollar word might be worth two thousand dollars.

A fancy word is like a fancy tie, expressive and bold. Fancy writing, though, is like being overdressed or wearing too much perfume; it's egotistical and rather pathetic. You'd be surprised at how many fancy words you use, usually to be funny. Here are common ones: *abode, attire, citizenry, communication, consume, converse, crave, dwell, edifice, evince, facility* (meaning building or toilet), *garment, missive, remuneration, repast, reside, trice, thrice, transpire, vanquish, veritable, visage,* and *weep.*

These words are well known and people understand why you might be tempted to use them. Such is not the case with foreign words, which are not so well known and which have to be used with extra caution. If they are well known they are not fancy, but clichés like *savoir faire, femme fatale, bon vivant, joie de vivre, idée fixe, raison d'etre, bête noire.* If they are not well known your audience may be embarrassed by its ignorance and resent your putting on airs. The Formal rule is: Don't use a foreign word or phrase if there is a good English equivalent.

Also, you have to decide whether you're quoting the word from the foreign language or whether you're trying to use it as a regular word in English. This affects tone and pronunciation. How should you pronounce *timbre*? as *timber, tamber,* or *tamb*? do you say *Gesstapo* or *Geshtapo, lawn jeray* or *lingerie, chaúffeur* or *chauffeúr, haute quizzine* or *la ote cuisíne*? The pronunciation depends on what your audience expects, not on whether you know the foreign language. As a rule, try to anglicize the pronunciations, since the foreign sounds are resented and since you may stumble in shifting languages. Of course, if you give the words English pronunciation you don't get credit for being able to speak in tongues. But you may get credit for English. And, as teachers love to say, you should know at least two languages—English and your own.

To sum up, fancy words, whether rare, foreign, or a foot long, must be used sparingly. Modern style is not showy and pointed, but verbose and low. In the past, writers could use fancy words like *ablutions, obsequies, repine, impecunious,* and *Weltschmerz,* but you can't anymore because of our shrunk vocabulary.

Only one kind of fancy word is still flourishing, and that is the euphemism. The term means speaking *favorably*. Euphemisms enable cars to become automobiles, drinks to become beverages, persons to become individuals. This is the Age of Euphemism, and advertisers and PR people make money as euphemists. Euphemisms, like works of art, protect us from the harshness of the world: we have hundreds of euphemisms for bodily functions, drunkenness, madness, and death. A horse may sweat, a man perspires, a woman glows. Since euphemisms are such an important, permanent feature of language, they cannot all be thrown out as dishonest or evasive. They are objectionable only when they don't work, because they are unnecessary or too fraudulent. Here's a little quiz on euphemisms.

What's a prison?	a penitentiary
a penitentiary?	a correctional institution
a correctional institution?	a rehabilitation center
a bombing raid?	a retaliation, an interdiction
What's firing people called?	rationalization, termination
What happens when a museum sells a painting?	It deaccessions it.
Where do you kill germs?	on environmental surfaces in your home
What's a hospital?	a health care institution
a store?	a supermarket
a supermarket?	a savings center
Then what's a bank?	an earnings center
What's a gym?	a physical fitness center
What isn't a center?	a comfort station
What's a slow student?	a slow advancer
a bribe?	a campaign contribution
a payoff?	an honorarium

If euphemism is allowed, so is dysphemism, or using bad names.

What's a homosexual?	a queer
a woman?	a broad
a person with standards?	rigid, elitist, a dinosaur
What's his class?	patrician, mandarin

Nothing happens to the language when words are used this way. They don't lose their meanings; the people who use such words may lose their meanings, that is, may deceive themselves. For every one who tells lies, there are countless sincere people who deceive themselves with their own words.

Formal is not squeamish, and avoids euphemisms when it can. It avoids dirty words too. Of course there are no dirty words, only dirty minds. To the pure all things are pure. But who's pure? People are weak, worried, repressed, and that's why dirty words should not be flung about. The only free speech is a madman's. Use dirty words with discretion.

Fad Words

If a newly invented or imported word is a good one, it will make its way into the language, and no amount of protest from those who don't like the look or sound of it will prevent its final triumph. The English speaking people, and Americans especially, do not show so much prejudice as speakers of other languages do against new and imported words. In fact, we welcome neologisms too warmly. Most of them are not useful, and lack the clarity and wealth of associations enjoyed by the old words they threaten to displace.

A new word may be a good one, but has to prove itself over a period of time, has to clarify its meaning before being used in Formal. To be Formal is to be conservative, and you should avoid new words no matter how much you dote on them. New words are often used aggressively, and may make the audience feel behind the times. Because new words are resented we like to use them with friends—to affirm our closeness by saying we're not afraid to use this new jargon or slang with each other.

There are three kinds of new words—fashionable words, jargon, and slang. Let's see why and how they are used, and try to decide if they should be banned from Formal.

Occasionally, fashionable words are new words for new things that everyone's talking about, but usually they are ordinary words that suddenly leap into the spotlight, words like *guide-*

lines thrust establishment liberation ongoing overview hopefully escalate image lifestyle. People object to fad words without knowing why. This is why: the words are echoing thru the air and are easy to catch. Since they're easy to use, using them marks the user as lazy. Also, the more a word is used, the more it's misused and the vaguer it gets. Fad words are new words or new uses of old words, and many people love the old and hate the new. The media of course love what's new, but that doesn't mean your audience does. So if an old word suddenly starts running around fast, stay away from it, it has a disease.

The usual objection to fad words is to their being faddish, but the proper objection is to their vagueness. A word on everyone's lips has to be vague to be well liked. Vagueness is the underlying fault when nouns are used as verbs. Just what is done when you *update, upgrade,* or *implement,* when you *customize* your house, *winterize* your car, *destabilize* a government, *personalize* your underwear, or *polarize* your audience? Do you *doctor* or treat? Do you *lawyer* or counsel? Do you ever *author, parent, eyeball, dialogue,* or *impact?* Are you *conflicted* and *problemed* about English? Using such verbs deprives you of the *old verbs,* which are the jewels of a language.

To believe that most new words are no good is not being stuffy. They aren't. Clear the mind of modern cant. Here's the rule to follow: if the word stands for a new reality—IUD, DNA, PVC, aerosols, polymers—don't hesitate to use it. If the new word stands for a new concept, don't use it. The experts who invent new concepts may not be illuminating your mind so much as blowing smoke in your eyes. We could well do without: *open marriage, affirmative action, behavior modification, child production, cognitive dissonance, counter culture, death instinct, double bind, dry skin, greening of America, halitosis, ethnicity, ethology, sociobiology, parapsychology, future shock, futurism, structuralism, male chauvinism, modernism, orientalism, imperialism, Caesarism, sexual politics, the work ethic, neoconservatism, the new hedonism, the new taurine excrement.* Stick with the older categories of thought represented by the older words. New words should not be embraced, much less trusted. The philosopher Hobbes said Words are wise men's counters—they do but reckon with them, but they are the money of fools. In short, new words and new fads in using words must be inspected. Let us not follow P T Barnum's sign This Way to the Egress.

Jargon

Jargon used to mean the song of the birds, and now it means the song of the doctors, lawyers, coaches, psychologists, dope addicts, and professors of English. (Not all of them.) Jargon is special language used by a group. Its main purpose is to save time, to enable the group to speak of its own concerns in a swift, precise way. Another purpose, a fishy one, is to promote the solidarity and the interests of the group by means of secret language. Any group has a right to all the jargon it wants, but they all seem to produce more than they need. Jargon becomes a problem when it escapes from the group and other people start using it. When that happens the words begin to lose whatever meaning they had. And outsiders prefer the jargon that has little meaning to start with.

Many new terms escape or are sent out from the academic disciplines, especially the social sciences, and find a wider popularity. Fortunately, academic jargon won't live very long, but since it is written as well as spoken, it lives longer than slang. The following jargon is objectionable because it is vague. Adjectives: *counterproductive, creative, culture bound, diametrical, interpersonal, preemptive, substantive, unilateral.* Nouns: *complex, conditioning, coöptation, dialectic, dichotomy, empathy, fixation, frame of reference, ideology, interaction, interface, interlink, interiorizing, mandate, module, trauma, value judgment.* Don't bother to look up these words.

If you look over the list you will see that most of the words are NG and VG rubber stamps. The more popular the jargon, the likelier it is to be some kind of stamp. *You're a revisionist. You're a teleologist. You're an epiphenomenalist. You're an anal retentive.* Anytime we label a person's thought or character we resort to jargon. It's all right to say that someone's a *leftie* but it's not all right to say that he's a *leftist.*

I'm not being fussy in warning you away from jargon. A good writer never touches it. If one can't remember a better word than *feedback, in depth, ongoing,* or *meaningful,* he should aim for a career in which jargon is rewarded and leave English to her poor but honest lovers. The trouble with technical sounding terms is that they aren't technical: plain English is more precise. The trick in technical writing is to use plain language.

When you're tempted to use an expert's word, welcome that as a warning: the poor word veils a fuzzy idea. Clarify the idea and the special word won't be needed. Back off, rethink the whole sentence or paragraph if you have to. If you're running short of time, consult a thesaurus. Be patient, remember there's always a way out. You can't paint yourself into a corner, since there are infinite ways to express your ideas.

Slang

Slang and jargon are similar in being special languages for special occasions. The jargon of golfing would be: *drive, slice, hook, birdie, bogey.* Golf slang would be: *hacker, sky shot, duffer's side, big mouth, rain bringer, smother, killing snakes, voodoo ball.* Slang is jargon with feeling.

The impulses to use slang are admirable: the desire to say things in a fresh way, to wake the language up, to be witty, youthful, exuberant, to increase one's intimacy with friends. The actual words produced by these good impulses are almost always disappointing. Using slang well is even more difficult than using Formal well. Like jargon and bad words, slang is overused, and since it's overused, it suffers a loss of meaning and is then mis-used. Misused words make the user look foolish. Also, slang terms die after a few bright years of life, and anyone using outdated slang looks foolish: she's no longer the *cat's whiskers, cat's pajamas, cat's meow,* she's not a *cool cat,* nor is she *in the catbird seat.* Also, slang is for the young, and if you use it and aren't young, you'll look foolish.

Slang communicates little meaning, since it's gaudy language that attracts attention to itself rather than to the message. On the other hand, it's useful when you want to talk and have no message. The few slang terms that stand for new things—like *sneakers* and *jeans*—are likely to enter the language, but most slang substitutes for conventional words. Because it does, there's always the suggestion that the user of slang doesn't know the conventional words. The same stigma attaches to slang that attaches to all fad words: the words are so popular that picking them shows laziness rather than vigor. Most slang terms are rubber stamps. *Gee. Wow. Crazy. Wild. Off the wall. Busted. Ice. She's getting off on doing a number on him and cracking on him for where he's coming from.* Carl Sandburg said that Slang is language that takes off its coat, spits on its hands, and goes to work. The truth is most slang takes off its coat, spits on its hands, and lies down and falls asleep.

Only a small part of slang is attractive and clever. *Vibes* for example. *Flicks. Threads. Wheels. Bug. Smokies. Corn. Hun, thou,* and *mil. Tube steak* for hot dog. *Slammer. Oreo. Flaked out. Goofy. Short fuse. Fast idle. Spinning your wheels.*

The slang of businessmen is falsely robust: *hard nosed, up front, in place, on the horn, on the blower, bite the bullet, ball of wax, balls and bears, hornets' nest, can of worms, witchesbrew, stonewalling it, stroking, bottom line, take a bath, the crunch, gut reaction, off the top, ballpark figures, hardball, groundrules, windfall, shortfall, tradeoff, killing, thrust, three pronged, trajectory.* As you see, slang often has an aggressive tone. Using slang can be an assertive act, implying that the user is more in the know or more vigorous than his listener. If you're assertive, use lots of slang. If you're mild mannered, stay away from it. Don't hit your boss with it, let him hit you.

We've now finished the lesson on diction. This was the least encouraging lesson in the course, because I told you mainly what not to do. You've been warned against using so many words you're probably wondering if you have any left. Sure you do. A normal, simple vocabulary is what's wanted in Formal. You have to be careful if you use a common vocabulary, because people will understand what you're saying, and so will you. On the other hand, you don't have to work at showing off. Some teachers advise using a *mixed* vocabulary of fancy and common words. An occasional word from a different language level will be allowed, but any real mixing of levels wrecks the tone. And the tone of what you say is a big part of what you say.

Don't worry much about diction. Everyone mischooses and misuses words. Diction is the basic step in expression but not the crucial step. Diction is only naming things—animals can do that. The crucial step is predication, expressing yourself in sentences.

In the next lesson, Lesson Three, I'll teach you to punctuate without having to know any grammar. Grammar is Lesson Four.

Lesson Three

Punctuating by Sound

Eye versus Ear

Punctuating is our way of showing in writing certain pauses and sounds in our speech. Just as the letters of the alphabet are signs representing sounds, so are the marks of punctuation. In talking about spelling I argued that the letters should represent the sounds better than they do, and I'll argue now that punctuation should represent sounds better than it does. Punctuation tells us what writing is supposed to sound like when it's put back into speech. It's like notes on a sheet of music and must be exact.

Punctuation marks were not invented by grammarians who laid down the rules for their use; the marks developed gradually over a long period and became distinguished from each other as they became associated with distinctive sounds. Their purpose was not and is not to help people read faster, by breaking up writing into pieces the eye can handle, but to help people read correctly and musically. The secret of punctuating well is to understand what sounds the marks really represent. Instead of learning countless rules of punctuation, instead of doing lots of exercises and drills, why not learn what a comma and a period sound like?

You don't punctuate pauses. There are frequent pauses in sentences—every few words, in fact. You punctuate sounds. Your teachers used to tell you to put a comma where you had a strong pause and a period where your voice came to a complete stop. This was helpful, but not helpful enough.

I'll teach you to punctuate not according to the pauses or the grammatical structure of the sentence but according to the melody in your speech. The best way if not the only way to discover this melody is to practice reading aloud with feeling and with proper attention to the marks. Unfortunately, many people have not had practice in reading aloud, and cannot read aloud and understand what they're reading. This inability to read well aloud is the main cause of the poor and confused punctuation that we see today. Most people, reading aloud, make a period sound when they come to a comma. Listen to your friends read a passage and see if this isn't so. But reading well aloud is easy with a little practice.

In school you were taught to punctuate for the eye of the reader, and were given many pages of punctuation rules. You were taught the eye method because it helped you in learning grammar and because students were always taught the eye method. But if you can use both eye and ear methods you'll have a way of checking what you do. The ear method is the better one; the marks do represent sounds. In school you were told the sound can help you punctuate, but you should rely on your knowledge of sentence structure. I say rely on the sound. I've put this lesson before the grammar lesson.

Let's look at examples of the difference in the eye and ear methods to see how unsatisfactory the eye method is. In the eye method, you're told to put a period at the end of a sentence. In order to do this you have to know what a sentence is. But no one knows. In the ear method I tell you to put a period whenever your voice makes the sound of the period. That is, the voice slows down, the *tone* falls, and the voice comes to a full, complete, solid stop. Like that. Did you hear the period? Read it aloud and then you will.

Another example. In the eye method, you're told to put commas between coordinate adjectives, that is, adjectives that are equally important. *The dog is a black, nervous poodle.* In order to use the eye method you have to decide how important each adjective is. In the ear method, I tell you to put a comma wherever there's a comma sound. *He was a dirty old man.* But, *he was a dirty, wealthy old man.* Did you hear the comma?

Another. In the eye method, you're told to put commas

around nonrestrictive clauses. *Carol wore a wig which shocked us.* Restrictive clause, *which shocked us,* no comma. *Carol wore a wig, which shocked us.* Nonrestrictive clause, use a comma. Can you always tell a restrictive from a nonrestrictive clause? I can't. In the ear method, you just put a comma wherever there's a comma sound. *My friend Lou, who was ill, watched TV.* Hear the commas? *My friend who was ill watched TV.* No commas.

The ear method will be used more and more in the future. Punctuation will be decided not so much by someone else's elaborate rules or style sheet as by the wishes of the writer herself. In many parts of the English speaking world, though not yet in the US, writers no longer automatically put commas between items in a series. *He loved every Tom Dick and Harry. Our flag is red white and blue.* The ear method says there is no rule, there can be no rule, about punctuating items in a series. If the writer wants comma sounds, she uses commas. If she doesn't, she needn't. *He quickly counted one two three four. But then he slowly counted one, two, three, four.* You heard the commas. *The wicked old president was replaced by the wicked new president.* But, *the wicked, old president was replaced by the wicked, new president.*

The comma is the only interesting and tricky mark of punctuation, and we'll concentrate on it. But we'll listen to all the marks. There are three kinds of marks. The first is the *full stop*, and there are four full stops—period, question mark, exclamation point, and semicolon. The second kind is the *half stop,* and there are four half stops—comma, and the other marks that can be considered varieties of the comma—colon, dash, and parenthesis. The third kind of punctuation mark is the *spelling* mark, which is not really punctuation since it does not represent any sound and is intended only for the eye. The four spelling marks are apostrophe, quotemarks, hyphen, and slash; these marks are more trouble than they are worth and most languages do without them.

Freedom to Punctuate

You've probably been taught many punctuation rules which you've forgotten. Here are typical rules taken from current grammar books. *Use a comma after a long introductory phrase. Use a comma before a coordinating conjunction that joins main clauses. Use a semicolon between items in a series that have internal punctuation. Don't use a semicolon before* and *or* but. None of these rules needs to be honored. Rules provide no help in those cases where you have a choice between several possible marks, and these are the majority of cases. There is only one useful rule in punctuation: choose the right mark for the sound you want the reader to hear. For the four spelling marks that have no sound certain mere conventions are followed, and I'll get around to them after the real marks.

Here's a typical sentence that can be punctuated in various ways: *I went to her apartment and I found him. I went to her apartment, and I found him.* You heard the comma? *I went to her apartment. And I found him.* You heard the period? Obviously, no one could help you punctuate this sentence. If you were speaking the sentence, you'd speak it in a certain way. Your job is to punctuate it the way you'd speak it.

If you say *I went to her apartment and I found him* the sentence is flat. If you say *I went to her apartment, and I found him* you're suggesting there's something odd; with the comma you've split the idea of the sentence into two ideas. If you say *I went to her apartment. And I found him,* you're showing surprise: the second idea is important and needs a sentence to itself. And if you don't like these choices, you try other punctuation or change the words.

Punctuation is sounds, the sounds make sense, and if they didn't, there'd be no reason for them. Punctuation has meaning, and using it involves all of your skill and judgment. It's not a mechanical matter like spelling. In times past, dictionaries provided rules of punctuation, but they've given up on that. Rules requiring us to analyze the sentence grammatically only distract us from listening.

You might want to protest at this point: if the ear method is so easy, why isn't it taught? Well, it's easy in one sense, but hard in another. If you know how your writing sounds, it's easy, because then you have no choice: you just put in the mark that represents the sound you want. If you don't know how your writing sounds, it's hard, because then you can't choose the right mark.

To convince you that you're free to punctuate, whether you like it or not, let's look at some wellknown sentences; guess how these sentences were punctuated, and then I'll tell what punctuation the original writers used.

1. Give us the tools and we will finish the job.
2. My father taught me to work he did not teach me to love it.
3. My theory is to enjoy life but my practice is against it.
4. Read over your compositions and wherever you meet with a passage which you think is particularly fine strike it out.
5. Better we lose the election than mislead the people and better we lose than misgovern the people.

Here are the answers.

1. Churchill in asking for help during the war did not say or write a comma after *tools*.
2. Abraham Lincoln wrote *My father taught me to work; he did not teach me to love it.*
3. Charles Lamb wrote *My theory is to enjoy life. But my practice is against it.*
4. Samuel Johnson wrote *Read over your compositions, and wherever you meet with a passage which you think is particularly fine, strike it out.*
5. Adlai Stevenson, a good loser, wrote *Better we lose the election than mislead the people; and better we lose than misgovern the people.*

I used this exercise to prove that no matter how much you know about punctuating, you can't punctuate someone's stuff for him. And if you can't do it for him, he can't do it for you.

Period

In discussing the sound of the marks, we'll first deal with the full stops: period, question mark, exclamation point, and semicolon. We start with the period, the most important of the marks, though the comma is the commonest.

You already know that you put a period at the end of a sentence. In Lesson Five I'll talk about what a sentence is. No one by the way knows exactly what it is; a rough definition is that it's a meaningful word or group of words; it makes sense by itself and is not part of a larger group of words. Listen to the following: After the ballgame is over . . . Enough . . . The president . . . You can hear that I've not been saying sentences. The thoughts were incomplete, and you knew they were because you didn't hear any periods. I now transform these same words into sentences by putting period sounds after them.

> When is it? *After the ballgame is over.*
> Two fingers enough? *Enough.*
> He wanted to be president. *The president.*

You can't tell from the words whether you have a sentence; you tell from the period sound. In school, your textbooks said that you had to have a sentence to use a period, but obviously you have to use a period to have a sentence. You have a sentence if you can get away with making a period sound, and you have a sentence fragment when you write a period where no one else would make a period sound. The writer of sentence fragments doesn't know the basic mark of punctuation. And if you write a comma where others want a period, you've made the dread mistake called a *comma splice.* If you miss a period you're in trouble. Ok: *Bob is cute, Carol is cute.* Comma splice: *Bob is cute, I love blonds.* Probably ok: *Bob is cute, he's a Leo.*

What is the period sound? You've been hearing it all your life without analyzing it. The final word in a sentence is generally stressed; that is, the voice becomes a little louder or rises in pitch or does both. (This prepares the listener for the end of the sentence. You don't want to shock him with a sudden silence.) And then the end of the sentence is signaled by a lowering of the voice, in pitch or volume or both, which is followed by a strong and complete pause. The voice doesn't just drop and stop, it distinctly drops and stops.

For practice in hearing the sound of the period, listen to a radio or TV announcer and whenever he makes the sound, say Period or scratch yourself. For practice in distinguishing pauses from commas and from periods, read aloud the following, over and over, until you hear the melody. Read expressively.

> one two three four five
> one, two, three, four, five,
> One. Two. Three. Four. Five.

The *soundless* period used in abbreviations (*Mr., St.*) and in acronyms (M.C.P.) is confusing, but luckily it's on the way out. You may now be able to omit the period after common abbreviations (*eg ie Ms Dr Mt etc*). Instead of asking your boss whether you still need a period after *Co Mo Ca Prof Prot* or need periods in CIO UFO and CIA, pretend you are your own boss and leave the periods out. Arguments about whether to put the periods in seldom arise in Formal because you're not supposed to abbreviate in Formal. Under cross examination at his trial, Oscar Wilde was asked whether there was any crime of which he was not guilty, and he proudly claimed that he had never been guilty of abbreviation. You must follow him in this example.

Question Mark

Somewhere in a question the voice rises in pitch and usually increases in volume. The sound of a question means that things are up in the air and something must be done. Like a suspended chord in music, a question wakes people up.

Only real questions, not things that look like questions, have to be marked with a question mark. Looks are deceiving. You can't tell a question by the way it starts off or by the subject and verb being turned around. Any word or group of words can be a sentence, and any word or group of words can be a question.

> You were in her apartment, weren't you.
> You were in her apartment, weren't you?
> Pass the mustard.
> Pass the mustard?
> I wonder will it come.
> I wonder will it come?

Why did he *do* it!
Why did he do it?
May we hear from you at your earliest convenience.
Would you be so kind as to send the check by return mail.
In the meantime what about her.

The writer decides whether any questions are being asked.
Sometimes the question sound occurs early in the sentence.
Will you please (?) *get in bed before my feet get frozen.* You may forget to put a question mark at the end of the sentence, since that's nowhere near the question sound. Some languages solve this problem by putting a question mark before the sentence. If the question sound is miles away from the end of the sentence, it doesn't matter much if you use the question mark or not, but still, if there's a real question sound anywhere in the sentence, remember to put a question mark at the end.

People forget to put in their question marks because most questions reveal themselves by reversing subject and verb: *You do, do you?* This makes the question mark unimportant, but you must remember to put it in anyway. Indirectly quoted questions have no question sound: *She asked who Bob was.*

Though the question mark is thought of as a full stop, you don't always use a capital letter after it. *Are you ready? she asked.* No capital *s* in *she. Will it rain? will it sleet? will it snow? Who knows. Who* starts the new sentence; capital *w* therefore in *who.* Little questions that are parts of a larger question do not begin with capitals.

Exclamation Point

To exclaim means to cry out. Whenever you write something that's cried out use an exclamation point. An exclamation can't be whispered or muttered. The exclamation point comes after words like *phooey, ouch,* and *Holy Smoke* only if they have been exclaimed. Like fortissimos in music exclamations wear a person out, and you should never use more than a few.

Though the question mark is put at the end of the sentence, the exclamation point goes right after the exclamation. *No! No!*

No! A thousand times no! Since an exclamation comes to so emphatic a stop, sentences do not resume afterwards; start a new sentence with a capital letter—except in *quoted* exclamations. *"Drop dead!" she shouted.* Small *s* in *she.*

A writer should rarely have any problem in choosing between an exclamation point and another mark, but if she does, she should lean to the calmer mark. The question mark can suggest shock, but the exclamation point cannot suggest a question. Hear the differences in the following: *Why did he do it. Why did he do it? Why did he do it! What have I done. What have I done? What have I done!*

Almost every exclamation, by the way, is a quotation. The reason is clear: other people exclaim, the writer doesn't, because she's sitting down and is not supposed to be yelling at the reader. Even when she exclaims, it sounds like she's quoting herself. When quotes are used, the exclamation point goes inside the quotes. Only once in a hundred years would you end a sentence with a quoted exclamation inside an exclamation, in which case you'd put the exclamation point either inside or outside the quotes, or else look up what to do in some wise book.

Semicolon

The semicolon, the last of our four full stops, is easily the most interesting of the lot. People think of it as a kind of heavy comma, but that's all wrong—it's a period. Call it a light period. It definitely represents the period sound. The difference between the semicolon and the period is that after the semicolon you don't pause as long as after the period. If the reader is going fast there's no distinction between periods and semicolons, and therefore no point in using semicolons.

Since the semicolon is a kind of period you can't use it unless you have a sentence on either side of it. You use semicolons to put two or more sentences together to make one sentence. But that one sentence must be one sentence; all its parts have to add up to a single idea. You cannot link unrelated ideas with a semicolon. You can't say *I will arrive there tomorrow; I like to fly,* but you can say *I will arrive there tomorrow; I'm catching the midnight plane.*

Here are examples of correct semicolons. See if you don't hear them as brief periods.

> He hit the serve as hard as he could; she returned it easily.
> I need a vacation; I haven't had one in ages.
> Carol wore a dress; everyone else wore jeans.

What would happen if we didn't have the semicolon? Nothing much. The period can substitute for it, or in short sentences with closely related ideas, a comma can be and should be used in place of the semicolon. *Carol wore a dress, the others wore jeans.* The semicolon, a recently invented punctuation mark, shows its function by its appearance—it's a compromise between a period and a comma. It's used eagerly by those who can't decide between commas and periods. Good writers are decisive, and stay away from semicolons. Amateurs and professors use far too many. The sound of the semicolon often appears in speech; some period pauses are brief. But the distinction between a brief period pause and a longer one is not important. The semicolon is not much needed, if it's needed at all, and it seldom appears outside of Formal writing. Since it's a sign of Formality, use it, but don't become addicted.

It's tempting to use as a device for making longer sentences. If your readers want longer sentences, use semicolons, and if they want shorter sentences, don't. The temptation to make sentences longer should be examined. Stretching the sentence out may be a way of covering up a weakness in the idea. Sometimes the writer figures that if she makes the sentence impressively long no one will notice anything missing. If you find yourself resorting frequently to semicolons, that probably means the ideas are weak. Though a semicolon allows you to pack a sentence, you know a sentence is not a bag. It's more like a stroke or blow, and you want it to be a sharp one.

Some handbooks say not to use a semicolon before *and* or *but.* You can do this, of course, just as you can use a period before *and* and *but.*

Bob left his wallet in the car; but he didn't worry about it.
I thought it would be a headache; and I was right.

Some people who have never been told about the sound of the semicolon put it in the wrong place. They associate it with words like *however, meanwhile, instead, nevertheless,* and when they see one of these words they toss a semicolon in, half the time on the right side of the word, which is the wrong side. The semicolon, as a period sound, can't come after these words that are joining new thoughts to the sentence. Do not write *He was tone deaf, however; he liked disco.* So, period or semicolon *before* words like *however, furthermore, likewise* and a comma after. Test by the sounds. Semicolons are not commas. Students are misled by teachers who tell them to use a semicolon if they can't decide between a comma and a period. A writer should know whether she's tacking things together with commas or separating them with periods. Fudging by using a semicolon is not smart.

There's one minor use of the semicolon that has caused people to get a wrong notion of what the semicolon is. This is the semicolon for the eye only. Sometimes, in long sentences with many phrases and clauses, semicolons are used to separate the major items from the minor items—even though these semicolons should be commas.

> Three uniformed men walked into the room: General Kachow, a graduate of West Point; Admiral Boom, a graduate of Annapolis; and Colonel Bang, a graduate of the Air Force Academy.

> These are my favorite recipes: beef with ginger, cooked in my wok; Peking Duck which takes a day to make; and lasagna, the tasty Italian dish.

This use of the semicolon is unnecessary and confusing. The reader would just as soon find commas used thruout for the comma sounds as find a mess of semicolons and commas that requires him to remember the big items with semicolons and the teeny items with commas. You don't look at a sentence to see what it says, you read it to hear what it says.

Comma

Now we move on to the half stops—the comma, and three special varieties of the comma—colon, dash, and parenthesis. There is only one rule for the use of the comma: When you have a comma sound, put a comma in. What is this sound? It's a lilt or lifting of the voice which is then followed by a pause. In pronouncing the word before the comma, the voice is stressed, it rises in pitch or volume or both, then falls down a little and comes up again. It goes up down up. By going *up* before the pause the voice tells the listener that the sentence is not finished, that the pause is not a period, and that more is coming after the pause. The comma means *more coming*. It warns the listener that the approaching pause is not serious and that something will be added.

Let's listen now to the song of the comma. In the following sentence there is a clear pause but no comma sound. *My friend Lou watched TV.* There was a distinct pause before the verb *watched*. Now listen to the commas: *My friend Lou, who was ill, watched TV.* You sang *Lou* and *ill*. Now read the following sentences aloud.

Please move over.	Please, move over.
Our flag is red white and blue.	Our flag is red, white, and blue.
Look up Bob.	Look up, Bob.
Sometimes he does what he wants.	Sometimes, he does what he wants.
Her work is in fact excellent.	Her work is, in fact, excellent.
That night I did not expect the vampire.	That night, I did not expect the vampire.
Just think snow.	Just think, snow.
O phooey.	Oh, phooey.
I was born March eleventh at noon.	I was born March eleventh, 1960.
Pass me the jam.	Pass me the jam, she said.
I haven't thought much of Lola since she went out with Bob.	I haven't thought much of Lola, since she went out with Bob.

You shouldn't need more evidence to convince you that commas have sound and meaning, and that you can't put them in or leave them out according to whim or according to a set of rules. My advice is to forget everything you've heard about commas, if you haven't already, and concentrate on listening for the comma sound. As I said at the start of the lesson, the way to learn punctuation is to practice reading aloud with feeling. You'll be surprised at how quickly you'll master punctuation by reading with feeling and melody. Another exercise is to say the punctuation marks as you read: *She said comma quotation marks I love submarine races exclamation point quotation marks.* If your own punctuation is really terrible, do not punctuate as you write, but do it afterwards, while you read it aloud slowly and expressively.

A word of warning now. There are two places in a sentence where commas are put in unnecessarily. There may be a significant pause before the verb and before the object of the verb which emphasizes these important words in the sentence. Don't mistake these strong pauses for the comma sound. Don't stick commas in before the verb or before the direct object. Occasionally, when the subject of the sentence is a mile away from the verb, you can put a comma before the verb: *What I've always dreamed of and want more than anything in the whole world, is to learn to punctuate.* You heard the comma before *is.* If you heard it, you get to use it.

You're not in charge of spelling, but you are in charge of how you want *your* writing to be read. Using the comma is an art and you are the artist. Punctuation is correct only when it correctly expresses your intention. If you write, *Today, the case is different,* someone might tell you that the comma after *Today* makes the punctuation heavy. Your answer should be that you want *Today* emphasized, and that he can jump in the lake with his theories of heavy and light punctuation. Another example. *I need to have my hair cut twice a year, for school.* By putting the comma between *year* and *for school* you're saying that both ideas are important. A different example: *In this cake I use butter eggs flour and sugar.* Someone might ask Where are your commas? Answer by saying you wanted to go faster than *In this cake, I use butter, eggs, flour, and sugar.*

If you write *Hey Stevie, come here,* do you need a comma before *Stevie?* No, though rulebooks say you do. If you write *I made the sauce, and surprisingly enough, it was good,* do you need a comma before *surprisingly*? No, though rulebooks say you do. What were you taught about punctuating a series? *Buy me root beer, french fries and a hamburger.* Do you put a comma after *french fries*? Most teachers say leave it out, most handbooks say put it in. What do you say? That you haven't been told the truth about commas, that they represent comma sounds. If you're asking for root beer french fries and a hamburger, ask for them your way. Of course, you have to figure out what your way is. What's your way here? *Women should stay home to cook, clean and raise children.*

A final reminder. Commas often come in pairs. These paired commas set off parenthetical elements in the sentence. *Parenthetical elements* interrupt, and are not essential to the basic meaning of the sentence. *Csonka, the fullback, is strong.* The basic sentence is that Csonka is strong. The parenthetical or unnecessary idea is that he's a fullback. *Put that bomb down, Achmed, before you get hurt. Achmed* is parenthetical and enclosed by commas. You can't tell what is parenthetical in your sentences by looking, you have to listen. You know you have one if your tone drops, telling the listener you're interrupting the main message for lesser stuff.

Parenthetical elements are set off by commas, dashes, or parentheses. If the parenthetical element comes in the middle of the sentence make sure you *enclose* it in a pair of marks. Don't forget one of the pair even though the sound is not so strong at one end as at the other. If the parenthetical element comes at the start or the end of the sentence of course you need only one comma or one dash. Unfortunately, you always have to use a pair of parentheses; you can't get by with one, which causes a problem about whether to put punctuation inside or outside the closing parenthesis. This problem arises because it's double punctuation, which is an impossibility, since no one can make two sounds at once, at least not with the voice.

Dash

The dash looks like a stretched out hyphen. When you type a dash you type two hyphens. But the dash is the opposite of the hyphen. The hyphen holds two pieces together, the dash pushes two things apart. The dash marks a sudden and dramatic break in the thought or a sharp change in the tone. Whatever is set off by dashes is emphasized. The dash has a distinctive sound almost impossible to mistake: the word before the dash is heavily stressed, for the break in the thought must be sharp. Then the pause is an unusually long one. The dash pictures its sound.

> I knew nothing about men—until I met Reggie.
> I knew nothing about men until I met—Reggie.
> I never said he stole—rubber bands?
> Then he sat down—on the Pekingese.
> I like English—muffins.
> My dear—he said, and couldn't go on.
> It was midnight—Carol was in bed—maybe to sleep.

The dash is such a useful punctuation mark, conveying excitement or surprise, setting up jokes, indicating long pauses, that writers are tempted to overuse it to make the writing livelier. You may have received—or may have written—letters gushing with dashes. Did you hear the dashes in that sentence? Were they justified?

The dash is overused for another bad reason: to substitute for other punctuation marks. Unsure writers trust in the dash because they can use it anywhere. Unfortunately, dashes slow sentences down.

If overusing the dash makes it less dashing, it should be reserved for special occasions. If you're writing Formally, you're supposed to be calm, not gasping. English professors say that when a writer is born she is given only a certain number of dashes to use in her lifetime—and shouldn't waste them.

Parentheses, Brackets, Ellipses

You can tell when you have parenthetical or inessential parts in the sentence because the voice distinctly drops down. It does so even when the parenthetical matter is important or exciting and set off by dashes. Listen. *He asked her—he couldn't resist—for a date. She gave him one—from the box on the table.*

Commas are used to set off parenthetical matter that is *close to the meaning* of the sentence. Dashes *emphasize* what they set off. Parentheses *minimize* what they set off. Parentheses, which always come in pairs like quotation marks, look like arcs trying to encircle what's between them. That's a good way to think about them: as the writer's attempt to draw a circle around stuff she's not happy about putting in the sentence. Parentheses confess the writer's embarrassment at having to insert what doesn't really belong. Dashes introduce something dramatic, parentheses, something dull. Both devices tempt the writer to dodge the work of arranging the thoughts and working them in properly.

Note how the voice drops way down and almost disappears to read what's within parentheses.

> William Shakespeare (1564 to 1616) was a middle class hetero-sexual. He married Anne Hathaway (a shotgun wedding) when she was three months pregnant. He had three children (Judy, Susy, and Hamnet) before he was twenty one. In his sonnets (written around 1595) he talks about an affair with a Dark Lady (dark meaning brunette and also unknown).

As you see, these afterthoughts are just sneaked into the sentences. A writer with a lot of parentheses is goofing off. Interruptions are annoying, especially when unimportant. Try not to write a parenthesis that's an entire sentence. (If you do, naturally the period goes inside the closing parenthesis.) Punctuation never appears before the opening parenthesis. (There the fact that the parenthesis has a sound is recognized.) Punctuation is added after the closing parenthesis (if it's needed). Did you hear your voice drop for those parentheses of mine?

Similar to parentheses are *brackets,* which are highly special-ized. They are sometimes used in place of double parentheses, or parentheses within parentheses, but most publishers find these brackets within parentheses ugly and have stopped using them. That suits me; there's no need for a sentence to look like a tool rack. Brackets are still used to enclose comments and corrections in *quoted* material. If you have to interrupt or explain while you're quoting, what *you* say is put in brackets.

The *ellipsis* is another rare but useful sign. It's easier to use an ellipsis than to remember its name. The ellipsis is a row of three periods that shows that something has been omitted from a quotation. A three dot ellipsis has no sound. A four dot ellipsis, or a period plus an ellipsis, has the sound of a period. Brackets are used to put something *into* a quotation, ellipses to leave something *out. This damned sole* [sic] *was guilty . . . of the sin of average* [sic].

Informally, the ellipsis is used in place of the dash to suggest . . . anything. *He and she sank to the couch. . . .*

Colon

At the end of my treatment of useful punctuation is the colon. Not so long ago, the colon was used interchangeably with the semicolon; it used to be a light period. Today it's distinguished from the semicolon, though some people still confuse them. The colon looks like a double period, but it represents a comma sound or a dash sound. Ladies use it instead of the dash. It is *conventionally* used in writing the time (*6:15*), in giving chapter and verse (*Matthew 5:7*), and after formal greetings (Dear Ms:).

When used as a mark of punctuation within the sentence, the colon means *as follows, here's the explanation or list,* or *here's what he said.* It tells the reader to pay attention to what's coming. It catches his eye and brings the sentence to a pregnant pause, as if it were a heavy comma or a light dash. It should be used only when exactly suited to the situation, only to introduce an explanation or restatement, or a longish list or quotation. With a short explanation, short list, or short quotation, do not use a colon— use a comma or dash. Examples of proper colons. *Here is the weather report for tomorrow: increasing winds, small craft warnings on the Sound, followed by rain and possible hail storms. There are four basic nutritional groups: meat and fish, milk and eggs, cereals, and fruits and vegetables.*

Here are examples of improper colons. *The weather report*

says: fair and windy. This is what people want: bread, love, and dreams.
The colon is too strong in these sentences. It usually is when it comes right after a verb. Don't say *All he could think about was: My theory is:* There's a good test for whether you're justified in using a colon. If you can insert the words *as follows* before the colon without making the sentence too heavy, the colon is justified. For example, you wouldn't say *This is what people want, as follows: bread, love, and dreams.*

Now let's learn unforgettably the difference between the semicolon and the colon. If you're adding a new idea to your sentence, use a semicolon to fasten it on. If you're restating or explaining what you just said, use a colon. Whatever comes after a colon refers back to what was said before the colon.

> Look at the rising sun; we have gotten thru another night.
> Look at the rising sun: it has turned the clouds pink.

> Two years ago there was a happy event; and they named him Bruce.
> Two years ago there was a happy event: Bob and Carol had Bruce.

> The meeting had little business; it was swiftly done.
> The meeting had little business: they had to decide on buying a widget.

Some people love to use a capital letter after the colon if a complete sentence follows. This newfangled usage confuses some readers who can't see the point in starting a new sentence inside an old one. Of course, if the colon introduces a quotation or something that sounds like a quotation, then you follow the colon with a capital letter.

> She proposed a solution to the arms race: Armies should fight with their fists.
> He was a man of principle: So many women and so little time.

Apostrophe

Now for the last and least of the punctuation marks, the *spelling* marks meant only for the eye. These are the apostrophe, quotemarks, hyphen, and slash. If you ever become a big shot, do us all a favor and refuse to use the spelling marks. The sooner these jots and tittles disappear from the language the happier we'll be and the more time we'll have for fishing. I myself don't use these marks. But my publisher has insisted that I at least put the apostrophes in, saying that the world is not ready to give them up. What do you say, world? So I put the apostrophes in. Writing is very much a give and take affair.

The apostrophe is used to show contractions and possessives. *There's the boys' gym.* You didn't hear those apostrophes, did you? I hope not. Apostrophes are sprinkled all over or neglected entirely because no one can hear where they belong. They are misused not because writers are stupid but because apostrophes are useless. Strong players in the Game of English love to find misused apostrophes and then laugh or scowl, as the mood strikes them, at the weaker players. You must learn about apostrophes not because they're worth knowing but to protect yourself. Handbooks have whole chapters on the apostrophe discussing where to stick it in *Bess's, bosses', Jack and Jill's, Jack's and Jill's, Cortez'* and so on.

The possessive apostrophe originated a few centuries ago as a mistake: some printers thought that *Bobs book* was a contraction of *Bob his book,* and since they used an apostrophe in contractions, they stuck one in *Bob's,* and it's been there ever since. You must perpetuate this error and indicate possession by putting in an apostrophe and an *s.* If the word already ends in *s,* you need to decide whether to add another *s* after the apostrophe. Decide first how to spell the word before inserting the apostrophe. (This is easy advice for those who write by hand but hard for those who are typing and have to leave a space for the apostrophe.) Think whether you have a singular or a plural. If you're writing about the *executives john* or the *drivers side* think whether it belongs to one executive or driver or more than one. (The right form is usually the plural.) If *a lady* has *gloves,* write *lady* and then add the apostrophe and the *s.* If you're thinking of *ladies gloves,* write *ladies* and then add the apostrophe.

The question arises, you've put the apostrophe after *ladies,* do you need another *s* after the apostrophe? Whether you need one depends on you, not on rules. No rules cover all the possibilities. If you want the reader to *pronounce* another *s*, put another *s* in. It's unlikely you want the reader to say *ladieses*. But you have a real choice with words like *Jesus' Jesus's, Hess' Hess's, Jones' Jones's, Davis' Davis's. This is Jesse James' Cave.* Or, this is *Jesse James's Cave.* Or, this is *Frank and Jesse Jameses' Cave.* Simple, isn't it? The constructions are logical and can be figured out, if you have the time. Decide how many *bosses* or *Moses* you're talking about, and write down the singular or plural form. (Where you can avoid a *special* plural form, do it: write *the Roberts' dog* instead of going crazy over *the Roberts's dog* or *the Robertses'* or *the Robertses's dog.*) In short, if you have a word that does *not* end with an *s* or *z* sound, write in apostrophe *s*. If you have a word that ends with an *s* or *z* sound already, write in an apostrophe, and then write in another *s* if you *want* an extra *s* for a zizzizz sound. (In England the rules are different: you can't write *Mrs Jukes' knickers,* you *have* to write *Mrs Jukes's knickers.*)

Remember never never use an apostrophe with the *pronouns its, his, hers, ours, yours, theirs,* and *oneself.* These pronouns show possession, the apostrophe shows possession, and if you show possession twice you will be fired. Washington, Jefferson, and others with wigs used apostrophes with these pronouns, but they were confused. Leaving apostrophes out shows your careless, putting them in wrong shows you're a nincompoop. You only use an apostrophe with a pronoun when you have a *contraction.* Test whether you're having contractions by letting them relax. When tempted to write *it's,* try *it is* and see if that works, for *they're* try *they are,* and for *who's* try *who is.* This rule isn't much help, since the misspellings are usually the other way around: *you are* is spelled *your, they are* is spelled *there.*

Only a few words in English are contracted, since we have such short words already, and they cause few problems. You should notice when you're using contractions since they're poison in *very* Formal situations. In Informal you regularly use contractions unless you want to emphasize the words by using their full form. The distinction between contracted words and their full forms is important: *I am* versus *I'm, I will not* versus *I won't, I'd* versus *I had* and *I would*. Do not avoid contractions because you're puzzled about apostrophes.

Though the apostrophe used for contractions is older than the apostrophe used for possessives, it is disappearing first, from headlines and *Dont Walk* signs and so on. Bernard Shaw did not use the apostrophe in contractions, and got away with it, but foolishly continued to use it with possessives.

Some people who don't have to teach apostrophes find them amusing, like these: *the president's wife's secretary's daughter's boyfriend's cat, this is the man who saw it on Tuesday's report.* Have you ever used the double apostrophe—*Tony's's the best pizza in town?*

To be fair, I must admit that I can think of an instance in which the apostrophe is useful: *These hamsters look like my parents'.* If I've told you more about the apostrophe than you want to know, the same goes for me.

Quotemarks

The next pitfall is the most difficult punctuation mark of all, quotation marks. Correct use of these marks, which always come in pairs and have no sound and are used inside and outside of real punctuation marks, is incredibly complicated, and that's why they play a grand role in the Game of English. As a test, why don't you send in your solutions to this question: how do you punctuate a quoted exclamation appearing at the end of a quoted question? For example, *Did Bob ask, Did she really say* Yes? Anyone sending in the right answer will receive a large prize. *Did Bob ask, "Did she really say* 'Yes!'?"?(?)

Luckily, the use of quotation marks is now becoming confused, which may bring about the collapse of the system. Some publishers are starting to leave the marks out, at the insistence of writers, and some are using single quotemarks, dashes, angles, or odd marks where they used to use the standard double quotemarks, our little old handwritten friends, 66 and 99.

We'll now run through some current conventions in quoting. Quotemarks are not used with long quotations, which are set off by being single spaced and indented. A long quote is more than four or five lines of prose or more than two lines of poetry.

In an *indirect* quote quotemarks are not used, even though some of the words are directly quoted. Indirect quotes read faster than direct quotes and cause no punctuation problems. *Groucho said he would never join a club that would have him as a member. Nixon said he was not a crook.*

Quotemarks are used with direct quotations after a verb of saying, as in *he said, they asked.* A verb of saying is followed by a comma if needed and if the quote is going to be short, or a colon, if the quote is going to be long. *He said "damn." He said, "Damn." He said: "Damn the torpedoes! Full speed ahead!"* After the comma or the colon comes the open quotemarks, then comes the quote, starting with a capital letter. At the close of the quote, period and comma go *inside* the closing quotemarks. Colon and semicolon go *outside.* Putting the colon and the semicolon outside the marks is logical enough (though ugly) because the sentence is being resumed. Putting the *comma* inside the marks is an illogicality in the present system, if the colon and the semicolon go outside; but that's the way it's done, and that's the way to do it. When the quote is an exclamation or a question, the exclamation point or question mark go *inside* the quotemarks. When the whole sentence in which the quote appears is an exclamation or a question, the exclamation point or question mark goes at the very end of the sentence. In England these rules are different—so don't go.

Say punctuation to remember how it goes.

He said comma 66 I am amazed exclamation point 99

66 Really question mark 99 she said comma 66 to think I missed it exclamation point 99 (Small *t* in *to think* because the quoted sentence is being resumed.)

66 The Chinese comma 99 she argued comma 66 are (small *a* in *are*) the best cooks period 99

66 Bob will go comma 99 she said comma 66 he likes parties 99 semicolon but she thought to herself comma Shall I go question mark

Words thoughts and questions *in the mind* are not put in quotemarks. *Should I say Thank you? She's asked herself time and again, Will I ever learn to punctuate?* In writing dialogue, what each person says is a separate paragraph. You can't have two people talking in the same paragraph.

If you have a quote within a quote, put single quotemarks around it. When single quotemarks and double quotemarks coincide, questions arise about where to put the real punctuation marks. Such questions can often be solved. Be patient and sort everything out. (Problems of quotes within quotes are avoided by making one of the quotes indirect and thus getting rid of one set of marks.) Here's a quote within a quote: *Did he ask, "Why did she say, 'What's in it for me' "?*

In Formal do not use quotemarks to be funny or sarcastic or because you're ashamed of a certain word. In Formal you're responsible for the words you write, and putting some wretched words in quotes won't excuse you. You can't write: *This swimsuit is "sensuous,"* or *This food is "organic."* Formal people do not sneer. Don't use quotemarks for emphasis—*underline*.

Titles of small pieces—stories, essays, articles, and poems—are put inside quotemarks. *Everyone loved Pinckert's essay "Quotemarks."*

Hyphen and Slash

The style book for the Oxford University Press says that if you take hyphens seriously you will surely go mad. We won't worry about that.

The hyphen used to be a small mark at the right hand margin of the page to show that a word was being split. This little bar was invented to hold together the broken pieces of a word. Once having used the hyphen this way, people extended its use to join two words together that looked like they might be one word or ought to be one word. *Mail - man* finally did turn into *mailman, volley - ball* turned into *volleyball, sun - bathing* into *sunbathing*. The hyphen seems to be a useful way of bringing words together, but it isn't. It delays the acceptance of new compounds. This use of the hyphen is chicken: the writer is saying I want to write these two words together as one word but I'm afraid to do it.

If you want to combine two words do it. All of us have a sense of what words can be combined and what words can't. Some words look right when combined, some don't. These would not look right as one word: *pocket billiards, racing car, fellow traveller, split level,* and *ice cream.* So don't worry about whether there *is* a hyphen in combinable words; either combine them or leave them separate. Do you like *diningroom* or *warthog*?

Another useless use of the hyphen caught on: to join words being used as a single adjective before a noun. *It's a well-organized move. He's an all-round dockwalloper. She gave me a don't-give-me-that-stuff look.* This use of the hyphen is inexcusable, particularly since these joined adjectives, when they appear after the noun, are never hyphenated. *The move was well organized. Her look was don't give me that stuff.* But for the time being you have to use the hyphen this way, since everybody expects it: *two-room apartment, mashed-potato sandwich, million-dollar baby, suspicious-looking package.*

Another wacky use of the hyphen is with compound numbers. *Donuts? I'll take twenty-seven.* This hyphen developed because compound numbers generally appear before a noun, where they're hyphenated as a single adjective. Happily, this hyphen used with spelled out numbers is disappearing, so be brave and use no hyphens with any numbers or fractions. Write out *thirty five* and *three fourths* without hyphens.

Sometimes a hyphen is used to attach a prefix to a word when not using the hyphen might cause the word to be misread: *re-entry, post-operative, semi-trailer, pre-selected, ex-mayor, all-embracing.* But if you left the hyphen out, the words wouldn't be misread. You can now write *cooperative, semicolon, oldfashioned, newfangled, selfserving, microphysics*—hundreds of such words all without hyphens, and nobody squawks. Once a year you may find a hyphen with a sound (*Take this little-used grammar book*) but that doesn't justify fooling with them for 365 days.

The slash can be dismissed in a few words. It has become

fashionable as a shorthand mark that means *and or or both,* as in *his/her, country/western, social/political.* As shorthand it's welcome, but the ambiguity it stands for is unwelcome. The writer doesn't know whether to push the two words apart or pull them together, and draws a picture of her problem. But she should conquer her neuroses and make choices, not present ambiguities. If the slash means *and/or* and if you can't use the slash, you can't use *and/or* either. Instead say... *or*... *or both.* The slash is also used to show where lines of verse end when verse is written as prose. Roses are red,/ Violets are blue;/ If you like these dumb slashes,/ That's up to you./

Underlining

There is one other kind of punctuation I've saved till the end—underlining. It's not generally thought of as punctuation because it's not a point but a line; it's a tone, the tone of emphasis. Underlining (in print, italicizing) directs the reader to stress the words in saying them. In most written sentences the important words are naturally stressed and do not have to be pointed out to the reader. But sometimes you *must* underline: a seven word sentence like *I never said Nixon authorized that burglary* can have seven different meanings depending on which word is emphasized.

Like any device to achieve emphasis—exclamations, questions, dashes, abrupt sentences—underlining loses its effectiveness when used too often. But the device is not forbidden to you, no matter how Formal the occasion. You may have been taught *not* to underline for emphasis, but that's one of those rules intended to dampen your spirits. Examples of legitimate underlining: *You may write a check, but I prefer* cash. *The duchess said it was a* damn *shame.*

Anything you offer as an *example* should be underlined. *Dot your* i's *and* cross your t's. Really foreign sounding foreign words should be underlined. *I sang it* con amore *after I ate chile con carne.* See if you can underline the following correctly.

Ain't you got no onions? I ain't said I ain't. I ain't ast you is you ain't, I ast you ain't you ain't. Now is you or ain't you got no onions?

Today, almost everyone follows the convention of underlining the names of books, publications, ships, operas, and other works of art. This convention, which directs attention unnecessarily to these words, arose from the need to distinguish real names from the names of works of art. For example, if you write *in Hamlet,* the reader is supposed to be confused whether you're talking about the man or the play. This is hardly a problem. If you wrote without underlining that you loved Madame Butterfly and went aboard Queen Elizabeth no one is likely to be confused. This underlining of names is not needed, but since everyone does it, you too should remember to underline book titles, names of newspapers and magazines, and names of works of art. Small works of art—songs, poems, and articles—these are put in quotemarks.

We're now finished with punctuation. Remember that the marks belong to you, they're your way of conducting the reader. But you must know how they sound. Allow no one to fool with your punctuation. When you want your reader to go slowly or dramatically you provide the cues, lots of them. If you want him to go fast, use a quicker lighter punctuation.

If you're having trouble punctuating while you're writing, that's a tipoff the ideas are a mess. You haven't gotten the ideas clear, and they're not making clear sounds. You'll remember what I said in the lesson before, I hope, that when you struggle for words the ideas are defective. When you have good ideas, sentences you want to say, the right words come and the sentences punctuate themselves. Good writers never give a thought to punctuation. Where there's bad punctuation, there's bad prose. When Oscar Wilde said he spent the morning putting in a comma and the afternoon taking it out, he was kidding. A good writer never chooses punctuation, she hears it.

For your final test in punctuation, read over these sentences to pick out the one you'd use for the most laughs.

Take my wife, please.
Take my wife. Please.
Take my wife—please!
Take my wife—please?
Take my wife—please.

I tested you to see whether you read the sentences loud enough for you to hear the punctuation. Did you? I myself prefer the second version.

Here's a tough passage for you to punctuate. Don't peek at the answer, which follows.

Is Here come the judge your joke he shouted
No came the answer it is Sammy Davis Jrs

The answer.

"Is 'Here come the judge!' your joke?" he shouted.
"No," came the answer, "it is Sammy Davis, Jr.'s."

If I were in charge, I would drop 17 of those punctuation marks!

Is Here come the judge! your joke? he shouted.
No, came the answer, it is Sammy Davis Jrs.

In our next lesson we'll take care of grammar, the Rules of the Game. You'll be delighted that grammar can be handled in one lesson.

Lesson Four

Rules of the Game: Grammar

Rules of the Game

In a sentence all the words are related to each other; grammar is the attempt to explain the relationships. It's the study of sentences, or human speech. Obviously, speech can be studied from many points of view—how it develops, how it's learned, what it is, what it should be. Grammar is a huge subject and the term is quite vague.

It wasn't always so vague. The word is related to *graphic, autograph, graffiti*—having to do with things scratched or written. Grammar originally meant the study of *writing*. Writing, since it can be corrected, has fewer mistakes than spoken language, and thus the idea of grammar includes the idea of correctness, or good grammar. Grammar began as the study of what should be done in writing, not what is done in speaking. When Latin was no longer spoken but written, it had lots of grammar. English was spoken and had no grammar. In an English grammar school, students studied Latin. How could English be studied? It wasn't even dead.

The way English is taught in schools today, it might as well be dead. It's taught as if it was a written language. The children are taught not only that writing is different from speech but superior to it. This idea has to strike them as weird; they begin to suspect that their teachers are trying to push them around. They're bombarded with terms. Do this, Don't do that. Don't

you want to get ahead? Don't you know objective from subjective? One more fused participle and I'll scream! Students hate
this bottomless subject. It's so tricky even the teacher is confused.
She talks about sentences, sentence fragments, and comma
splices as if she knew what they were, but no one knows what they
are. She doesn't teach English, she teaches mistakes in English,
and she doesn't know what a mistake is. The students catch her
confusion, become anxious about using their mother tongue,
and some of them decide never to dare to write again, not even
letters.

Maybe I can help you change an old attitude toward
grammar and writing, and help you see that they are not so
threatening as all those Rules suggest. I'll try to show that there
aren't so many useful rules as you may have supposed. The good
rules, the basic rules, you learned in your crib, and needn't worry
about. The not so good rules, the arbitrary ones always being
changed by the mysterious Rules Committee, have to be followed, but there aren't many of them, and there's no cause ever
to be scared by them. If someone accuses you of syllepsis,
zeugma, or anantapodoton, laugh and say the construction is
common in Shakespeare.

There are as many rules as anyone wants to find. Luckily,
only a relatively small number of rules can be enforced. If few
people have heard of a rule, it's not much of a rule. On the other
hand, if *many* people have heard of a rule, it's not much of a rule
either: you don't get much credit for *not* saying *ain't,* but you get a
lot of credit for not dangling a participle—among those who
know a dangling participle when they see one.

An honest discussion of English grammar, grammar in the
sense of what has been done and what can be done in the
language, would require many volumes. But a description of the
language is not what people are looking for. They want a pre-
scription of what should be done. They want someone to speak
with authority and clear up the mess. They're looking for a
miracle. Any treatment of grammar that tries to be honest as well
as useful has to strike a balance between describing and pre-
scribing. I am not honest. I prescribe. I prescribe Formal (and
use Informal). I did not invent this Game.

To prove it's a game look at just one well known rule. Where's the mistake in these sentences? *No one loves her like he does. She treats me like I was her mother.* The supposed mistake is of course the use of *like* as a conjunction, which means, using *like* to begin a clause. These sentences are forceful and cannot be improved, but they are taboo—and have been ever since the poet Tennyson told Prince Albert that using *like* as a conjunction was vulgar. Since then, those who hate vulgarity have refrained from using *like* as a conjunction. Where did the rule come from? The Committee invented it. Is it a good rule? No. Must it be followed? Yes.

A mistake in grammar is an infraction of a rule, and it makes no difference whether the rule is defensible or whether you like it. Your audience decides when you've broken a rule. Just as any utterance can be a sentence, depending on whether the listener hears a sentence, so any utterance can be a mistake. Since you are at the mercy of your audience you had better think about what they expect, and forget about what is Right and Wrong under the Eye of Eternity or the eye of Miss Thistle-bottom.

Homers in one ballpark are easy outs in another. If you say to the delivery boy *I wish it were time for lunch* and *These frankfurters are for whom?* and *I am a better tipper than she,* he will think you sound pretty funny. If you say to the Duchess of Exurb *I wish it was lunchtime* and *Who are these hotdogs for?* and *I'm a bigger tipper than her,* she may never invite you back.

In this lesson on mistakes, I'll be talking about mistakes that will be discovered by the wrong people, who are in this case the Right People. There won't be any point in my trying to sort out big mistakes from little ones: all mistakes are big. According to one way of thinking, if you say *I brang the beer* or *I brung the beer* that would be a little mistake because you did not offend against meaning and got your point across. But most audiences would consider that a much worse mistake than if you said *I have conveyed to this place the carbonated, slightly alcoholic malt beverages.* A mistake is a mistake, whatever it is.

If a mistake is something that others think you're guilty of, it's not likely that you'll be able to avoid them. But the point of writing is not to avoid mistakes. I've made a thousand mistakes in these lessons, mistakes in English—I'm writing in English. It's good to make mistakes. Everyone should be willing to take his lumps. It's not good to go around thinking you're safe from mistakes. So don't get all upset by the uncertainties of grammar. I wouldn't want, and I don't think you would want, a situation in which certain people made no mistakes and others made all of them. A person who really knew grammar would not be fit to talk to.

What Good Is Grammar?

Not much. Grammar is largely negative and analytical. Some enlightened teachers of composition refuse to spend one minute talking about questions of grammar. Composition is putting things together, and is hard to teach. Grammar is taking them apart, and is easy to teach. Grammar goes on forever. Teaching it has always offered job security. The demand for grammar, like the demand for medical attention, is unlimited. Grammar is the perfect subject, since anyone can teach it and no one can master it. It is even being taught to a large number of apes, who have in fact been getting good marks. Though there are apparently no slow learners among these anthropoids, none has as yet come up with a striking sentence, much less a good essay.

I'm not giving you a grammar lesson because it's easy for me. I think you have to know a little grammar and from time to time have to review your knowledge of it if you're going to catch mistakes when you revise and proofread. It's hard to know what a mistake is if you have no idea of its name or why it's thought to be a mistake. A piece of advice like *Cut modifiers, conjunctions, and articles* isn't much help if you don't know what they are. Questions of usage focus on words, questions of grammar on categories. For some people the categories of grammar are too abstract, and they don't want to learn them or they soon forget them. We walk, but don't have to name the muscles we use. Why should we name the parts of speech?

If you asked a graduate student in English to name the parts of speech and the parts of the sentence it's unlikely he could do it. But this minimum of grammar is needed; these terms are your tools for taking a sentence apart. Everyone must be able to explain what each word is doing in a sentence. Analyzing sentences used to be called *parsing,* but few know this word, since parsing is not regularly done in schools anymore. Even *syntax* is dead, the thought of a tax of sin being too depressing. The poet Cummings says: Who pays any attention to the syntax of things will never wholly kiss you.

If a sentence can't be analyzed, questions of correctness can't be solved. You can generally trust what *looks* or *sounds* right, but not always. What you're used to may not be correct, especially in Formal. Some people are lucky and without knowing much grammar seldom fall into mistakes. They don't know it, but their subjects and verbs *agree,* their pronouns have clear *reference* and are in the proper *case.* Some people don't even know they're speaking prose. But almost everyone, including me, will benefit from the following review. I promise to hold technical terms to a minimum.

Grammar Quiz

To find out if you can skip this grammar lesson, why don't you take a little quiz and see how you do? Each of the following sentences is unacceptable in Formal. I bet that if you can pick out the error in each sentence you can name it or explain why it's an error, and if you can't name it or explain it, you can't pick it out.

1. As far as time, we have a whole hour.
2. Jim told Bob he was wrong.
3. I have more trouble with spelling than grammar.
4. Bob approved of Carol going.
5. I do not care whom she said did it.
6. For we women to back down would be silly.
7. He was in the Marines, and his son wants to be one too.
8. Is this enough questions for now?
9. Standing on the bridge the island looked dark.
10. The Senate along with the House of Representatives have adjourned.

11. I wrote to RSVP on the invitation.
12. I wish I were born in England.
13. He manages to occasionally change the oil.
14. First lie on the floor, and then you should jump up.
15. To shut the dog in, the gate should be closed.
16. Dress warm when you go out.
17. He was late so I left.
18. California's Governor Brown is cute.
19. I should have planned to have gone to the party.
20. It shouldn't take only ten minutes.
21. The chances of the car skidding or you losing control of the steering is great.

Now I'll give you the answers, using a few technical terms which will be explained later.

1. *As far as time, we have a whole hour.* A mistake in *diction.* The conjunction *as far as* has been confused with the preposition *as for.*

2. *Jim told Bob he was wrong.* The mistake is in the *reference* of the pronoun *he.* The reference is *ambiguous.* The sentence should be *Jim told Bob that Bob was wrong* or *Jim told Bob that Jim was wrong.*

3. *I have more trouble with spelling than grammar.* That should be *I have more trouble with spelling than with grammar.* This fault is a lack of *parallel* structure; the preposition *with* should be repeated to make the parallel clear. Similarly, the famous ad should be *Winston tastes good as a cigarette should taste.*

4. *Bob approved of Carol going.* This should be *Bob approved of Carol's going.* A mistake in *case;* the possessive case, *Carol's,* should be used before the emphasized noun, *going.*

5. *I do not care whom she said did it.* This should be *I do not care who she said did it.* A mistake in *case. Who,* in the *subjective* case, should be used, since *who* is the subject of the verb *did.* In choosing the pronoun, see how it's used in its own *clause.*

6. *For we women to back down would be silly.* Another mistake in *case.* This should be *For us women. Us* in the *objective* case is the object of the preposition *For.* Pronouns in the front of the sentence may look like subjects but often aren't.

7. *He was in the Marines, and his son wants to be one too.* This should be *He was in the Marines, and his son wants to be a Marine too.* A

mistake in the *reference* of a pronoun; *one* cannot refer to the plural *Marines*.

8. *Is this enough questions for now?* That should be *Are these enough questions for now?* This mistake is a lack of *agreement*, between a plural subject *questions* and a singular verb *is*.

9. *Standing on the bridge the island looked dark.* Should be *Standing on the bridge, we thought the island looked dark* or *As we were standing on the bridge, the island looked dark.* The mistake is a *dangling participle, standing.* Participles, like verbs, require subjects. The island isn't standing on the bridge; someone has to be standing. Hemingway wrote this sentence, but he knew what he was doing.

10. *The Senate along with the House of Representatives have adjourned.* That should be *has adjourned.* A mistake in *agreement* between subject and verb. *Senate* is the subject. Similarly: *The hammer along with three thousand tacks is over here.*

11. *I wrote to RSVP on the invitation.* Should be *I wrote on the invitation to RSVP.* The fault is a *misplaced modifier.* The modifier, the phrase *on the invitation,* should be closer to the word it modifies—in this case, *wrote.*

12. *I wish I were born in England.* That should be *I wish I had been born in England.* A mistake in the *tense* of the verb.

13. *He manages to occasionally change the oil.* Should be *He occasionally manages to change the oil.* The fault is a *misplaced modifier.* The adverb *occasionally* modifies the verb *manages,* not the infinitive *to change.* You *can* split an infinitive with an adverb, but not with one that belongs elsewhere.

14. *First lie on the floor, and then you should jump up.* Should be *First lie on the floor and then jump up.* The fault is a *shift,* in the verbs, from the imperative *lie* to the regular *should jump up.*

15. *To shut the dog in, the gate should be closed.* That should be *To shut the dog in, close the gate.* To shut the dog in is a *dangling* phrase. This *infinitive* phrase needs a subject.

16. *Dress warm when you go out.* Should be *Dress warmly when you go out.* A word usually considered to be an *adjective* has been used in place of an *adverb.* Here you want an adverb to modify the stressed verb *Dress.* (You could probably get away with saying *I am dressed warm.*)

17. *He was late so I left.* Should be *He was late and so I left.* A mistake in *usage.* In Formal *so* is not permitted as a conjunction. *And so* is ok.

18. *California's Governor Brown is cute.* Should be *Governor Brown of California is attractive.* California doesn't own Brown, so the *genitive* form *of California* is better than the *possessive* form *California's.* (And *cute* isn't Formal.)

19. *I should have planned to have gone to the party.* Should be *I should have planned to go to the party.* A mistake in the *tense* of the infinitive *to go.* You need the present tense after a verb like *plan.*

20. *It shouldn't take only ten minutes.* Should be *It should take only ten minutes.* The *should not* and *only* are a *double negative,* thought of as an offense against logic.

21. *The chances of the car skidding or you losing control of the steering is great.* That should be *The chances of the car's skidding or of your losing control of the steering are great.* This sentence had three mistakes. *Car skidding* and *you losing* are *fused participles.* The subject of the sentence *chances* should *agree* with the verb— *chances are.*

If you caught all of the mistakes, skip this lesson, unless you love grammar. I hope you got a kick out of spotting the mistakes. What could be more enjoyable than the mistakes of others? In *Informal,* every one of these sentences, with the possible exception of *Jim told Bob he was wrong,* is perfectly acceptable. If you were alarmed by some of the terms I used, don't be, because I'll explain them.

Eight Parts of Speech

Nouns are words that name persons, places, and things. Whatever exists or can be said to exist is a noun (or *substantive,* as it used to be called). Nouns can express action, like walking, swimming, thinking, but express it abstractly. Verbs call for an agent to perform the action.

For some reason *pronouns* are always named as a separate part of speech even though they're nouns. A pronoun is a noun that stands for another noun. There aren't many pronouns—*we, they, mine, hers, each, myself, which, that, another,* etc—but they cause a lot of trouble.

An *adjective* modifies a noun. Modifying means describing, qualifying, telling something about another word. Modifying is not a good term, since no word is actually changed by a modifier; another idea is simply added to it. Here are two adjectives: *a silk* dress. *Silk* is a descriptive adjective that modifies the noun *dress*. *A* is a limiting adjective, a special kind known as an *article*. It limits the number of dresses being talked about.

The *verb* is the most important part of speech. It's the word that allows us to make a sentence. It's needed for the predicate, or what is being said about the subject. A verb expresses action (he *ran*) or a state of being (he *is*). Verbs have tense and tell what happens in time. Nouns exist independently of time. Only humans are aware of time, only humans know verbs. When an ape makes a sign for a verb, like *eat,* he is really thinking about the noun, *eating,* and if you don't believe me, ask him.

Many words refer to action without being verbs. How would you tell if the word *swimming* is being used as a noun or as a verb? If it's a noun you can put an adjective in front of it (*good* swimming) and if it's a verb you can put an adverb after it (I'm swimming *well*).

The *adverb* is a versatile part of speech, since it can modify verbs, adverbs, and adjectives. Like a pair of pliers, it does a lot of jobs and is overused. Any modifier that's not modifying a noun has to be an adverb. *Slowly, Freudianly, very, too*—these are adverbs. An adverb tells where, when, how, or how much.

The *preposition* is a word that's placed in front of a noun (*pre*-posed), and shows the relationship of this noun to other words in the sentence: *for* a ride, *into* the river, *behind* bars, *off* the top, *in* the way, *with* pleasure. Prepositions are these familiar little words indicating direction that are placed before nouns. The noun that follows the preposition is called the object of the preposition, and the two words form a prepositional phrase.

The *conjunction* is used to join one word with another, one phrase with another, or one clause with another. Coordinating conjunctions are *and but or nor* and *so.* Coordinating conjunctions do not join similar things, they join similar structures. You can say *bacon* and *eggs,* you can say *bacon* and *motorcycles,* but you can't say *bacon* and *after breakfast.* You can't say *My car gets poor mileage* or *like it burns money.*

Coordinating conjunctions join words, phrases, or clauses. Subordinating conjunctions only join clauses, clauses that are not equal in importance. A phrase is a group of words doing one job. A clause is a phrase that contains a subject and predicate. Subordinate clauses—*after I left, who she was, because he snores*— these have to be joined to main clauses with subordinating conjunctions in order to make sense.

The last and least part of speech is the *interjection: ah, well, gee, ouch, um.* Interjections aren't at all interesting, since they have no relationship to anything in the sentence and are just thrown in.

Now you remember the parts of speech: noun, pronoun, adjective, verb, adverb, preposition, conjunction, and interjection. These terms from Latin sound a bit remote, but they're easy to understand. Everything in a sentence, whether it's a word, phrase, or subordinate clause, is being used as one of the eight parts of speech. The subject of a sentence has to be something being used as a noun. The predicate has to contain a verb.

Sentences would be easy to analyze if words were used as only one part of speech. But many words function as different parts of speech. *Round,* for example, is used as a noun (*round of drinks*), verb (*she rounds the turn*), adjective (*round table*), adverb (*all year round*), or preposition (*round the clock*). Usually it's easy to figure out what part of speech a word is being used as, but sometimes it's impossible. In *dress designer* is *dress* a noun or adjective? Is the possessive form of a noun (*Bob's*) a noun or adjective? In *It cost a dollar,* is *dollar* a noun or adverb? If you can answer these questions, you shouldn't be taking this lesson. But then, no one can answer these questions.

Parts of a Sentence

Every sentence has to have a subject, in the ordinary sense of the word and in the grammatical sense. A sentence has to be about something, and some thing has to be a noun. When you're looking for the subject of a sentence, do not just hunt for nouns—the sentence may have lots of fascinating nouns. Look for the noun the predicate is about. What is being said about the subject is called the predicate; that fancy word means *what is being said.* Therefore, you can't pick out the subject unless you've been thru the predicate. You can't start at the front of the sentence.

The predicate contains the verb. To find the subject and its verb you look for them both together. If you can't find the subject until you've found the verb and if you can't find the verb unless you know the subject, you had better find them both at the same time. You should hear or feel that collision of subject and verb. In good sentences this is easy to do, but in some it's difficult because the predication is so feeble. Some sentences are busted because the speaker forgets the subject. This accounts for the frequency of faults in *agreement* between subject and verb. The worst fault in grammar is to fail to make a sentence with a subject and verb, and the second worst fault is to have a subject and verb disagree. In the good old days we had missing verbs (*Kojak with his lollipops*). Today we also have missing subjects (*In choosing a career calls for a lot of thought*).

Sometimes a sentence has more than one subject and verb. Each separate subject and verb forms a clause. When a clause makes good sense by itself (*he laughed*) it's a main or independent clause. When it makes no sense by itself (*after she laughed*) it's a subordinate or dependent clause. Once you've found the main subject and verb of the sentence you look for phrases (groups of words that go together) and for clauses, which are phrases that contain subjects and verbs. Page long sentences are not hard to analyze; you just find the main clause or clauses and then take the lesser clauses one at a time and see what they're up to.

Subordinate clauses are used as nouns, adjectives, or adverbs. Here are noun clauses. I don't care *who said it.* I want to know *how he found out.* That is *why I'm angry. When he comes home* is no concern of mine. Here are adjective clauses. Here's the number *where you can reach him.* She's the one *who gave it to me.* Here are adverb clauses. *Since he left* I've been glad. *When he came back* I was furious. I took him back *because he's Bob.* You can't tell what kind of clause it is by looking at the first word. You can't tell

what anything in a sentence is by looking at it: you have to find
out what it's *doing*.

You want to recognize clauses right off, since many rules
concern them. You're not supposed to string many subordinate
clauses together. Problems arise about where to put the clause in
the sentence and about the tense of the verb in the clause. In
Formal, noun clauses are not supposed to start off like adverb
clauses, or vice versa: *I wonder whether* (not *if*) *she's going. The reason
is that* (not *because*) *I'm going too. The best part comes when* (not *is when*)
she says yes.

A verb can be one of several kinds. A *transitive* verb requires
an object to complete the meaning. *I put . . . I laid . . . I sliced. . . .*
Transitive verbs require direct objects that receive the action
named in the verb. (The object can be named or implied.) An
intransitive verb doesn't have an object. *I danced. I sang. I read.*
Most verbs can be transitive or intransitive, depending on the
sentence. *I danced*—what?—*a solo. I sang*—what?—*a song.* The
direct object answers the question What? The verb can also have
an *indirect* object. I danced a solo for *him.* I sang *her* a song. A few
verbs are always either transitive or intransitive. *Fall* is intransitive (you can't *fall* something) and *make* is transitive. Dictionaries
tell whether verbs are transitive or intransitive so we can avoid
mistakes in usage. *Lay, raise,* and *set* are transitive, but not *lie, rise,*
and *sit. Hens rise after setting and laying.*

A special kind of intransitive verb is the linking verb: *am, is,
were, have been*—all forms of the verb *to be.* They link the subject to
the part of the predicate called the *subject complement: The dinner
was* beancurds. *I will be* an evangelist. After the linking verb the
predicate is *completed* with an adjective or a noun.

There are a few special linking verbs besides the forms of
the verb *to be.* It's good to know them since they require the use of
an adjective after them instead of an adverb. He *became* hungry.
The lobster *looked* good. It *seemed* silly not to order it. The price
sounded cheap. The lobster *tasted* good, but soon he *felt* sick.

However long and complicated a sentence is, the basic
parts are simple: a subject and a predicate. The predicate contains a verb. The verb can be followed by nothing, by an object
complement completing the sense of the verb, or by a subject

complement referring back to the subject. Everything else in the sentence modifies some part of the basic sentence. All modifiers are adjectives or adverbs.

Subject and Verb Agree

Subject and verb have to agree, which means that a singular subject takes a singular verb, a plural subject a plural verb. Mistakes in agreement are common in speech but unforgivable in writing. Often the speaker is merely interested in naming her subject and then she aborts the predicate, or gets so excited by the predicate she forgets her subject. If she remembered that both are needed and framed the sentence in her mind before saying or writing it, she wouldn't make faults in agreement. Examples of the fault: *The woman with all those cats* live *in that house. The value of these fine Victorian homes* keep *going up.* You check the following: *All we heard at night were crickets. There are five years' difference in our ages. What has been, the doctor asked, the results of the tests? This book as well as four others have fallen into the bathtub.* Whenever you write a sentence with an inch or more between subject and verb, you better check whether the two agree.

If you can think of your subject as a number of separate *items* or think of it as a single *group,* then *you* decide whether the verb should be singular or plural.

> The arm and the hand (is, are) held out straight.
> Here (is, are) pencil and paper.
> A variety of drinks (was, were) offered.
> Two and two (is, are) four.
> The memoranda (is, are) on the desk.
> The family (is, are) sitting down.

No one can guide you in these choices; you have to guide your audience. You don't often have this freedom. You can't say *they is* and *one are.* And unfortunately your options have been limited in some cases by the Rules Committee cracking down. In Formal you have to use a singular verb after *either, neither,* and *everyone.* You cannot say *Neither of them are there.* Also, you say *There are more than one,* not *There is more than one.*   The Committee is trying to make *none* singular (*none is, none was*), but this pressure can still be resisted.

When you have a double subject separated by *or* or *nor,* and one of them is singular and the other plural, which verb do you choose? *Either the president or his advisers is mistaken.* Should you use *are* mistaken? Use the subject closer to the verb to determine the verb. *Either the president or his advisers* are *mistaken.* You can do the same thing with different forms of the verb: *Either he or I am going crazy. I am the one who is going crazy.* (Don't say *I am the one who am going crazy.*) Also, *not only we but Carol is going crazy.* If that sounds clumsy say *Not only we are going crazy but Carol is too.* If you don't like that keep plugging away. You're expected to have lots of time to do things right.

Getting Tense

Only foreigners make serious mistakes in verbs, and they are forgiven because we understand how complicated our system of verbs are. (Catch that mistake?) Some supposed mistakes are made by dialect speakers using their standard forms. *He come, she fooling me, I be surprise.* Dialect speakers have to shift to the dialect of the ruling class, or become the rulers theirself.

Native speakers who are not burdened with a dialect cope miraculously with English verbs despite their unusually complicated system of tenses, moods, and voices. We can say such things as *If I were to have been being beaten, I would have had to protest* or *Bob, when Carol had had* had had, *had had* had; had had *had had the teacher's ok.* No one can choose the right tense by looking in the rulebook. *I find I like English, I find I liked English, I found I like English, I found I liked English.* Rules tell us the right form for the right tense, but can't tell us what tense we want. We have to feel tense. When we're writing a sentence and have to think about the tense, there's something fishy. Simplify the thought to avoid an outlandish verb phrase.

We won't review our verb system but I will warn about two popular mistakes. The verb *would have* is threatening to replace had. *If he would have been there, this would not have happened.* (Should be *If he had been there. . . .*) *Would* and *could* sneak in to replace *will* and *can. By proofreading we could* (should be *can*) *catch our mistakes. If you look closely, you would see* (should be *will see*) *why TV is called the Boob Tube.*

Here are some sentences that test your feeling for the right tense.

> The people had cheered when the Pope (had passed, passed) by.
> He (has made, made) so much money he bought a station wagon.
> (Finishing, Having finished) his writing, Bob collapsed.
> The market has been dropping because the buyers (have been, are) scared.
> If I (were, had been) living then, I would have been drafted.
> I'm exhausted, (being, having been) awake all night.
> We should have asked him to (have sponsored, sponsor) us.
> After she gave up Perrier, she (feels, felt, has felt) better.

In these sentences, the first choice was wrong. You probably discovered that if you think about the tense you get confused and are tempted to pick the more complicated one. But the seat of your pants is right in telling you to choose the simplest, easiest verb. Check the tense by making sure that if one thing happens *before* another, it's put in an earlier tense, if it happens at the *same* time, the tenses agree, and if it happens *after,* it's put in a later tense. All tenses look good, so don't look at them—*say* them.

Shifts

When subjects or verbs are unexpectedly and unnecessarily changed inside the sentence, we have what's called a *shift* in the point of view. Shifts are very common—unnoticed in speech, but noticed in writing. They are borderline faults, since a writer is allowed to change subjects and verbs. It's only when she does it needlessly, jerking the reader, that she's committed a fault. Sentences with shifts *look* ok, and to catch the mistake you have to hear it.

Everybody should wash your hands before eating.
Catfish caught the ball and then throws it home.
She was a polite girl, or so it had always seemed to me.

In the first sentence *Everybody* shifts to *you*. In the second, past tense *caught* shifts to present tense *throws*. In the third, the subject *she* shifts to *it*.

Shifts to the present tense are common, since thinking is always in the present. In the historical or literary present, past events are viewed as happening now or as always happening. *Hamlet picks up the skull. At the concert Mozart plays beautifully.* This literary present tense is not used so much in English as in other languages—which is fine, since it's confusing. Stay away from it, and use it only for a synopsis. Don't know synopsis? Where's your dictionary? Give me twenty pushups.

The use of the present tense is also complicated by what's called the eternal present. *He believed all men* are *created equal.* In Formal, a truth is expressed in the eternal present and an untruth is put in the past. *He thought marriage* was *a trap. He thought the world* is *round.*

There are needless shifts in the *voice* of the verb. In the active voice: *Catfish caught the ball.* In the passive voice a word that ordinarily would be a direct object is made the subject, and then receives, passively, the action of the verb. *The clock was wound. I'm being stung by a bumblebee.* Don't shift between the active and passive voices as some dope does here:

Carol shopped all over, and the widget was finally purchased.
I hate writing, and am made sick when I have to do it.
The football was kicked and went seventy yards.

Also, don't shift between the moods of a verb:

Give me a drink, and then you should read this sentence for me.
Carol is offering the appetizers when she drops them.
He takes a break when he is doing his homework.

Do not change the subject within a sentence unless you have to. You can change it of course, if you can justify having different subjects in one sentence. Here are sentences in which the subject is shifted and the gears stripped.

> This medicine will help you, and you will feel better instantly.
> The hunter entered the clearing, and the leopard was spotted.
> I read science fiction; it's exciting to me.
> *Hamlet* will be read by each student; then you will write a report on it.
> Your hair should be shampooed and the shampoo should be rinsed thoroughly.

For practice you might like to repair these sentences. You have enough trouble with your own? I understand.

Dangling Verbals

Some words look like verbs, are made from verbs, have a couple of tenses, take subjects and objects like verbs, but really aren't verbs at all. They are not used as verbs, but as nouns, adjectives, and adverbs. They are *verbals,* and come in three kinds—gerund, participle, and infinitive. The gerund is the form of the verb ending in *-ing* that's used as a noun. *Dancing is healthy.* The gerund *dancing* is the subject of the sentence. *I like dancing.* The gerund *dancing* is the object of the verb *like.*

The participle is a verbal used as an adjective. *Dancing too fast, I fell.* The participle *dancing* is an adjective that modifies the noun *I. I am happy dancing the tango.* Here the participle *dancing* trails the noun it modifies, *I.* The present participle, like the gerund, ends in *-ing.* A past participle uses—guess what? the past participle of the verb. *Having swum the channel, I am tired. Swum* is the past participle. If it's not clear what noun the participle modifies, we have the hilarious dangling participle. *Born in 1564, his birthplace was Stratford. Born,* a past participle, cannot modify *birthplace. Being late to work the boss fired me. Being late* does not modify *boss. Eating our lunch, the cow came toward us.* This is wrong, since the cow already had lunch. *In the bushes sighing softly, she felt the breeze. Lying in the hammock, it struck her that Bob was ok. Law Protecting Sailors Attacked by Admiral.*

The third kind of verbal is the infinitive. The infinitive is the word *to* plus the infinitive or timeless form of the verb. *I want to dance. To dance* is the infinitive used as a noun. *To dance is fun. To dance* is the subject. *That's a long time to dance.* Here the infinitive is used as an adjective modifying *time. To dance you need good shoes.* Here the infinitive is used as an adverb modifying *need*—need *how.* There's a past infinitive for prior action (*to have danced*), but it's rarely used.

These verbals—gerunds, participles, and infinitives—often join with other words to form verbal phrases, as *walking to work fast, filled to the brim, to dance all night.* You'll recall that to exist a verb needs a subject (named or understood), and the same is true of verbals. It must always be clear what subject is performing the action. If there's confusion, you have a *dangling* verbal. Here's a dangling gerund. *By walking to work, a half dollar was saved.* A dangling participle. *Walking to work a half dollar was saved.* A dangling infinitive. *To save a half dollar, work is in easy walking distance.*

You only have dangling verbals when you speak of actions to be performed by a particular agent. If the action is general or impersonal, the verbal doesn't dangle. *Considering the difficulties, the results aren't bad.* Here *considering* does not dangle, because no one in particular is supposed to do the considering. Similarly, the following are ok: *Speaking frankly, the Yankees can't win. Weight can be lost by eating only hotdogs. To be brief, grammar is duck soup.*

Similar to the verbal phrase is the elliptical clause. In an elliptical clause the subject is left out: *if awakened, once aroused, while on duty, until exhausted.* An elliptical clause dangles when its subject is not the same as the subject of the sentence. *While walking my dog, the fire alarm sounded. When tender, turn down the flame. Beer cannot be bought if under twenty one.*

Prepositions: Problems of

A verbal phrase is used as a noun, adjective, or adverb, and so is a prepositional phrase. The prepositional phrase is almost always an adverb, telling us where, when, how, or how much. *I walked in the rain. In the rain* is a prepositional phrase used as an adverb, and modifying *walked*—walked where?—*in the rain. For coming in late, I got the sack. For coming in late* is a prepositional phrase used as an adverb modifying *got*—got how. *A man with a moustache rehired me. With a moustache* is used as an adjective modifying man—what kind of man. *In the lounge is not a safe place to hide. In the lounge* is used as a noun, the subject of the verb *is.*

You'll be pleased to know that the only mistake you'd make with the prepositional phrase is to misplace it. Since most of the phrases are adverbs, and since adverbs can easily be misplaced, you will, from time to time, misplace a phrase, as is done in the exciting sentence, *Throw mother from the train a kiss.* Here are other misplacements. *With his strength, the coach made Csonka the fullback. The teacher told us on Monday to do it. She served him in pajamas on paper plates. She kissed him in the narthex. She stuck her tongue out at him thru the window. These cats have short tails with blue eyes.*

Phrases starting with *with* are often misplaced because it's hard to figure out what they modify. *I like swimming and tennis, with tennis my favorite.* What does *with tennis* modify? *With* can be a fuzzy word expressing a fuzzy connection of ideas. *He goes swimming with a swimsuit. Think about Bob along with Carol.* In Formal watch out for loose *with phrases,* and never write a long *with phrase.*

Since a preposition indicates direction and implies movement, the noun in the prepositional phrase is thought of as an *object.* Don't say *For* we *to do that would be wrong.* Say *For* us. *With Bob and I* cooking should be *With Bob and* me *cooking.* You want to recognize prepositional phrases right away in order to use *objective* pronouns with them.

That you shouldn't end a sentence with a preposition is one of those rules no one understands but everyone has heard about. There, I just ended a sentence with a preposition—*about.* Or did I? Actually, *about* is part of the verb, *heard about,* and not a preposition at all. People confuse prepositions with verbal particles. *What are you looking for? For* is not a preposition but part of the verb *are looking for. This is the kind of nonsense I won't put up with. Up* and *with* are part of the verb *put up with.*

So what's the fuss about ending sentences with prepositions? What's objected to is constructions in which words that should be together are torn apart. In *What did you give me that book to be read to out of for?* the real objection is to the separation of *for* and *what*. Other examples. *This is the man whom I spoke to you on Tuesday about. I admired the ease which he wrote with.* These ugly sentences are easily repaired. *This is the man about whom I spoke to you on Tuesday. I admired the ease with which he wrote.* You get the idea. Instead of saying *whom blank blank about, which blank blank with,* say *about whom, with which.* Also, you run into no problems with witchy *which* or treacherous *whom* if you change the sentences to get rid of them altogether: *The man about whom I spoke* becomes *the man I spoke about, the ease with which* becomes *his ease in.* There are ways to skin a cat, and you keep trying until you find one you like or until you give up.

When you're ending a sentence with what looks like a preposition, think whether this forlorn word is needed. *I want the donut with the hole in* becomes *I want the donut with the hole. Which tree was it the cat climbed up?* becomes *Which tree did the cat climb? What did he want to say that to us for?* becomes *Why did he want to say that to us?* And check whether the word does not belong where it is. *What are we supposed to talk about? About* belongs with *talk.* You wouldn't say *About what are we supposed to talk? Which steps did he walk up?* You wouldn't say *Up which steps did he walk?* Usage, whether Formal or Informal, should always sound like English. You don't want people to laugh at you just because you're obeying orders.

The Case of Six Pronouns

One of the blessings of English is that nouns are not inflected as they are in other languages; that is, the form of the noun is not always being changed according to the way it's used in the sentence. English plurals are formed regularly by adding *s*, with a few exceptions such as *ox oxen, leaf leaves, sheep sheep.* Possessives are formed regularly by adding *s*—Carols, Bobs. (In writing some people add apostrophes.) All these *s*'s in plurals and possessives add to the geeselike hissing noises English makes.

With pronouns we run into a few problems of inflection,

which unfortunately play a major role in the Game of English. Nouns in a sentence are subjects, possessives, or objects; the three uses of the noun are called *cases,* subjective, possessive, and objective. The possessive case is no problem. And with the hundreds of thousands of nouns in English, there are no problems with the subjective and objective, since they're the same! We're so unused to thinking about case we resent it in foreign languages and fall into frequent errors in using the few pronouns we have that show it.

Only six words in the whole language show the objective case. These six are *me, him, her, us, them,* and *whom* (*whom* includes *whomever,* which is nearly kaput). If you can use these six words without making a mistake, skip this lesson. Still with me? I thought so. Everyone is puzzled by *whom.* Wishful thinkers have been telling us for ages that *whom* is dying, but this is not the case. The faster it dies in Informal, the livelier it gets in Formal.

We'll get to *who* versus *whom* in a minute, but let's do the easy pronouns first. When a pronoun is an object, *direct, indirect,* or *prepositional,* for goodness sake use the objective case. When it's a subject use the subjective case. Even if you can't tell objects, you can tell subjects, because they have verbs.

Rule number one is pay no attention to the position of the pronoun in the sentence. Just because it comes near the start of the sentence does not mean it's a subject, and just because it comes after the verb does not mean it's an object. Most Americans now say *Between you and* I and *With* we *girls* and *Among* we *students.* These errors arise partly from illiteracy, but mainly because the position of words in English sentences is so important for the meaning.

Here are examples of the correct choice of the *objective* case: *Along with* us *taxpayers, he voted for the budget. Besides you and* her, *who is going? The teacher wanted Bob and* us *to learn.* If you're puzzled by these objective pronouns, figure out why they're objects, of what verb or preposition. In *Let's you and* me *learn this grammar, me* is objectively correct; *you and me* is another way of saying *us,* the object of the verb *let.*

Here are examples of the correct choice of the *subjective* case. *It is* I. *It is* he. *This is* she. In these sentences *I, he,* and *she* are another way of saying the subjects *it* and *this*, and that's why they're in the subjective case too. Informally, everyone says *it's me, that's him, it was her, there were us and four others.* Formally, you should say *It is I, it was she, there were we and four others.* Answering the phone at home, you'd probably say *That's me,* but at the office you'd say *This is she.* Since this kind of switching about is so common, when people find themselves in Formal situations they try to change every objective pronoun they find into a subjective pronoun, and are guilty of what is known as overcorrectness, as in these examples: *The boss wants we secretaries to call him Buddy. The editor would like she and I to revise the article.* English teachers have fits about overcorrectness, thinking it to be social climbing, but it's quite unconscious. Since compound subjects are more common than compound objects, people assume that a pronoun that follows *and* has to be subjective. They say *He told Bob and I,* though they would never say *He told I.*

The following examples are also *incorrect.* Figure out why. *If it had been* her, *I would have smiled. We'll do it, you and* me. *Going there does not appeal to you or* I. *Toys are* us. *A number of we grammarians find this fun. It was hard for them*—she *and Bob.*

Whether you use the possessive or the objective case before a gerund (*she watched* his *dancing, she watched* him *dancing*) depends on what you're emphasizing—the action or the doer. *Bob approved of* them *going instead of him. Bob approved of* their *going instead of staying. He was sad to see* them *leaving. He was sad to see* their *leaving so soon.* You decide which meaning you want. In Informal, the possessive is never used with the gerund, even when there's ambiguity: *Your husband is against* me *smoking.*

Conjunctions are often interpreted as prepositions, which confuses the choice of the pronoun. *I'm taller than* (she, her). *He will do it, or* (they, them). *Everyone liked it but* (I, me). *She drives as fast as* (I, me). If you choose the subjective pronouns, that means you feel the presence of a silent verb or else you love subjective pronouns. The objective pronouns sound more modern and Informal. In the past, *than, as,* and *or* could not be interpreted as prepositions, and you had to use subjective pronouns with them. Some old clubhouse pros may try to bring this rule back into the Game, so watch out.

For Whom Are You Looking?

The choice between *who* and *whom* is confusing for several reasons. One reason was already mentioned: people have been told so often to use the subjective pronoun (*It is* I, *This is* she) they tilt to *who*. Another reason is that whenever this pronoun is heavily stressed in speaking, the choice is *who*, and never *whom*. You want *who* to come? You gave it to *who*? In writing, this heavy stress can't be heard (unless the writer is brave enough to underline), and *who* reverts to the calmer *whom*.

The main reason why *who* replaces *whom* is that it's interpreted as the subject of a silent clause, *who it is*. Instead of saying the correct *Guess whom*, people say *Guess who*, meaning *Guess who (it is)*. Instead of saying *Whom do you want?* they say *Who do you want?* meaning *Who (is it) you want?* Instead of saying *Whom are you talking about?* they say *Who are you talking about?* meaning *Who (is it) you are talking about?* Instead of saying *I know whom we think we want* they say *I know who we think we want*, meaning *I know who (it is) we think we want*.

You may want to scream at this point and say Why are you telling me how these mistakes arise? Just tell me what to do! I'm telling you. Use *who* whenever you hear the silent verb after it. If you do this you're not making a mistake. You can't hear the silent verb where you really have to use *whom*. You say *With whom?* because you wouldn't say *With who (is it)?* You say *He loved whom?* because you wouldn't say *He loved who (is it)?* You say *I am looking for whom, it was given to whom, it was liked by whom,* because you do not think of these whoms as beginning clauses. That's the solution to *who* versus *whom*. It's the solution you've been using unconsciously for a long time. The ear is now the test for correct *whoms*.

Educated people overuse *whom* as uneducated people overuse *who*. They choose *whom* in *error* when it is followed by expressions like *I think, they know, we saw*. Errors: *He's one* whom *they say won't let you down. It was Bob* whom *she said started the fight. We'll ask* whomever *we find knows the way*. Check the case of the pronoun by how it's used *in its own clause*.

Finally, try not to separate *whom* from its preposition. Say *from whom, of whom, about whom,* and don't say *Whom did you get it from? Whom are you asking the favor of? Whom are you talking about?* These sentences are awkward because they start with *whom* in the subject position and because the phrases are split. Informally you say *Who are you sitting with?* Formally you say *With whom are you sitting?* Avoid *Whom are you sitting with?*

Fatherless Pronouns

Pronouns save us much time and effort. When we're doing a piece on Transylvanian vampire researchers we say *they* and *them* and save lots of time. Pronouns are so lovable they are used even when they shouldn't be, when it's unclear what they refer to. Faults in the *reference* of pronouns are common as Kleenex; proofreaders need to check every pronoun. If the antecedent (the noun the pronoun stands for) is too far from the pronoun, if there's confusion about which noun the antecedent is, or if the pronoun doesn't match the noun—for example, a singular pronoun for a plural antecedent—the poor little pronoun is off on its own, and its parent must be found.

Faults in reference are common because the writer has a clear idea of the antecedent, but the reader doesn't, and can't get it from the pronoun. In speaking, faults in reference seldom occur, because we don't frame long sentences requiring lots of pronouns, and we make antecedents clear by emphasis in the voice. We can say things like He told *him* what he owed to *his* mom, but in writing, the pronouns have to be sorted out.

Here are examples of lost pronouns.

Each team member should decide whether they want to play.
We should feed those who need it.
There's a fly in your soup; do you want another?
A hermit is happy, but it's hard to make a living at it.
To Bob's way of thinking, he knows everything.
To his way of thinking, Bob knows everything.

Faults in personal pronouns are not as annoying as faults

in the use of *this, it, that, which,* and *such.* These are often used in a broad, vague way to refer to more than one antecedent. They can refer to a whole list of things, but not to two different things. The reader must never be forced to go back:

> He used to take the bus, but now it doesn't appeal to him.
> She told him she loved him, and gave him a flower, and this made him happy.
> I didn't wash my hair last week, which I never do.

This one may be ok:

> In the third quarter they fumbled twice, and in the last quarter they missed three field goals, and that's why they lost.

Faults in reference are akin to shifts: the writer forgets what she's said (prompting us to do the same). *If everyone doesn't pay their taxes, they'll get you. Everyone* and *no one,* by the way, are followed in Formal by singular pronouns (*he, his, him*) and in Informal by plural. Formal: *Everyone loves* his *mother.* Informal: *No one loves* their *mother all the time.* And while we're still on pronouns, remember in Formal to avoid saying *you* when you mean *one.* One *should never pour with his left hand.*

Conjunctions and Parallels

Coordinating conjunctions are the simple little words *and but or nor so for yet* that join words, phrases, and clauses. What is on one side of a coordinating conjunction must balance what is on the other by having the same grammatical structure. When the sides are not balanced, the fault is called a *lack of parallelism.* Some non parallel structures are easy to spot. *Betty loves swimming and to play tennis.* Some are hard to spot, because the sentence is complicated or there's a long list in it. Did you just spot mine? I should have said: *because the sentence is complicated or because there's a long list in it.*

The two things being coordinated by the conjunction don't have to be *like* each other; they only require the same structure. You can say: *Lying on the table are the oranges, bananas, and penguins.*

You can't say *Lying on the table are the oranges, bananas and I can't tell what those funny birds are.* You can say *He is dark, handsome, and over thirty. Over thirty* is a phrase, not a single word, but it's an adjective like *dark* and *handsome.* You can't say *He is dark, handsome, and snores.*

Informally, no one ever worries about parallelism. Informally anything can be joined to anything with the magic glue—*and. She said that she wouldn't go, and if I wanted to and she knew I was going that would be ok.* In Formal that would be *She said that she wouldn't go and that if I wanted to go and if she knew that I were going that would be all right.* In Formal, words have to be added to show the parallelism. This helps in a courteous way to make everything perfectly clear, even at the risk of wordiness: *The artist lives in agony and ecstasy.* That becomes *The artist lives in agony and in ecstasy.*

To give you practice in drawing parallels here's a little drill.

> Life is a welcome burden and like a huge crumb of cake being carried by an ant.
> Life is a welcome burden like a huge crumb of cake . . . or
> Life is a welcome burden and is like a huge crumb. . . .

> She said she would not go but to pick her up anyway.
> She said she would not go but we should pick her up anyway.

> Tell the driver to drive fast and when you have to be there.
> Tell the driver to drive fast and tell him when you have to be there.

> I boiled the potatoes and macaroni for salad.
> I boiled the potatoes for potato salad and the macaroni for macaroni salad.

Do these yourself:

> Americans believe two things: that there is no free lunch but you can get 40,000 miles on a set of tires.
> By walking I save money as well as getting exercise.
> She is a woman of great beauty, and who has great wealth.
> I want to laugh and to sing and make love.

Some of these revisions may have struck you as fussy, but

Formal is fussy. People love to fuss. If they didn't we wouldn't always be saying Don't go to any fuss.

Comparing Adjectives

No big problems arise with adjectives, which is one reason people love them. Adjectives are the fourth most common part of speech, after nouns, pronouns, and verbs. Unlike nouns, pronouns, and verbs, adjectives are not inflected, except for a handful that change their forms in comparisons: *hot hotter hottest good better best, few fewer fewest.* The comparative form is usually a simple matter of inserting the word *more,* as in *more beautiful,* and the superlative form is a simple matter of inserting *most,* as in *most beautiful.*

Occasionally you'll wonder whether to try an *-er* or *-est* ending or fall back on the regular use of *more* and *most.* Should you say *redder, leafiest, blunter, slenderest, ruggedest*? In Formal, if you don't feel confident with an *-er* or *-est,* play safe with *more* or *most.* It's hard to err with *more* or *most,* but easy to make your audience think you're being cheeky if you say *cloudier, joyfullest, uncleaner, backwardest, hopefuller, stupidest.* With long or uncommon adjectives and with participles, don't use *-er* and *-est* (*tireder, laughingest*).

Another little problem arises with adjectives, and people get excited about this one since it has to do with logic. Certain adjectives are not supposed to be compared because they already have an absolute meaning: *infinite, complete, virginal, supreme, vital.* You've often heard about these absolutes, that you mustn't say *more exhausted, emptier, more full, almost pregnant.* But people say illogical things all the time, to speak forcefully. Jesus, for example: He who has nothing will have taken away from him even the little he has.

Since Formal tries to be logical, show that you are trying, and do not say *very unique, increasingly comprehensive, less fatal.* On the other hand, don't be upset that these Informal exaggerations are constantly used. People just don't have the time to choose words with the most perfect precision. (Catch *most* perfect?) Adjectives ending in *-able* and *-less* should not be compared: *harmless, powerless, destructible, inflatable, unable.* In Formal, you can't use the Mad Ave comparative—better tasting, longer, smoother, milder—because no one knows what's being compared.

Of course, the main problem with adjectives is not misusing them grammatically, but overusing them stylistically. Adjectives are only words about words. But verbs, ah, verbs live.

Where to Put Adverbs

Since an adjective only modifies a noun there's no trouble in putting it alongside its noun, but since an adverb modifies different kinds of words, and phrases, and whole sentences, it's often misplaced. It splits infinitives when it shouldn't and misses its cue in verbs. *He had been* always *helping* instead of *He had* always *been helping.*

One reason why adverbs are misplaced is that many of them are useless, and no one knows or cares where they belong. Called on to intensify expression, they often make it weaker and vaguer. *I am* very *happy to meet you. I was* really *hurt not to be invited. He is* highly *praised for his omelets.* When you say you don't know *too much* about cars, how much is too much? As the adjective can be the enemy of the noun by distracting attention from it, so the adverb can be the enemy of what it modifies. Some adverbs are *infinitely* annoying and *literally* drive me up the wall.

The position of adverbs is no problem in speech, for they can be stressed or left unstressed wherever they are, but in writing care must be taken in placing them. Certain adverbs modify two or three things at once or have a general effect on the whole sentence. *Just, only, even, ever, never* move around rather freely in a sentence. But in Formal, they should be placed as precisely as possible. *I only shop at Woolworth's* should be *I shop only at Woolworth's. I just want a cigarette, I want just a cigarette. I never will learn, I will never learn. He not only made a living but a fortune, He made not only a living but a fortune.*

A special kind of adverb comes near the start of the

sentence and modifies everything that follows: *luckily, happily, apparently, significantly.* Since this kind of adverb neatly tells the reader how he should respond to the sentence, it's overused by writers who lack confidence that their sentences speak for themselves. *Logically,* these adverbs dangle, since what they modify is unclear. *Interestingly, x plus 2y equal 3z over x square.* What's going on *interestingly? Hopefully, we can find the square root, though no one has ever seen a square root.* Who is hoping or who is hopeful? *Most importantly, she adores me.* Most important of what?

Adverbs can be emphasized by taking them away from their normal place in the sentence (Loudly *she snapped her gum*) or by letting them split closely related words. *I want never to see you again.* Here *never* splits the verb and its object. *Bob, during lunch, saw Carol.* Here the adverb phrase *during lunch* splits subject and verb. *This is a wild, skinny, very hungry cat. Very* splits the series of adjectives. *He had been quietly eating hotdogs.* Normally the order would be: *He had quietly been eating hotdogs.*

If it's kosher to split phrases with adverbs for emphasis, why not split infinitives too? You *should,* when you want to emphasize the adverb. When you don't want to emphasize it, you shouldn't. Here are the infinitives that probably shouldn't have been split.

I want you to carefully turn around.
The weather is to always be taken into account.
She likes to quickly walk to work.
My cat seems to never be hungry.
You should try to, if you want to quickly get ahead, learn to not
 split infinitives.
I hope I don't have to, because I split infinitives, lose my job
 with the bank.

The infinitive should be split when the adverb is important.

I want you to entirely forget what I said.
He used to constantly chew tobacco.
You have to deeply water your mango.
It is rather for us the living to be here dedicated.

If there weren't a rule against splitting infinitives, if they weren't awkward, you couldn't emphasize the adverb by splitting the infinitive. Let's hear it for the rule. Just as there's a reason for every mistake, there's a reason for every rule. Rules aren't so bad, if breaking them and observing them allows us to express ourselves.

Lying behind the objection to split infinitives is a well founded dislike of adverbs. Adverbs, get lost! *To finally resolve* should be *to resolve. To quickly go* should be *to speed, to run, to hasten. To flatly forbid, to completely drain, to thoroughly baffle.* For every adverb you don't use, you don't have to worry about where you put it.

Adjectives versus Adverbs

Another problem with the adverb, one that brings anguish to the nervous and amusement to the confident, is the choice between adjective and adverb *forms.* Before getting deep into the question, let's have a snap quiz. Pick the correct form.

feel bad,	badly
land soft,	softly
made wrong,	wrongly
weigh heavy,	heavily
fit loose,	loosely
sing different,	differently
go gentle,	gently

Which did you prefer—the *-ly* forms or the ones that seem to be adjectives? I recommend you use the first versions and avoid the timid *-ly* forms. These are associated with Formal in the minds of some people, but shouldn't be. Formal prefers the older, shorter, more vigorous forms. Here highbrow usage is the same as lowbrow; only middlebrows say things like *the dress looks well on you, slice it thickly, the engine ran smoothly.* Middlebrows avoid what seems vulgar, and vulgar usage ignores adverbs: *I paid him good, she talked excited, he hit it perfect, that was real nice.* But the vulgar avoidance of adverbs doesn't mean they're good for educated people.

In the quiz, the first versions—*bad, soft*—should be interpreted as adjective adverb mixtures. In *she made it wrong, wrong* can be thought of as modifying the noun *it* or the verb *made.* These double purpose words come in mighty handy (not mightily handily).

Remember too that adjectives, not adverbs, follow the special linking verbs mentioned earlier—*feel, sound, look, turn, become. Feel bad, look bad.* Some borderline linking verbs are *dress, treat, behave, act. Dress cool. You treat me unfair. You behave mean to me now but you used to act sweet.* In Formal play it safe and keep away from the border.

The notion that adverbs are elegant has led to some incredible coinages: *doubtlessly, thusly, overly, muchly, importantly, lastly, firstly, diametrically, icily, uglily.* Climb all over anyone who uses these words.

Not many adverbs appear in speech, but writing is heavy with them. In speech we say *I'm TIRED* and get the message across, but when we write *I'm very tired* no one knows how tired we are. We can therefore omit nine out of ten *verys toos greatlys reallys actuallys extremelys quites rathers slightlys fairlys* and *somewhats.* If you're using lots of these, your writing needs more than these vitamin pills, it needs life itself, the sound of your real voice. Good adverbs are those that modify verbs (*Old folks walk* about, *not* to *and* from). Bad ones modify adjectives, or everything, or nothing.

Adverbs are essentially vague, like *essentially: said happily, immensely rich, endlessly entertaining, sometimes, later.* They'll trip you up when you write *rather appalled, very necessary, almost overwhelmed.* They'll sap your strength and you'll go around muttering *more or less, by and large, in general, on the whole, to a certain extent, to all intents and purposes,* until you're off to the hospital.

Pep Talk on Grammar

Grammar is a wide subject overlapping usage on one side and style on the other. Style is taken care of in our final lesson. I've put off till then some questions that could be treated as questions of grammar, such as the use of the subjunctive (*If I were*), absolutes (*The game over*), the reference of the pronoun *we,* and choices between *which* and *that, of which* and *whose,* etc. Faults in logic are sometimes considered grammar faults, but resist classification and are hard to talk about. They include *non sequiturs,* or ideas that do not follow (*It was raining and I lost my virginity*), and impossibilities or contradictions: *Look at the rat between the three garbage cans, Take your hands out of your pocket, There's lots of square space here, Crime on the subways is improving, Empty the water.*

Problems in grammar are like problems in diction: you have to choose between *perhaps* and *maybe* in diction, and choose between *It was they* and *It was them* in grammar. Some people deny that such freedom exists where grammar is concerned, but it does. Some would argue that *perhaps* and *It was they* were fussy; some would argue that *maybe* and *It was them* were too Informal. Having prejudices in these choices can hurt your chances of persuading your audience. Of course, the more Formal the occasion the less choice you have.

It's a pity that people get so caught up in questions of grammar and usage when they should be concerned about what is being said. A bad mistake is not so bad as a poor sentence, and a poor sentence is not so bad as a foolish or false one. Why search for grammar faults in a pile of manure? Because what's manure to us may be someone's fertilizer. To attack someone's language is to attack him. We may have to do it indirectly, by referring to his misunderstanding of certain words, his lack of parallelism, his dangling verbals.

When others get after your grammar, it may not be the grammar they're after, it may be what you said or it may be you. That's why your grammar must be invulnerable. And you can always distract attention from your grammar by having something to say. With something to say you have faith in, you'll not be scared, and you'll say it passably. Faults of expression arise from having nothing to say. In the rest of these lessons we'll concentrate on finding things to say.

Before moving on to our next lesson on Good Sentences let's look at some puzzles to test your mastery of grammar. Which is correct? There are no nails and hammer, There is no hammer and nails, There is no hammar or nails, There are no nails and no hammer, There is no hammer and there are no nails. I'll give you the answer in a minute. Here's a tougher one. *She lay sobbing. I sat smoking. Drop dead.* What part of speech is *sobbing, smoking,* and *dead*—verb, adverb, adjective? The answer is that no one knows. You see why some professors get fed up with the traditional parts of speech and invent new systems for analyzing sentences. But this does no harm and keeps them off the streets.

Here's your last puzzle. Which is correct? Bob and Carol blew their nose, their noses, his nose, his and her nose, his and her noses, his nose and her nose, his nose or her nose, his nose and hers, his/her nose, his and/or her nose, his and/or her nose or noses, his and her nose respectively. There are dozens of ways of expressing this idea. Maybe there is no Right Way. Sometimes you find yourself in a no win situation. When this happens, don't panic—try to enjoy the predicament. If you can't figure out what to do, whatever you decide won't make much difference. If you're anxious—let's say you're taking the bar exam—and won't commit yourself to anything less than perfect, cast the sentence a new way. The obvious solution to Bob and Carol's nose problems (or Bob's and Carol's noses problem) is to recast the sentence: *Bob blew his nose and Carol blew her nose.* But no one would have been puzzled if you had used the original version—*Bob and Carol blew their nose.*

Many grammar puzzles are illusions. They're like those knots you pull and the knot disappears. If one fourth of the people say *For whom are you looking?* and three fourths say *Who are you looking for?* whichever you say, you'll be in good company. When usage is divided and there's no compelling argument in favor of one usage (what is traditional is not compelling), then choose what you like and stick by it. Do *you* like *There are no nails and hammer?*

Lesson Five

Good Sentences and Paragraphs

The Heart of the Sentence

You'll be pleased to know you don't have to learn the definition of a sentence. There isn't any; a sentence can't be exactly defined. It's a word or group of words that somehow makes sense. Anything spoken can be a sentence, depending on what's said before or after, and depending on whether the listener hears some kind of complete or satisfactory message. A single word like *banana* can be a sentence, if what is being said about the banana is understood, such as *I want the banana* or *Here is a banana*.

Handbooks spend time trying to define the sentence, because they have to warn people not to make the mistake known as a sentence fragment. It's easier to say what a fragment is than what a sentence is. A sentence makes sense, but just how it does is a mystery. A fragment is not mysterious—it's the mistaken use of a period where no one wants a period sound. *She's his neighbor. Who sings too loud. Grandma snores. Because she's stopped up.* If you know what a period is, you won't be guilty of this fault.

A different construction, the sentence lacking a subject or predicate, is incorrectly referred to as a sentence fragment. In speech, such sentences are common. They're not common in writing, since writing, which lacks the resources of the voice, has to spell out the meaning slowly and carefully. Here are examples of sentences lacking subjects or predicates. *Never in a million years. Which is true. A ballplayer who can do everything. Gone fishing. Two million dollars. A hundred years later.* These expressions make sense, and should be distinguished from real fragments caused by misused periods. Can these expressions, called clipped sentences, be used in Formal? Not in *very* Formal. Clipped sentences appear more frequently in writing today, giving it a fast pace and intimate tone. They're quite effective, but like any device, if overused they'll seem phony.

Sentences used to be called *periods*. This word *period,* meaning a *cycle*, reminds us of what the sentence should be. A sentence moves, and stops. A subject is announced, the listener assumes that something will be said about it, something is said, the predicate is completed, the voice falls. A sentence has one job to do: one big subject and one big thing to say about it. Of course the subject can be a compound and the verb can be a compound and the sentence can have a number of main clauses, but no matter how much is said, all must add up: the sentence must have unity. You can't say *George Washington was our first President and had a set of false teeth made of ivory.* Here are two ideas, two sentences are needed. A sentence is not a bag into which words and ideas are thrown, not a clothesline on which items are hung. It's an act. During its moment of life, it can only do so much, and the more it tries to do the less it gets done. A very good sentence is like a slap in the face. The reason transitions between sentences are so hard is that each sentence is a completion and each new sentence is a new start.

A sentence is a proposition that others will accept or refuse. To offer a sentence is to stick your neck out. You're saying Here's my subject and here's what I'm telling you about it. The sentence arches up over the magical moment when you link the predicate to the subject. There's often a heavy pause before the verb because this is the moment everyone waits for. Sentences are created. Creation itself began when a subject met a verb: *Let* there *be* light. If the speaker lets her audience down, by offering them a dud predicate, she has no feeling for a sentence. Here are some fizzlers. *The hydrogen bomb is very dangerous. The Pope is in favor of the Church. Othello got mad at his wife. Two billion dollars was made by Octopus.* The subjects are *the hydrogen bomb, the Pope, Othello,* and *two billion dollars,* yet the sentences are awful. What's said about the subject is what's important, not the subject. This applies to the most common subject of them all, the perpendicular pronoun I.

Interest in a sentence does not depend on the verb either, though verbs are more important than subjects. Vigorous verbs are always welcome, but a sentence is more than its verb, or even the sum of its parts. A sentence depends on how the subject is treated in the predicate. In poor sentences the link between subject and predicate is lost. The subject becomes the focus, and may be buried under a heap of modifiers, or the predicate becomes the focus, and may be sapped of its strength by modifiers and afterthoughts. If a sentence has a job to do, it should be stripped for action. Words devoted only to the subject or predicate, rather than to the treatment of the subject by the predicate, drag the sentence down. Any word not helping predication should be cut, any detail not serving the point of the sentence should be cut.

Here is a sentence from *The New York Times* in which predication has been buried:

> If that time is used aggressively to overhaul drastically the grossly mismanaged Hospitals Corporation, it may be possible to save some jobs that otherwise would be lost.

That should be:

> If the mismanaged Hospitals Corporation is overhauled quickly, some jobs might be saved.

Whoever wrote that sentence for the *Times* did not know how to write or was being paid by the word. Write like that only if you get paid.

Here is a sentence from a letter to the *Times* explaining why city buses come in groups:

> Having become more heavily loaded, they must stop more frequently to let off passengers, so there is both a first and second derivative positive feedback to the progressive clustering of independent vehicles.

That should be:

Buses bunch up because the ones in front lose time in picking up more passengers and in letting them off.

Instead of thinking about building a good sentence the writer of that bad sentence was thinking about the jargon he was dying to use. But a thousand socko words do not have the punch of a good sentence. A fault in American prose as compared to English is that Americans are colorists rather than draftsmen. They get excited about the words and forget the structure. This fault has been aggravated by advertising, which uses words, phrases, suggestions rather than sentences to get its effects. But the best ads have been sentences: *Pepsi Cola hits the spot, Wouldn't you rather have a Buick, Duz does everything, Winston tastes good.*

Here's another example of writing done with words rather than sentences. It's a brief review of the movie *Grease* from *The New Yorker.*

> The grease is the Elvis Presley sort of hair grease, the society is proudly sexist and ritualistic, the film's commercial calculation is obviously shrewd. The movie runs on pure ozone, good times, and an easy homesickness for a past decade that the people who lived through it will not find particularly missable.

This is that, this is that. I doubt it.

What Should Be Put in a Sentence

I've warned against overloading the sentence, but obviously we can squeeze extra details in without wrecking predication. Details do not always have to be relevant. But they should not be distracting. In deciding what details to use, the writer takes tone into account. In serious writing, with powerful predication, you want stripped sentences. In unserious writing, you toss in extra details. If you were writing about a ballgame, could you write like this?

> Curly headed Bob Firecracker from Chillicothe Missouri knocked the white horsehide pellet into the newly painted bleachers in

the bottom of the ninth to put the rampaging Cardinals over the .500 mark, even though he broke his bat when he did it.

You could write that, but you would write better if you left out the distracting details. They should go somewhere else, even if the only place for them to go is the wastecan. This is better:

In the bottom of the ninth, Bob Firecracker put the winning Cardinals over the .500 mark when he knocked the ball into the bleachers—with a broken bat!

The following sentences lack unity, though they offer fascinating information:

My boyfriend lives two floors above me and he's a Sagittarian.
After eating a big dinner of tacos, tamales, and refried beans, Bob asked Carol to marry him.
Last Tuesday it was raining and I caught a cold and I was late to work.
The explosion flattened the fireworks plant, which was built in 1960 by the Sperber Construction Company, a firm which has been in business here in Fernwood since 1880.

These sentences were silly, their lack of unity was so obvious. But it's surprising how many sentences, if examined for unity, are found lacking. Many sentences have no main idea, or have several ideas. Sentences lacking *point* are found in writing done under pressure—the pressure of deadlines or course requirements. Forced writing betrays itself in sentences that are about everything and say nothing.

The impulse to tell everything, a welcome, generous impulse when we're with friends, who dote on our every word or seem to, leads us to use extra modifiers—*There was this big huge truck*—and to bring in irrelevant details even when they interrupt. *Then I went to the butcher's—Jim, you know Jim, he's the redheaded one—I've always liked redheads—well, this roast we needed—he asked how big it should be, and I said for ten, but I didn't really know if three of the people would be able to make it—Bob and Carol and Mary.* This flood of thoughts must be dammed in Formal writing. There we show we are energetic and friendly by saying as little as possible. Speech pours out, writing comes drop by drop. Speech should be slowed down and writing speeded up, so that they're more like each other and less like parodies of themselves.

We sometimes feel it's economical to make a number of points in one sentence and stuff the sentence good and tight. This doesn't work. The more points a sentence tries to make, the less significant they become. Sometimes when the writer makes a number of points in one sentence, she has a notion of how they're related, but her mind and the reader's work differently. The relationship of the ideas may have to be spelled out for him. If the writer has a reason for saying in one sentence that George Washington was our first President and had false teeth made of ivory, she better tell her reason right away. It's not enough to clear up confusion in the next sentence or two. The next sentence is too late, the damage has been done, the reader has raised an eyebrow.

Young writers come up with *amputated* sentences. *Hamlet had certain problems. She's a Terpsichorean. The devil is an angel. Bob looked for his glasses. Carol never ate hotdogs.* When a sentence raises a question, the writer should at least begin to answer the question in the same sentence. Sometimes a sentence omits the explanation of how the ideas are related. *Bob is a Leo and Carol is a Scorpio, but they get along well.* Revised: *Even though Bob's a strong willed Leo and Carol's a strong willed Scorpio, they get along well.* Another: *I grew up in St Louis and I can't stand hot weather.* Revised: *I grew up in St Louis, which is so hot, I can no longer stand hot weather.* Another: *He talked to the committee and they adjourned.* Revised: *He persuaded the committee to adjourn.* The connection between ideas or events should be explained—it only takes a word or two—if the connection is not obvious to *everyone.* Frequently, intelligent people do not write well because their minds are quick and skip over the connections between ideas that need to be laid out for the reader. The good writer thinks like her readers. This gift of sympathy and imagination is more valuable to her than intelligence.

Kinds of Sentences

If a sentence has one main clause, that is, one subject with its verb, it's a simple sentence. *Carol sneezed.* If a sentence has two or more main clauses it's a compound sentence. *Carol sneezed and Bob said Bless you.* If a sentence has a main clause and a subordinate clause it's a *complex* sentence. *Bob said Bless you when Carol sneezed. Carol sneezed because she was allergic.*

Which kind of sentence is best depends on what you're saying. For stories, simple sentences are best, giving a fast tempo. For creating an aura of importance, compound sentences are best, the ideas being linked with no explanation as to why they're linked. Compound sentences are poetic and suggestive: the Bible is loaded with them. Complex sentences are best for discussion. In them ideas are related to each other and the relationship is named—*because* so and so, *when, which, after, although, unless.*

See how the effect of the sentence is changed by the kind of sentence.

Simple	I went to her place. I found him.
Compound	I went to her place, and I found him.
Complex	I went to her place, where I found him.

Many are called. Few are chosen.
Many are called but few are chosen.
Although many are called, few are chosen.

She walked home. Her feet hurt.
She walked home, and her feet hurt.
Since she walked home, her feet hurt.

In simple sentences each idea is separate and important. In a compound sentence the ideas combine to form one idea that's more important than the separate ideas. In a complex sentence one idea is emphasized at the expense of the other idea, which is subordinated to it.

Beginning writers use simple sentences because they feel that every idea they have is important. Too many simple sentences is kindergarten style, where nothing is sorted out and everything is equally emphatic. Compound sentences may be overused when the writer is trying to keep a narrative going or is aiming at a cumulative effect. *I got on my bike and I rode down the street and I reached the corner and I saw the fallen tree in the road.* Too many *complex* sentences gives an impression of timidity; the ideas all seem to require help.

Thus the three kinds of sentences have advantages and disadvantages. Notice what kind you're writing because the use of one kind for too long gets tiresome, and the effectiveness of that kind is lost. In revising, you shouldn't just patch mistakes and change words, but change a number of sentences to a different kind. Choppy simple sentences suggest a simple minded attitude, stringy compound sentences suggest haste or fatigue, and puffy complex sentences suggest the writer is a mouse. Proust expressed how feeble he felt and how complicated everything was by writing such long sentences that one, as Joyce reported, could fill an entire magazine.

Of the three kinds of sentence I praise the complex, since it is the most useful and should be the most frequent in Formal writing. Complex sentences are not awfully common in speech, and writers aren't using so many of them today as they used to. In the past, excessive subordination of ideas produced overloaded and overrefined sentences. Today, we do not find as much subordination as would be useful.

The more Formal the writing, the more ordering and relating of the ideas is required. In Formal, the writer sweats to make everything perfectly clear. She changes many simple and compound sentences, that would be natural in Informal, to complex.

Compound	He's an ex drunk and he's our mayor.
Complex	Though he used to be a drunk, he's now our mayor.
	My first boyfriend was Bob and he was a freshman.
	My first boyfriend was Bob, when he was a freshman.
	Try this on Carol. She needs practice.
	Try this on Carol, who needs practice.

Do this one yourself: *Consider the ant, thou sluggard, and be wise.*

Complex sentences, despite their name, are clearer. When teachers nagged you to write longer sentences, they meant clearer.

Ordering the Ideas

To write a complex sentence one of the ideas has to be subordinated. *I went to the movies, where I saw* King Kong. *When I went to the movies I saw* King Kong. If you can't tell which idea is more important, going to the movies or seeing *King Kong,* then coordinate by saying *I went to the movies* and *I saw* King Kong. But usually, when there is more than one idea in a sentence one of them is the main idea, and the others should be put in their place, or they will be insubordinate.

It's more important to be able to use subordination than coordination. We could do without most *ands* and *buts* between main clauses. In revising your work, you'll find yourself taking out unnecessary *ands* and *buts.* The *and* between main clauses is never really needed, and *but* relationships are often understood without your having to use *but.* Subordinating conjunctions, on the other hand, are much more instructive than coordinating conjunctions. Coordinators make sentences smoother and faster, subordinators make them smoother and *clearer.*

No subordination. *The used car salesman approached us. He was very smooth and he told us he would give us a deal on a 1980 Mouse. It had good tires and low mileage, and he was only asking ten thousand.* With subordination. *The used car salesman, who was very smooth, approached and offered us a deal—a 1980 Mouse with good tires and low mileage for only ten thousand dollars.*

Another example. *Last night I was driving my car and I missed the evening news, but I did see the morning news.* With subordination. *While driving last night I missed the evening news, but I saw the morning news.*

Another. *I graduated and I went into the Army, and then I worked in a store, and so I saved enough to get married.* With subordination. *By*

going in the Army after graduation and then working in a store, I saved
enough money to get married.

Change main clauses to subordinate clauses, change clauses to phrases, and combine sentences. You may be surprised at how much of this revision is possible and how it improves what you've written. A lot can be done, because in what you've written—just as in what you say and what you think—the ideas are connected somehow. Subordination clarifies the connections.

We'll now review the ways of making subordinate clauses.

Start them off with the relative pronouns, *that, which,* and *who.* Instead of saying *Tightening my prose is a problem. It's bothered me all my life* say *Tightening my prose is a problem that's bothered me all my life.*

When you're stumped in thinking of a way to follow up an idea, be inspired by the following list of conjunctions (or the list of connectives on page 140). Connect the ideas in terms of

TIME	Use the conjunctions *after, since, before, when, while, as,* and *until.*
PLACE	Use *where, wherever.*
PURPOSE	Use *so that, in order that.*
COMPARISON	Use *than, as, as if, as though.*
CONDITION	that is, one event depends on another. Use *if* or *unless.*
CONCESSION	Use *although, though, even though.* Some people sense differences in these, but I think you can use any of the three depending on the sentence rhythm.
CAUSE	*Because* is a little more emphatic than *since. For* and *as* also express cause relationships, but they are weaker and can be ambiguous, especially *as. As he looked at her she looked at him.*

Other conjunctions can get you into trouble. *While* can be ambiguous. *While he looked at her, she looked at him. So* can be ambiguous. *He looked at her, so she looked at him.* At least four other conjunctions besides *like* are now taboo—*being as, being that, plus,* and *let alone.* If you use these your goose is cooked. *Being that Bob is a Satanist, plus Carol is a Baptist, they argue like hell, let alone they don't speak to each other.*

Arranging the Sentence

Most people have never heard that position in the sentence is important, but it is. Should a main clause go before or after a subordinate clause? It depends. Usually the speaker or writer automatically puts the subordinate clause in the right place, but often she doesn't. Sometimes there's no choice; for example, you say *Don't stand up until the judge stands up;* you do not say *Until the judge stands up, don't stand up.* But generally, in Formal, try to put the subordinate clause *before* the main clause.

> After he missed the shot, he threw his racquet.
> Because he paid no tax, they called him in.
> As the tornado struck, he thought of his insurance.
> When you're out of Schlitz, you're out of beer.

These sentences would be weaker if the subordinate clauses were put after the main clause: *You're out of beer when you're out of Schlitz. He thought of his insurance as the tornado struck.*

When the subordinate clause comes after the main clause it can sound like a mere afterthought.

> You must have the car inspected, when the time comes.
> I have a widget, which is why he asked to borrow it.
> I detest hotdogs, though right now I'm very hungry.

Sometimes you will want a falling or cadenced sentence for a funny or sad effect.

> I never watch the soaps, although my canary enjoys them while drying off.
> We never go to that place in the country any more at this time of the year.

You may have heard of the rule that you should try to put what is important in the sentence at the end of the sentence, because the end of the sentence is the position of greatest emphasis. This rule should be explained. The position of greatest emphasis has to be the predicate, and whatever is important in the sentence should be in the predicate of the main clause. The reason is obvious. Whatever comes after the predicate is an anticlimax. You can write sentences in which you say the important thing first, and then add a lot of extra stuff, but you should not write many sentences like that. Sentences that end when the predicate ends are strong. (Like that one.) Putting as much of the sentence as you can *before* the predicate strengthens the sentence. (Like that one.) Anything put in the sentence after the predicate is weakened, and will in turn weaken the sentence, for no sentence is stronger than its weakest part.

These instructions run contrary to your general experience, in which you're always being told to be brief, say what you have to say, get to the point. But a sentence is supposed to build up, not fall off, not fall from a cliff, as these do.

> Someone at this table is a werewolf, he said as he sat down and arranged his napkin in his lap.
> The world is coming to an end, according to Reverend Swain, pastor of the First United Church at the corner of Locust and Vine.
> The suspect turned out to be a man, which was disclosed by the matron who ran from the room where the suspect was being searched after being arrested for possession of a suspicious looking cigarette.

Arranging the sentence for emphasis is the master trick that separates pros from amateurs. In speaking we all tend to say the important thing first and tack on extra stuff. In writing, the modifiers and the subordination should be put at the front of the sentence. This arrangement is a sign of Formality, and the more frequently it is done, the more Formal the expression.

Do not open a sentence with a bang. If you have a bang in a paragraph, save it for the end of the paragraph. If you have a big bang to set off somewhere in the composition, save it for the finale. All writing should have some bangs, or it drones on like a textbook.

Sentences that do not build to a climax are called loose or accumulated sentences. In speech, loose sentences are fairly short, and no one minds them. In writing, loose sentences can go on and on and be very tedious. Loose, shapeless sentences are a disease of modern prose. In Latin and in German, where the verb is often put at the end of the sentence, the sentence can build to that climax. In any language, though, emphasis is achieved by doing things in an abnormal way, and that is why you *should* write sentences that build. *If it looks like a duck, walks like a duck, and quacks like a duck, it must be a—duck.*

Clauses that trail along after the predicate are bad enough, but trailing *phrases,* participial and prepositional, are even worse. Here are trailing participles:

> The teams played an evenly matched game, resulting in a scoreless tie.
>
> She couldn't resist ordering a widget for herself, thus overextending her credit.
>
> He had the good sense to take a cab, enabling him to be there for the appointment.

Here are trailing *with* phrases:

> The stock market soared, with the result that he celebrated more than he should have.
>
> Carol enjoyed smoking the huge cigar, with Bob watching her closely.
>
> Bob likes all the flavors, with blueberry ripple his favorite.

Maybe you don't find anything wrong with those sentences. If you didn't, it's because they reflected our normal way of talking. But the normal way is not the best. It's bad enough to have normal ideas, but to say them normally is worse. What's the point?

Cute Tricks

Writers seldom think about arranging their sentences because the words usually come to them in the right order. *Carol kissed Bob goodby when he left for work.* That loose sentence need not be changed to a climactic sentence: *When Bob left for work Carol kissed him goodby.* The normal word order is *usually* right. But striking effects are achieved by breaking the normal pattern of the sentence, inverting the natural word order, throwing in interruptions or questions, and falling back on the passive voice. Here are striking inversions.

You'll always have the poor.	The poor you shall always have with you.
She wore a pants suit to the wedding	To the wedding she wore a pants suit.
We don't have real evidence.	Real evidence we don't have.
I have devoted my life to Yale, to country, and to God.	I have devoted my life to God, to country, and to Yale.
To begin with, Marly was dead.	Marly was dead, to begin with.

Similar to inversions are interruptions.

The movie was, if you must know the truth, a disaster.
This criticism, the more you say it, strikes me as unfair.
Her he chose, from all his girls, to do his shirts.
Out of the water we fished, dripping sinisterly, a book on—what was it on?—grammar.

Here are examples of the passive voice. Note the difference between active and passive.

Carol punched Bob.	Bob was punched by Carol.
The bride wore a white satin dress.	A white satin dress was worn by the bride.
The Army discharged me when the war was over.	I was discharged by the Army when the war was over.

In the switch to the passive, the object of the verb is thought to be more important than the subject, and takes its place. The subject does nothing then and is passive. The passive voice is used when what is being done is more important than who is doing it. *The car was stolen. We were gypped. He's tanned. Trash was thrown. The war was ended.* What about *I'm asleep*—active or passive?

All too frequently, though, the passive is used to cover up a mystery about who is doing what is being done. *It is thought.* By whom? *Data has been gathered, trespassers will be shot, he is considered, it has been suggested, it was decided, they are known.* When the verb is vigorous, putting it into the passive voice can sound ridiculous. *My nose was punched by you. Hotdogs are hated by her. The tree was struck by the car.* In short, the passive voice may be used (I just used it) when the verb is unexciting and the agent unimportant or unknown. In good writing these conditions don't often occur, and that's why the passive voice is seldom used. (I did it again).

Seven Tips on Sentences

Let's go over the requirements for an acceptable written sentence. It has unity, or a single main point. No point, no sentence. Everything needed to make the point is in, everything not needed is out. Whatever is unclear or distracting is out. The ideas that are left have been weighed, consciously or unconsciously, and have been coordinated or subordinated. The sentence is built around the main point.

A sentence is like a juggling act: all goes up and comes down at the right time in the right place. The inexpert juggler sends stuff up, like a subject, forgets about it, then grabs anything that's handy and sends it up too. Sentence juggling is not easy, but gets easier after years of practice. The expert juggler has the sentences arranged in her mind before letting them fly.

A good written sentence has stricter requirements than an acceptable spoken sentence. It's hard to compose a decent sentence and harder to compose a forceful one. But if it was easy, it wouldn't be worth doing or be so well rewarded. Good sentences can get you into the White House or even Westminster Abbey. The essential talent for a writer is not intelligence, wit, knowledge, or personality, but a feeling for sentences.

Here are seven tips to help you build sentences.

Keep the sentences brief. In any art, energy and force derive from economy of means, and not because the artist has different ends and different means. Shakespeare tried to entertain, Mozart wanted to write good tunes and score musical comedy hits. They achieved their results more swiftly and easily, and thus more powerfully, than their rivals. You should write the shortest possible sentences using the shortest possible words in the shortest possible paragraphs, not because people are dimwits or because they're busy—they're not that dim or that busy—but because force comes from the elimination of the inessential. T S Eliot said, Artistic creation proceeds by a series of destructions. In the next lesson I'll encourage you to destroy what you've written. A brief sentence does not mean a baby sentence, but a stripped sentence. A hundred word sentence that's clear and worth saying can seem short, but a dull four or five word sentence can seem interminable. Nixon: *Death is always inevitable.*

Vary your sentence patterns. Use simple, compound, and complex. Using all of them preserves the special effectiveness of each. Try to write climactic sentences, even though they sound a bit unnatural. Here's a pointed sentence by Dr Johnson: *No man but a blockhead ever wrote, except for money.* Today that sentence would be edited: *Everyone writes for money except blockheads.* Another kind of sentence to try is the balanced sentence. *I seem to see blankety blank, I seem to see higgledy piggledy, I seem to see dickery dockery. Men think, women know. Men do, women are. Men are men, but man is a woman.* Balanced sentences are for Sundays and holidays.

Mix up short, normal, and long sentences. Short sentences are a dozen words or less. Long sentences are, say, thirty or more words. The average written sentence is fifteen to twenty words. Most of your sentences should be around the average. Anyone can write short sentences by turning clauses into separate sentences or write long sentences by tacking sentences together with coordinating conjunctions and by adding clauses with subordinating conjunctions. Ho hum. But the reader expects sentences of normal length just as he expects normal words. If he didn't expect them you couldn't surprise him with a long or short one.

Wake the reader up, if you want him to be awake. Use questions, exclamations, asides, commands, interruptions, and inversions. Unless you're doing pure reporting, all of these devices are available to you. You can address the reader. It's silly to always pretend you don't exist and he doesn't exist. But guard against saying *you you you.* He may not want to get involved, or think he's listening to his mother.

Be brave and strong. As St Paul says, If the bugle does not sound a clear call, who will prepare for battle? Don't overqualify what you're saying. Speak what you feel, not what you ought to say. When writing is dull, it's because the writer is timid. Don't stall, don't be nice. Avoid the passive voice. Throw out the adjectives and adverbs. Make the nouns precise, the verbs forceful. Remove the copulatives: don't say *He is distrustful,* say *He distrusts,* don't say *She's a good writer,* say *She writes well,* don't say *I am hungry,* say *I hunger.* Look at each negative statement, and try to recast it as a positive statement. *He did not agree, He disagreed. She did not accept it, She rejected it. She did not take her purse with her, She left without her purse.* The word *not* is strong in speech, where it can be stressed, but weak in writing.

Combine sentences. This tip seems to contradict *Keep the sentences brief,* but both tips are intended to smooth the reader's way. Combining sentences may or may not save words, but often makes the reading easier. Young writers, erring on the side of short sentences, should try to combine them. When two or three sentences in a row have the same subject, combination is possible. *The factory is at 1500 Ohio Street. It is an old, red brick building. Repairs are badly needed.* Combined. *The factory, an old, red brick building at 1500 Ohio Street, badly needs repairs.* When a pronoun keeps reappearing, combinations are possible. *He used to lose a lot. Now he's given up playing poker. This has made his wife happy.* Combined. *Since he lost so much at poker, he's given it up, which has made his wife happy.* Sentences that follow each other are related by time, purpose, comparison, etc, so combine them using the appropriate subordinators.

Don't distract attention. Avoid devices that draw attention to themselves. In writing, the right hand shouldn't know what the left hand is doing. Writing is best as a window, not a painting. Don't dote on any trick or mannerism, because you'll start using it for its own sake instead of the better purposes of your writing.

Don't like what you wrote. Admiring what you have down beclouds your judgment. The sentences you're fond of, you'll probably have to get rid of. A writer is ruthless: she cuts down and hauls away great armfuls of brush and weeds, and flowers go with them. If you're having trouble with a sentence or a paragraph skip it and move on. You'll discover you didn't need it, and that's why it gave you trouble.

What's a Paragraph?

The word *paragraph* originally meant *outside mark.* It was a mark— a star, hand, leaf, dagger, or the special paragraph mark (¶)— that a writer or printer put in the margin of the page to show that a new subject was being introduced and to help the reader mark his place. Today these little marks aren't used. Paper being cheap, white space is used: the paragraph is indented.

Some publishers love white space so much they insist on short paragraphs, and divide the writing up not according to the ideas but according to the desired paragraph length. But a paragraph should not only be a convenience for the eye but an aid to the understanding. Paragraphs should help the reader follow the argument by offering the ideas in groups.

How long should a paragraph be? One sentence or one word paragraphs are possible. In dialogue, each speech by each speaker gets a paragraph to itself. But in other kinds of writing the paragraphs should not be too short, for this gives a choppy, hard breathing effect, just as short sentences do. A paragraph should normally be from three to ten sentences long. Readers now expect two or three inch paragraphs.

In the past, much longer paragraphs were common. Long paragraphs were and are a sign of Formality. But remember that the paragraph is a device of writing, not of speech. Since less reading is done nowadays and since writing is becoming more like speech, the taste for long paragraphs is disappearing along with the ability to read them. It's a good idea to break up a four or five hundred word paragraph into three, and allow the modern reader to rest his weary eyes. Paragraphs are getting shorter, but if they get too short they'll slow the reader. When you paragraph keep in mind the expectations of the audience and the natural divisions of the discussion. Sometimes you negotiate between the two demands.

I won't spend much time talking about *the* paragraph. Since paragraphing is only a device for the eye, it's of minor importance. When handbooks talk about developing a paragraph, they're really discussing the big problem in composition—joining sentences. All of the sentences in a paragraph should be related to each other—that's true. But that's not saying much, because we know that all the sentences in the composition should be related to each other. How we divide the sentences into groups is often arbitrary.

Paragraphing can be done two ways: the sentences can be grouped after the whole composition is written, or the paragraphs can be written one by one according to a plan as little compositions in themselves. The writing comes easy with a good outline that lists subtopics of the right size for each paragraph. But good outlines are hard to get, and most writing is done without them, as we know. It's not enough to be a master of diction and a master of the sentence. Another skill is needed: the ability to develop an idea thru a paragraph and thru the whole composition. The choice of words and the shaping of sentences require thought, but paragraphs require planning. The ability to work with the larger structures, with the design, is a special skill and the one most often neglected. Many writers choose words well and write strong sentences, but get lost in the paragraph. They're like tennis players who master several strokes but have no serve. In a paragraph the sentences must follow and in a composition the paragraphs must follow. Nothing follows anything unless there are controlling ideas for paragraphs and the composition. Composition means putting things together, and you can only put things together that go. Where do they go? Where are you going?

Pursuing an Idea

The hardest part of writing is writing consecutive sentences. In writing poetry this is no problem because the poet has a license to flit around. In writing narrative or description this is no problem because the writing simply follows time order or space order. In writing discussions and arguments, this is *the* problem—making the thoughts follow. The mind does not come up with consecutive thoughts unless it has been disciplined to do so; there's a great difference between the way the mind naturally works and the way sentences have to follow each other like elephants holding tails. Since this is the main problem in composition, I'll talk about it here and pursue it thoroughly in the next lesson.

There are two ways of proceeding: the way of the painter and the way of the composer. The painter begins with a design and fills in the details. The musician begins with a phrase and then elaborates it into a grand design. Some compositions call for the way of the painter and some for the way of the musician. Few people are good at both. Young writers should use the painter's method and work from a design. But because they lack experience it's hard for them to come up with good designs. The reason they don't plan their compositions is they don't know how. Planning is in the next lesson. Here we'll look at the musician's way of building. Speech and music have much in common, since both proceed in a linear way through time. Rhythm and tempo are as important in writing as in music.

Most people have had little practice in pursuing ideas. They have an idea, and then they have a different one. Here, for example, is a writer working on an essay about hotdogs. She starts with an ordinary idea: *Hotdogs are pretty good sometimes.* (The first idea doesn't matter, any idea gets you started.) Next idea. *I had a good hotdog the last time I was at the stadium.* Next. *That was some game.* Next. *I wish I was there right now.* Next. *That cheerleader was cute.* You see what has happened. Instead of moving in on the first idea, the mind has moved on. What was the first idea? *Hotdogs are pretty good sometimes.* Let's stay with that. Why pretty good? Are they good or aren't they? Why sometimes? On what occasions are they good? What makes them good? What makes them bad? By pursuing these few questions one could easily develop enough material for the essay. Though people think about themselves, they're not in the habit of questioning themselves. That's what pursuing ideas is, questioning oneself about the topic.

Maybe the writer has to do an essay on cats, and starts

thinking: *Cats are not as demanding as dogs.* Next idea. *I only see my cat Reggie about once a week.* Next. *Reggie is a good old boy, a real tom. A ginger cat.* Next. *He has a big piece out of his ear.* Next. *I wonder how that happened?* Once again, the mind of a writer is not supposed to move *on,* in a natural browsing way, but move *in,* in an unnatural gnawing way. *Cats are not as demanding as dogs.* Why not? Should they be? Are dogs too demanding? Are cats not demanding enough? What is being demanded? How does a cat demand? How does a dog demand? What is better? Why? You see, this is the way to pursue an idea and develop a paragraph—not by putting down thoughts as they come but by asking questions about each statement you'd like to make. The procedure seems slow, destructive rather than creative, going backwards instead of forwards. But that's what thinking is—driving into the subject, not bouncing off and moving on.

Don't think of a paragraph as a collection of ideas on a subject, whether it's hotdogs or cats. Think of it as something to build, piece by piece, on the first idea. You could have a million thoughts about hotdogs, but you can't write a six sentence paragraph with a million thoughts. You've got too many thoughts. In fact your mind is like a beehive. What you have to do is to stay with the thought you started with, then stay with that thought and the next, then with those two and the next, and so on. It's hard, but gets easier with practice.

Do *not* proceed this way: *Reggie is my cat. He's a ginger cat. Some people call them marmalade cats. One called Morris used to be on TV. Reggie is a tom who really gets around. He has a piece out of his ear. His right ear.* Instead, proceed this way: *Why did I name my cat Reggie? I suppose I thought the name sounded elegant and debonair. Reggie lived up to his name and still lives up to it. He doesn't look so elegant and debonair as he did ten years ago, when he was young, and not missing so many pieces of himself—such as his right ear. But now he is even more elegant and debonair in his manner. He enters a room as if he were Louis XIV, the Sun King of France. But Reggie is only Moon King of Nyack. Every night he holds court,* etc.

Each sentence picks up an idea from the previous one and works with it. The mind stays focused by asking questions about the previous sentence. If what you've put down gets you nowhere, scratch it and try something else. The reason writing takes so much time is that a train of thought can stop after you've been following it a while, and then you have to start another and follow it to see where it's going. You don't have to go far; you only need five or six sentences for a paragraph, and once you've gotten them you'll have a number of ideas to pursue in the next paragraph. You'll make countless false starts. Writing is like panning for gold—lots of time and effort, but then there is the gold.

If pursuing ideas is hard for you, get practice this way. Have someone give you a sentence, then force yourself to write three or four sentences about that sentence. Doing this will convince you you're wrong ever to say you have nothing to say. When you get a sentence down, it automatically begins to suggest a critique of itself. Whatever is said has to be incomplete. A statement cries for help, needs to be explained or improved, either by adding an idea or taking a bit away. The sentence is a thesis. The next, if it follows the first, is an *and* or a *but* sentence. You add to or subtract from what you've said. There's nothing unnatural in this; it's the way thought proceeds. Thesis, antithesis, synthesis. Yes, but, and. Some thinkers have said that's how history proceeds. Whenever you put a sentence down, somewhere in the wings is the next sentence talking back. It's there all right—just call it forth. Its cue is *but,* the most wonderful word of all. *I will give it to you but. . . . I love my wife but. . . .* Use this priceless word all the time. It was Ibsen's dying word. Get your sentence down, say *but,* and see what happens.

Paragraph Form

Young writers are told that a paragraph should have a beginning, a middle, and an end. They are told that a paragraph should have a topic sentence near the beginning, and maybe a thesis or concluding sentence at the end. They're told that a paragraph should start with a transitional expression to link the paragraph to the previous one.

This advice is not helpful, and I wish I hadn't mentioned it.

Paragraphs are not written according to a model. Good writers don't think about paragraphs, they just write. As they write of course they keep their topic in mind, but they don't worry about topic sentences or the arrangement of the paragraph. A paragraph doesn't have to build to a climax or open or close. If you look at your books in which you've underlined important sentences, you'll see that these sentences come anywhere—at the beginning, middle, or end of paragraphs. If you can skim a book by reading the first or last sentence of the paragraphs, there's something wrong with the writing. In good writing, each sentence is important, and you can't pick out the ones to underline. You don't need a topic sentence in a paragraph, but you better have a topic. If you have a clear idea of your topic, you'll have a hard time not coming up with a handful of topic sentences.

It would be nice to write paragraphs full of tricks, little compositions in themselves, with beginnings, middles, and ends. But thinking about *form* while writing only distracts you. Questions of form may be considered once you've done a draft. Then you can divide what you've written into paragraphs of the right size, rearrange sentences, and maybe add little touches to show that you're opening and closing the paragraphs.

Only advanced and fluent writers come up with whole paragraphs that have not been previously planned for. Others need a clear or controlling idea for each paragraph in order to keep from straying. A plan has many benefits and no risks. No one needs to follow a plan exactly, and any plan can be left behind when the writer gets hot. Sad to say, most young writers have neither fluency nor plan; they can't use the musician's method or the painter's. They need to learn both, learn to draw up a design and to follow where the ideas lead. Writing calls for alternating the methods, allowing the thoughts to flow, while checking them according to the design. One can have a good design, but the writing can be dead, lacking fluency. And one can write fluently, but wander off the topic. Writing is an art like the others—a balancing of conscious form and unconscious inspiration. Too much form means dullness; too little form, the work is shapeless, pointless.

Paragraph beginnings are no problem. Did you notice that

I just started a new paragraph? Probably not. Which shows that one can start a new paragraph without preparing for it in the previous paragraph and without sticking in a transitional idea or expression. Paragraphs *should* open with sentences that sound like beginnings. Questions or definitions get the paragraph off to a good start, as in these examples: *There are three basic types of hotdog. The cat is man's best friend. What is a hotdog? The cat is a domestic feline; that says it all. The hotdog is a frankfurter or wiener sausage on a soft roll.* When you're revising, check whether your paragraph beginnings sound like beginnings. You needn't pay special attention to the closing sentences of paragraphs. Paragraphs are not long, and don't have to be brought around. They can stop abruptly, without closing chords. Don't sum up; summing up is tedious, except when it's a relief.

If you can join sentences you'll have no trouble with paragraphs. When you start a new paragraph you're allowed to. You're not likely to talk about cats in the first paragraph and hotdogs in the second without explaining how you got from one to the other. (When you have to explain what you're doing, something's fishy.) You move easily from one paragraph to the next if the paragraphs are subtopics under the main topic of the composition. Connecting the paragraphs does not depend on clever transitions but on having a design for the composition which includes these paragraphs.

Making Transitions

If the paragraphs are related to each other through planning and if the sentences follow each other by staying on the topic, the writing goes merrily along. The problem of transitions is the whole problem in writing. Writing is joining things. It's not like the song of a bird, it's like engineering, bookkeeping, bricklaying. It can be taught *or* it can be learned: it can be done.

When the writer has her material and her building plan, she won't have trouble with transitions. But sometimes a little work has to be done on some of the pieces to fit them in, and that's where tricks come in handy. One trick in making the writing appear to have more coherence is to repeat a word used in the previous sentence. The repetition of just one word makes a connection between sentences that are about quite different things. Pronouns link sentences. Another trick is to stick with the same subject through the sentences. *He does not believe in democracy. He has not cut his hair in two years. He eats alfalfa. He never wears shoes.*

The easiest trick in linking sentences is to use transitional expressions like *meanwhile, furthermore, on the other hand, similarly, as a matter of fact, in other words.* The English language has a great store of these expressions called *connectives* or *conjunctive adverbs.* They are used all the time in writing and are signs of written and Formal style. If you use too many of these glue words you run the risk of making the writing sound artificial and lacking the tone of speech. Beginning writers do not use enough of these words; academics use far too many. Professional writers stay away from them.

Some of them are so stuffy, they are nearly unusable: *accordingly, rather, nevertheless, moreover, indeed, to be sure, thereupon,* and *in sum.* Don't use these smug words unless you want to sound like a professor. *However* is particularly overworked, and I never touch it myself. Use *but* or *though* instead. Give your reader credit for being able to see connections between ideas, and don't steer him by opening every paragraph and every other sentence with a connective. No one wants to be lectured to with a lot of *thuses, thens, therefores,* and *howevers.*

A *few* well chosen connectives do add grace notes to your writing. (See how I managed to start that sentence without *however?*) I'll now tick off the connectives that are still useful.

If you're *adding* another thought, use *besides, also, then too, what's more, and then,* and *furthermore.* If you're *listing* thoughts use *first, second, third, in the first place, in the second place, next, finally, last.*

If *comparing* use *similarly, in the same way, likewise, equally important, equally so and so. By the same token* is pretty tired.

If *contrasting* use *yet, and yet, still, however, in contrast, on the contrary, on the other hand, to be fair, otherwise, still, or else, alternatively.*

If showing a connection in *time,* use *earlier, afterwards, later, before, at that time, then, since then, meanwhile, in the meantime, subsequently.*

If *summing up* use *in brief, in short, to repeat, as I have said, once again, in other words, as has been said.*

If offering *examples* use *for example, for instance, as follows, that is.* Be careful with the Latin abbreviations *e.g. (for example)* and *i.e. (that is).* In Formal you don't use abbreviations. And if you don't say *e.g.* and *i.e.,* that's a reason not to write them.

If you want to point out a *cause* relationship, use *so, and so, hence, thus, then, as a result, consequently.*

If you want to intensify the next idea, use *in fact, after all, of course, surely, certainly, in any case, at any rate, to tell the truth, to be sure, whatever the reason.* But these don't help much.

This list of connectives, like the list of conjunctions on page 125, reminds you of ways to develop ideas. Connectives are similar to conjunctions, but conjunctions (usually) follow commas, and connectives follow periods or semicolons. *Carol has her problems; for example, Bob loves hotdogs. But she cooks them. After all, she's his wife.*

A problem with these glue words, besides being tempted to use them too often, is that the glue is weak. The ideas have to match up. Success in making transitions depends on the ideas. You can say *The Germans love music and eat sausages.* You can't say *The Germans love music and began the war.* You can say *She has freckles on her but I love her.* You can't say *she has freckles on her and I love her.*

A writer's skill is shown in the smoothness of her transitions. You can tell a good writer just by the way she uses *and* and *but* and leaves them out. *But* is the great word for writers. *And* is the troublesome word, causing no end of logical problems. *The world is a closer place* and *Stud deodorant is a part of it. She's a Scorpio* and *all three of her sons married Scorpios. I am an American,* and *I am proud of it.* You can begin a sentence with *and,* of course, but you'll have a sneaky feeling that the new thought should have been worked into the sentence before. *He still likes girls. And he's 96 years old.* In Formal that should be *Even at 96, he likes girls.*

Putting in the conjunction or leaving it out is important. Take the saying *Love me little, love me long.* If this idea were not put so well it wouldn't have become a proverb. It might have been put *Love me little, and you will love me long* or *If you love me little then you will (or I hope you will) love me long.* This last way, the clearest way, would be right for Formal. Sometimes the clearest way is a little dull.

If you can dispense with a conjunction or connective (or anything) without a serious loss in smoothness or clarity, do it. Writing that's crawling with *and, buts,* conjunctions, and connectives is condescending to the reader or fishy. These words cannot paper over cracks in the thought. How to think without cracks, without stopping, that's our next two lessons.

Lesson Six

Writing: Before, During, After

The Need to Plan

There are three steps in writing: planning, actually writing, and revising. Young writers must put a lot of effort into what they do before and after writing. As they gain experience they can spend less effort on planning and revising. These are the steps in writing that need to be taught, and these are the only steps that can be taught. First, the plan.

Your parents probably told you there were at least two ways of doing a job—the easy way and the hard way. The easy way is planned. Writing is a job like any other, it just differs in requiring a shocking amount of effort. Even great writers squawk about having to write. Dr Johnson said I wonder that so many people have written who might have let it alone. In view of the strenuous work, it's surprising that so many people do not plan their compositions to save themselves effort while writing. They'll draw up a neat plan for a birdhouse, but won't plan a paper or report that could affect their careers.

The main reason they don't plan is that planning is even harder than writing. It requires prolonged and concentrated thought, and that's hard for everybody. Also, they may feel that a plan will inhibit them as they write and halt the flow of ideas. This notion is silly, because the plan assures a steady flow of ideas and saves the writer from drowning in them.

Some people have to start scribbling right away. They need to get something down. Engineers say they need paper to talk with—talking paper, they call it. A certain woman who loved to write everything down once said How do I know what I mean until I see what I say? The critic Harold Clurman was asked what he was going to say about a play he had just seen, and answered: I don't know yet, I haven't talked to my pencil. It's true that right things to say, lovely things, come once you begin to write. But if you have many things to say, you need a plan to sort them out.

The hard way to write is to begin scribbling away. You may get fifty or a hundred good sentences down, but when you try to fit them together—they're like pieces from different puzzles. If you know the tricks of making transitions you can fit almost anything together—as you can make clothing fit by opening seams and taking in and letting out material. But that's work. Make things to size. The easy way is to refrain from writing as long as possible, and spend your effort in thinking and planning. That way you don't commit yourself to sentences and paragraphs you have to fiddle with or throw out later on, or that you keep, even though you shouldn't, just because you've sweated over them.

Most people write the way a musician composes, by making a start and going on from there to the finish. I tout the painter's method, making a design and then filling in the details. I may have contributed to the notion that writers go from small to large, work up instead of down, because that's the way I've gone in this course—from word to sentence to paragraph, and now to the whole. Maybe I should have started with what the writer should start with, the plan. The writer of course chooses the words and sets them down one by one, but without some notion of where she's going, the words don't come. The words, the details of writing, make it succeed, as details make every art succeed, but they do so only by contributing to the overall design. When you find yourself blocked, skipping from subject to subject, fumbling for words, wrestling with sentences, that means the plan needs work.

In planning, you have to start at the finish and work backwards. Thinking sometimes feels that way, that you're moving backwards or sinking. Hard thought can make you dizzy. This feeling of going backwards is common among writers, because they, unlike other thinkers, start with the conclusion—an attitude, a belief, a thesis, a story they want to persuade others to accept. The writer has to go back in her own mind to find support for what she is presenting to the audience. She has to keep an eye on three things at once—herself, the subject, and the audience. She handles the subject, questions herself, and deals with others. Scientific problems are easy in comparison.

Writers have trouble beginning because the beginning is farthest from the end, which they already know. The plan has to be worked out backwards and written forwards. The real work of writing—everyone knows it—is getting ready. The severe discipline lies in what must be done before the sentences appear. Once the typewriter keys or the pen starts moving, the battle is over, the writer breathes easier.

Thinking and Writing

Thinking is like certain other words—*art, poetry, grammar*—in that it stands for a category of activity and also for the ideal type of that activity. We may wonder what our cat is thinking, but whatever it is, it's not what IBM wants us to do when it gives us signs saying THINK. Thinking covers all kinds of mental events—jumbled up sensations, perceptions, images, concepts. Some of these can be steered in the right direction and some cannot. In the general sense of the word, thinking is equated with consciousness. In the ideal sense, it refers to the ability to control thoughts, follow them up, and communicate them.

When the mind is working well, directing the thought, it works in an impersonal way duplicable in other minds. When mathematicians see an equation their minds analyze it in the same way. They're thinking. When musicians read a score and follow the music in their heads, they're thinking. When you express yourself clearly in sentences, you're thinking, and when your audience follows what you say, they're thinking. As a sharable and impersonal activity, thought seems opposed to *creativity* and *originality.* Thought is strictly controlled by form; its forms are called languages. Our ability to use our primary language, the language of words, is usually considered the best indicator of our ability to think.

Like it or not, we're judged in this world according to our intelligence, which is judged by how we use our tongues. The word *dumb* means not only silent but stupid. Beautiful but dumb blondes do not marry millionaires, they marry other dumb blondes. One may wonder why intelligence is so highly prized, if it doesn't make people happier. That it doesn't pay to be too smart is proverbial. Psychoanalysts are smart, and commit suicide at ten times the normal rate. Apparently happiness is not so much our goal as is success. Intelligence brings *success.*

When people buy books on English, they're not just seeking to avoid mistakes but trying to become more intelligent. They know that the powers of the mind and the powers of expression are functions of each other, and grow or decline together. This view is not an error, though it is an error to suppose that one can get smart fast, or that if he uses the new, magic words he'll take over the company.

I've talked about thinking for this reason: if you're going to write, you should admit what writing is, and what it is—let's have no secrets—is thinking. If you can't think you can't write. Learning to write is learning to think. Everyone knows this, but pretends it isn't so, for though they want to write, they feel they can't improve their thinking. But of course they can. If writing were not thinking, not such a serious matter, then people wouldn't be so afraid of it. They know that by writing they expose their minds to others. It's pride that silences the would be writer. The reason writing is not taught in schools is not that writing can't be taught, it's that feelings can't be hurt. Don't worry about hurt feelings. Get the stuff down, no matter how bad it is. So it's not *Hamlet,* at least it's yours. A jabbering monkey is more fun than a silent genius. And every genius used to jabber.

Many words can flash in our mind while the trained part of the mind selects the right word. Many sentences can be framed and rejected while the chosen one is being spoken or written. Mental events are electrical, but sentences are slowly built. People speak and read only about a dozen sentences or a few hundred words a minute. Going faster than that becomes a meaningless trick.

The mind spends much more time composing written sentences than spoken. Written style can be elaborated into something very slow and artificial. That's often what's wrong with writing, and that may be why most people don't like to read, however much they love to talk and listen. Written words, put together like cars in a freight train, are far removed from the flashing thoughts in the mind.

The writer should try to speed up the writing, making it less slow and unnatural and more like talking. Though writing is read a little faster than speech is spoken, it seems slower and duller, and it is. The writer should try to write as if she were dictating. This is the best way to write, and it's a way of getting you to write. You're used to talking. Writing should flow, and slow down, and race like speech. Put the stuff down fast. Later on it can be tidied up.

Inside the mind it's like a silent movie—images, words, phrases are flashed, all is dim, jerky, chaotic. The writer has two jobs: to control this circus through articulate speech, and to get the little black marks on the paper to speak. With experience she has more and more thoughts that are *sentences,* and she stops writing down *things* she would never say.

Concentrating

What happens when people think who aren't much used to it? They let anything pop into their heads. Their minds, instead of working like a machine, stand there like a blackboard on which anything can be written by an invisible hand. The student reading a discussion of the causes of the Civil War keeps turning her thoughts to her boyfriend, or worries about the soap opera that's on television while she's reading. A businessman at a sales conference keeps thinking how much the ties cost that the other men are wearing. A voter listening to a politician is not really listening—only a few key words get thru—because he's thinking of how the politician looks and whether he can win. No one's mind is always under control. A human being is not a brain kept in a glass jar. Our needs and emotions are fierce and keep breaking in on us, stopping the train of thought before it goes anywhere.

Concentration, the ability to keep the mind from being interrupted, is not a hard skill like playing the violin, but an easy one, like meditating, relaxing, or swinging a golf club. The first thing to do in getting the knack of concentration is to eliminate distractions. Internal distractions of the mind—worries and desires—are bad enough without having to cope with external ones. Turn off the radio and TV. Shut out noise. Don't answer the phone. Stay away from members of the opposite sex. Stay away from members of your own sex.

If you worry you can't concentrate. But look at it the other way—if you concentrate you can't worry. Sit down and concentrate, and don't get up until something is accomplished—a chapter read, an outline planned, two pages written. If the mind starts to wander, catch it before it goes very far. Referring to a plan reminds you of what to focus on. Concentration will break from time to time, but don't be anxious when this happens. Don't start thinking about yourself—*I* can't think, *I* can't think—but get back to the subject. An English wit, Sydney Smith, said that he never could find any man who could think for two minutes together. But a lot can be done in under two minutes if one is thinking well.

Once you're off the track, getting back takes effort. You feel frustrated, feel you've been wasting time. That's why it's better to stray as little as possible, by following a map—your plan. We seldom notice just when our minds begin to wander, since everything happens so quickly in the mind. Wrapped up in what it's doing, it forgets where it's going. It's most liable to wander at the moment the thinking gets tough. But that's the crucial moment; that's what you watch for. Real thought only begins when the mind meets an obstacle. Most people give up or try a detour around the obstacle, and the detour takes them away instead of around. The obstacle should be faced: Why can't I think this thought? What don't I know? Maybe the obstacle can't be climbed, but if you try at least you'll know how far you can get. For the climb the will has to help and provide the power of concentration. All advice on writing is useless if one cannot learn to concentrate, and stay with a question the way a dog stays with a bone.

Everyone concentrates from time to time, and does it unconsciously when the work is interesting. So try to get interested in what you're doing. Convince yourself you want to do what you have to do. Some minds are stubborn, though, and need to be subdued, as some dogs need to go to obedience school. The mind has to learn *NO*. When it wants to wander off yank it back. This sounds easy, but it's hard, because people are not in the habit of watching what their minds are doing, since they are their minds. Here then is the trick of concentrating: dividing the mind into one part that works and another that watches.

The best way to divide the mind is to start a dialogue between the parts. Let the will question the intelligence and boss it around: What do you mean by that? What's this word? How can you say that? Back to the subject, please. Look at the problem a different way, you boob; you're getting nowhere. Break the problem into parts. Let's do a diagram to get the picture. What are other ways to look at it? What would a scientist say? an historian? a child? the devil? a conservative? Why are you stuck? What are you stuck on? Are we barking up the wrong tree? What's up there? Do we have a case or not? What are the facts? Stop moving off the topic. Why are you moving off? Do you know what you're talking about? You want a break? Eat a donut? Smoke? I'll let you if you state the problem clearly.

The will disciplines the mind by firing many such questions and orders at it. The will can coax and tease the mind or, if necessary, badger and crossexamine it. Writing is the result of this dialogue. People who go around talking to themselves aloud are considered odd, but people who sit around talking to themselves, whether silently or aloud, are thinkers. They are the ones who become articulate and win the Game of English. Athletes and performers are always muttering and giving little lectures to themselves. Why shouldn't a writer do the same? especially if writing is the most difficult game. Writers tend to view what they've done as a collaboration, maybe between their inspired self and their critical self, or maybe with their Muse or an imaginary reader over their shoulder. Maybe that's why they're so fond of saying *we* and *us,* when no one knows who *we* is. Writing only looks and sounds like a monologue; it's really a condensed dialogue.

Let's say you want to write an attack on privilege, on the tax benefits of being wealthy. How do you write it? Do you just tell what the tax law is and what privileges it provides? Do you just offer a series of facts? What you're expected to write is what *you* want to say, and you have to think about the subject in relation to yourself. You have to concentrate on you and the subject. You are part of the subject. The thinking that writers do must include thinking about themselves.

That's why you should get used to questioning yourself as if you were two people. This does not mean that when you write you're expected to write about yourself. But you have to think about you, you have to think about what you're thinking. Here you are working on your piece on the income tax. To start, you could ask: What result do I want? Why am I talking about the rich? Do I envy them, admire them? What should I think about them? What do they do with their money? Do they deserve it? Do I deserve my money? What does *deserve* mean? How did they get rich? Can I get rich too? Should I? Why? Why not?

Here are enough questions for a lifetime. You may only have time to work on a few of them and maybe you'll find them unanswerable. But you have to work on hard questions like these, though they may strike you as leading away from the topic of the tax laws. They are really leading you into the topic. How can you talk about *inequities* and *privileges* unless you examine what *you* mean by these words? Any subject that involves right and wrong involves personal judgments and thus involves you.

If you can't find answers to your questions, then what do you write about? You write about how far you got into the questions, how they might be answered, whether they can be answered. You'll have plenty to write without having plenty to say. Thinking proceeds by asking good questions, and a good question is one whose answer is unknown. Thinking is done with questions, not with answers. When you say I'm thinking of the answer, that means you don't have the answer. An answer can only be remembered.

Very little writing is straight reporting, and personal judgments are involved in deciding what should be reported. Writing cannot be totally impersonal, although most Formal writing tries to sound impersonal. How it sounds is one thing, but how the writer thinks is another. There's no way for her to stay completely out of the picture. If she has to think, and not just remember, she has to think about herself, and question herself in regard to the topic. It's hard to do this. When people question themselves, they come up with answers they don't like. But if they don't like them, who will?

Every subject can be as hard or as easy as you want to make it. There's no end to the thinking to be done on any subject. You can't run out of questions. The supply of *why* questions alone is inexhaustible. *You* are an especially handy inexhaustible subject. Let's say you're doing a piece on the sex life of the praying mantis. Why? Start with *you,* before going on to *it* and *them.*

Gathering Ideas

Gathering ideas, strange as it may seem, is fun. As a matter of fact, some people pay others to listen to them do it—analysts are paid to listen to their clients free associate, and that's what gathering ideas is. When a group gathers ideas they *brainstorm* to get a torrent. Arranging the ideas or planning is work, but gathering ideas is fun, like picking a bouquet.

In gathering ideas you want a big sheet of paper for jotting down whatever comes into your mind on the topic. Jot down words, abbreviations, phrases, slang, anything. Don't write sentences, because that slows you down. And besides, you wouldn't use these sentences in the composition anyway. In gathering ideas the aim is to get a big bunch without worrying how good they are. Do not list the ideas. Scatter them all over the paper. Put them in groups if you like. If you list the ideas, that may suggest a plan for using them, and you don't want a plan yet.

Ready with the sheet of paper? Our topic is hotdogs. Pretend you have to write an essay on hotdogs. Take five minutes now to gather ideas about hotdogs, and I'll do the same. Start.

Here's what I jotted down: are they hot   where dogs   hush puppies   hotfoot   dogfish   dogwood   dogdays   dogpatch color: pink   red   brown   gray   juicy   dry   wrinkled   short 3 to 12 inches   bun size   flat buns   soggy buns   toasted buns   buns too short   too long   fall apart   buns vs rolls   where from   who invented   why   how popular other countries   where eaten   ballparks   picnics   kids   whats in em   yuck   dont ask   cereal   fat beef   pork   chicken   spices   flavoring   chemicals   what parts of animals   best to know   best not to know   why want to know   rely on taste   who likes em I dont   why kids like em   dont taste like meat   kids not like meat   easy to eat   hold in hand   reason for bun shape   whole thing   what else   mustard   yellow   brown kinds of mustard   how much mustard   sauerkraut   Coney Island with chile   ketchup   pigs in blanket   hot dog on stick   deep fried frankfurter or wiener   skin casing   artificial casing   snappy chewy skin   past present future of hotdog   big future meat substitute

You get the picture. My list was probably more thorough, more wide ranging than yours, with more questions to pursue. That's understandable because I'm the teacher and have to show off. As in every task, a lot depends on motivation. When writing comes hard, there's lack of motivation. Deal with that problem first. Maybe you didn't want to write on hotdogs. Maybe you didn't want to write. Then why'd you buy this book? Who are you not to write on hotdogs? Somebody has to. Are you the teacher? Not everybody gets to be teacher.

I've put down several dozen ideas or hints about hotdogs. I can sort these ideas; I see that they fall into groups that would make good topics for the four or five paragraphs or sections I want to write. First paragraph: What's a hotdog and what good is it? Second paragraph: Where, when, how eaten. Third: Reasons for hotdog success. Fourth: Past, present, future of hotdog. Fifth: The Ideal Hotdog. With a plan such as this, writing a good essay shouldn't take anyone more than half an hour. You could write a whole essay on why hotdogs are called hotdogs, without having the foggiest idea of why they are. You don't need *ideas* if you have questions. Questions are ideas.

Let's try another topic. Ready? This one is not cats, it's

earthworms. Dig the earthworm for five minutes. Back already? Here's what I jotted: fishing   putting worm on hook   all fish seem to love   irresistible   what a way to die   worms dont seem to mind or do they   handling worms   can of worms   dirt in can   where dig   rotting vegetation best   eat worms   Im gonna eat some worms   why do kids eat em   must look good   I used to dont anymore   why not   used to play with em   appearance disgusting, movement disgusting?   people dont like   or pretend not to wheres head   wheres tail   worms crawl in worms crawl out   do worms crawl   do snakes crawl   night crawlers   snakes and worms   worst worms like snakes   snappy muscular worms   cost of worms   raising worms big money   usefulness of   aeration of soil   leveling of lawns   how many worms   how many species sex life of worm   top speed   length of worm   robins vs worms how robin catches worms   looks listens   other birds   early bird catches   why   worms in city   worms on sidewalks

Here are a number of ideas to work with without my having to read any articles about worms, and there's no law against reading an article or two before gathering ideas. With these ideas five or more paragraphs could easily be written. First paragraph: Worms and fishing. Second: Finding and keeping worms. Third: Appearance and activities of worms. Fourth: Bad things about worms. Fifth: Good things. If I knew a lot about worms and fishing I'd write the whole essay on that. This gathering of ideas is awfully easy once you're used to it. If you want more practice, gather ideas for these topics: *a perfect dinner, watching baseball on TV, checking out at the supermarket, the ideal vacation, collars and ties, the weirdest person I know.* Practicing with easy topics prepares you for the other kind.

This technique of snatching any idea from anywhere should be used for even the most rarefied topics. The writer is expected to think deeply through concentrating and questioning, but is also expected to think widely and inclusively, to make sure that what's interesting or important will not be ignored. This technique of ranging thru a field like a hunting dog may seem at first rather wasteful, but saves time in the long run, and brings a lot that you can work with within reach. You needn't worry about finding enough ideas. There's an infinite supply of them— questions. Every subject can be seen and handled from different points of view. Every subject is related to others, and these can be brought in. Really, couldn't you talk about any subject? If you were asked to write on vodka, couldn't you move on to drinking? If you were asked to write on differential calculus, couldn't you talk about why you never got that far in math? No one is required to be an expert on everything. You can sneak off the topic to topics nearby. Knowledge is supposed to be a seamless web, or one big subject. An old definition of an educated person is one who can talk indefinitely on any subject. She can do this, not because she knows more than the uneducated person, but because she can articulate or join what she knows. Being educated means being skilled in listening talking reading and writing.

Focusing Your Topic

Choosing a topic is probably the most fun there is in writing, but it may take work—candidates for the doctorate can spend years looking for a topic—and it may take luck—white sharks and godfathers pop up from nowhere. But you shouldn't agonize over the choice of topic. Any topic can be handled interestingly. The poet Cowper wrote an epic about a sofa. Hemingway wrote well on boring, silly topics—shooting big game, killing bulls, war.

You're part of the subject, and that's how you make it exciting. If you're bored, you'll be boring. If you've been assigned a topic, at least you're not responsible for choosing it. And there's no need to fret at having to write on a disagreeable topic; it's good discipline. Greek and Roman students were trained to write on both sides of a question and made to praise baldness, suicide, obedience to tyrants.

You might consider shying away from topics you have strong feelings about. Your feelings will show, and no one cares about them, except your mom, sometimes, and you're not writing for her. As a judge withdraws from a case in which he has an interest, writers should perhaps do the same. It's hard to write about AstroTurf and the designated hitter when you're foaming at the mouth.

Pick those topics you have your own ideas about, for

nothing is more stimulating to the writer than the belief she's saying something for the first time, and nothing more discouraging than the feeling that all she can offer is a rehash. Writers plagiarize when their topics are too ambitious. Check whether you have the knowledge or experience to handle the topic. You wouldn't write about life on a commune without having been to one.

The narrower, more limited the topic, the easier the writing will be. To inexperienced writers this seems like nonsense, for they assume that the bigger the topic the easier the writing. But the work of writing does not lie in accumulating a certain heap of words or in thinking easy thoughts on big topics; the work lies in thinking of things for you to say, and whether you say anything depends on whether you can narrow a focus and put outside the focus the infinite number of things that might be said. *Everything* is a topic on which nothing can be said.

Inexperienced writers should not tackle grand, abstract topics like patriotism, education, punishment, equality, justice, freedom. It may be that these are the only subjects worth talking about, but you run risks in talking about what you don't know about. Big topics are the worst. General ideas—*loyalty, capitalism, God*—these are either boring or inflammatory. Are you inflamed? See what I mean?

For a five hundred word article you'd work on a topic like Dinner at Chicago's Best Restaurant, for a thousand word article, a topic like Chicago's French Restaurants, and for a book, a topic like A Guide to Chicago's Restaurants. But focusing is not so easy when the topics loom. Asked to write on inflation or the French Revolution, you might very well feel threatened.

To narrow your focus on a topic, work right away on the question of tone, weighing what you can say and would like to say with what the audience wants you to say. Do not think about a *title.* Wait until the writing is finished; titles are too important to be chosen quickly, and they must be accurate. (Since the audience wants to get the tone from the title or the first sentence or two, snappy titles and openings are not always appropriate.)

Your focus on the topic will remain unclear if you are thinking of the writing primarily as *self expression* or as a *study* of the subject, and neglect what the audience wants. It's always tempting—and always a mistake—to forget about Them, who make the writing *work*. Thinking about any of the three separately—you, it, and them—wastes your time. In thinking about hotdogs mull over what you can say about them and what the audience is willing to hear. You *could* go on for hours about hotdog facts and put everyone to sleep. You *could* deliver a jeremiad against hotdogs and infuriate all the hotdog lovers.

If you solve the problem of tone, you don't have to worry about the other nagging questions that writers are supposed to ask themselves, such as: What's my point? What's the big idea? Why am I telling them all this? Forget these questions. When you write, you don't have to have a single purpose or main idea or thesis. Ideas are for inventors, messages are for Western Union. Writing is discourse, or talking about a topic. If you want to talk you just talk. You don't have to defend yourself, or say I am now writing about the widget because people are not sufficiently aware, etc, or In this paper I intend to prove, etc.

If the audience doesn't have to know the writer's purpose, she doesn't either. Did Shakespeare understand his purpose when he wrote *Hamlet*? The writer's purpose in discussing the topic need be nothing more than to discuss the topic. She doesn't have to *say* anything, but needs to hit the right tone. If she has something to say, she's in luck, because her job will probably be easier. It would be harder only if the audience doesn't want to hear what she wants to say—which happens. If the writer winds up saying nothing, but saying it with the right tone, she will be doing exactly what most writers have always done. You can write a wonderful piece on hotdogs without deciding what they are, what they should be, whether they taste good, whether people should eat them, whether you like them, etc.

The message in writing is often overvalued, because its presence is what distinguishes writing from the related arts of painting and music. But writing is primarily a formal art like the others, and a good writer is one who has done her lessons and learned the form. Audiences looking for *instruction* are hard to find. If your audience ever starts asking What's your point? Why are you telling me this? they're doing so not because you have nothing to say, but because you don't know how to say nothing. You have no tone.

Thinking How to Do It

In any composition the larger the part the more important it is (word, sentence, paragraph, chapter, the whole) and the more important it is, the more attention it should get. When the unskilled writer hears the command Write! she immediately starts thinking of words and sentences and gives no thought to the paragraphs and the whole. Writing is done with words and sentences but it's not about them. It's about you, it, and the audience. What can you tell them about it? What do you want to tell them? What do they want to hear?

Sometimes the topic *determines* the tone. If you're speaking over a coffin or writing a dissertation you can't clown around much. Or the audience determines the tone. When the audience is all important and the topic is of no importance, the writing is called *academic.* When the writer's personality determines the tone the writing is *stylish.* Tone can be anything—ironic, deferential, lascivious. There's even the solemn tone of no tone, which for some reason is thought to be ideal for the reporting of news.

As you decide on the tone, think about the basic mode of the piece. Is it going to be telling, describing, explaining, or arguing? Telling and describing are usually associated with fiction, explaining and arguing with non fiction.

Telling can be narrative or dialogue, a report of what happened or what was said. Telling is the easiest kind of writing, for there's no problem in arranging the material; it's arranged according to time. But since telling is the easiest and commonest mode, it's the hardest to excel in. Most great literature is telling.

Describing is another easy kind of writing, a listing of impressions that does not attempt to go below the surface. The material is arranged from the large to the small, from the whole to the part, or from the general to the particular. Describing is thus a narrowing of focus, and is often anticlimactic in its effect. Straightforward description gets tedious quickly, and a writer usually tries to inject it with some dramatic interest or create a little excitement in *moving* from one part to another. Readers skip description, so writers can do it too. Mark Twain once inserted into a description the words *a solitary esophagus winging its way into the sunset* and apparently no one noticed his little joke.

Explaining is more complicated. Explaining is presenting information, and interesting questions arise as to how the information can best be presented. It's usually arranged in one of the logical ways I'll get to in a minute.

Arguing is a special kind of explaining. Explaining and arguing often overlap; behind every exposition is an argument, in the sense of a point that the writer is trying to make. The word *argument* is used in two senses: as the design or purpose of a piece of writing, and as the attempt to persuade. The word is ordinarily used in this second sense and has bad connotations. *Don't argue with me. No arguments during dinner.* Because argument is disliked the cleverest kind doesn't look or sound like argument.

The four modes of writing seldom appear in their pure form. Exposition pops up everywhere, in narrative, description, and argument. Narratives and descriptions can conceal hidden yet powerful arguments. If the modes are always getting mixed, why bother thinking about them? Because, the less you mix up the modes, the better your chances of maintaining the tone. In going from mode to mode you confuse the reader. What are you up to? Are you describing or are you telling a story? Are you explaining what happened or saying it should never have happened? It's poor tactics to interrupt a hot argument for a cold explanation, or slow down a narrative with description. Modes in writing like modes in music set up the proper responses in the audience and get results merely by being sustained. So when you tell, tell dramatically, when you describe, describe vividly, when you explain, explain carefully, when you argue, argue convincingly.

Planning

There's a lot to do before you get to write—gathering ideas and pursuing them, focusing the topic, deciding on the tone, finding the facts, drawing up the plan. These are not separate steps and do not have to be done in order. The mind doesn't work that way. It spends time on one job, switches to another, then back again. I've talked about what has to be done as if there were separate steps in order to impress on you all the work that needs to be done before you go onstage to perform. Organizing the material and drawing up the plan is the hardest part of writing and thus the part most often skipped.

Planning is hard enough without having to put the plan in the form of an outline. Most students have been asked to submit outlines that follow a form. There's a topic outline and a sentence outline. The sentence outline is the sillier, for how can you write sentences without knowing what's before or after them? These formal outlines have Roman and Arabic numerals, capital letters and small letters, and there has to be at least two of everything. It's hard enough to think in advance of what you're going to write without having to fool with alphabet soup outlines. An outline belongs to you. Do it how you want. See it as a friendly time-saver, not as something to turn in to the teacher for your punishment.

Those who complain they can't write don't have an outline. They don't lack things to say, but try to say everything at once. The point of an outline is to let you do all the things you want to do one by one in good order. You take an outline or shopping list to the store; if you're used to the store, you put the items on the list in a certain order.

There are different ways of ordering the items in an outline. The obvious way of proceeding when writing about events is to use *time* order. *Goldilocks fell asleep on the bed, and then. . . .*

The second obvious way of proceeding is to use *space* order. Things are described according to where they are in relation to other things. *In the first row sat the sleek professors. In the next row were the twitching instructors.*

Ordering the items logically is more complicated. There are four basic ways. You can use *examples. Women are naturally superior to men: they bear children, live longer, and do not lose their hair.* In giving examples—facts, figures, illustrations—you can assert something and then give examples of it, or use the more unusual and effective way of giving the examples first and then saying what they are examples of. Whatever you say that's disputable should be backed by examples.

Another logical way is to explain *cause and effect* relationships. You can talk of causes first and induce the effects, or talk about effects first and deduce the causes. The deductive way is preferred. People talk about causes first when they don't know the effects. *Bad people go to Hell. If Viet Nam goes, all of Southeast Asia will go.*

Another logical way is to *analyze,* or break the subject into its parts. *There are five kinds of ape: gorilla, chimpanzee, orangutang, gibbon, and man.* You can go from the whole to the parts or from the parts to the whole. The better way is the way these lessons are ordered.

The last way of proceeding is by *comparison.* Comparisons are risky since no two things are exactly alike, so far as we know. They're only alike in certain respects. A remote comparison is an *analogy,* a close comparison is a *definition.* Comparisons are more prevalent in writing than is generally supposed, since definitions are comparisons. Overt and extended comparisons are tedious. Definitions are tedious. Implicit comparisons are better, and are unavoidable, if every common word, standing as it does for a class, involves comparisons. *Roy Cohn is a lawyer.* Here Cohn is being compared to other men called lawyers. Contrasts are easier to do than comparisons, but are even less interesting, since it goes without saying that things are different. This accounts for the weakness of negative statements: *Blank blank is not blink blink.* So?

In drawing up your plan don't make it too elaborate or detailed. It should have a topic for each paragraph you're going to write. Paragraphs vary in size, remember: you can have an item in your plan that you may be able to handle in one sentence, or one that you'll want to extend thru two or three paragraphs. The most helpful kind of plan is one that includes *ideas,* as jotted propositions or questions, rather than just *names* of topics. This gives you a clearer idea of how to develop the paragraph.

Here's a good outline (all outlines are good) for an essay on beer cans: *billions of cans, colors, collectors, aluminum, popup rings, litter, back to bottles.* And here's a better outline: *See cans everywhere, billions, US becoming garbage pit. Some cans beautiful, well worth collecting, should be more collectors to pick them up. Aluminum cans may be the answer, since they're returnable, but the price for returns is still low. Popup rings dangerous and double the items littered.* You can do the rest. It's not hard to do outlines once you've done a few. But just as the writing won't come without an outline, an outline won't come without thought.

In drawing up a plan try to use climactic order. People read what keeps them in suspense. Don't announce your purpose (readers might not like it). Keep your cards close to your vest or whatever. Don't think about opening or closing. These are easily added afterwards, if needed. Short compositions needn't open or close. In long compositions you may want some little formalities in getting under way and in concluding. Conclude only if there's something to conclude. Don't explain what you've done, don't apologize, don't sum up, don't repeat. First impressions count, last impressions last.

Finding the Facts

By now you should feel confident you can handle any topic. You can discuss any topic merely by reflecting on it. But sometimes mere reflections will not satisfy your audience or you. You'll want to hunt down some facts, not because knowledge is an end in itself, as they say, but because you don't want to get caught making a mistake in a question of fact. A mistake in grammar is a misdemeanor, but for a mistake in fact you can be up on a felony charge.

You can't keep from making some mistakes. No one has a monopoly on truth, no one can check out everything that's supposed to be a fact. But you can steer away from embarrassing mistakes by offering as few facts as possible. (Facts by themselves, remember, quickly become boring.) And you shouldn't present as fact what you dimly remember or what you think really ought to be a fact. At least ninety nine percent of the opinions in the world are thought to be facts, and that's a fact.

Few writers are bold enough to invent their facts, they let their subconscious minds do it for them. Facts are so esteemed by the public they are often imitated. The media are filled with pseudo facts, which tip off their falseness by sounding a little too precise: *Shakespeare had 190 IQ, study shows homos happier than heteros, cave has six and a half million bats, cat urine increases gas mileage, orgasm machine shows masturbation more satisfying than intercourse.* What sage was it who said there were no facts?

If you present something as a fact, that means you can back it up, that you have someone to blame the fact on if it turns out to be wrong. You don't have to check every fact. The facts you assert as your own experience are not going to be questioned. Facts that are commonly known are not going to be questioned. Facts that are not commonly known have to be checked. You can say that hotdogs are delicious or that they vary in size, color, and taste. But you can't say that Americans ate two billion hotdogs in 1980 unless you have someone to blame this statement on. You can say George Washington was the greatest American or that he was married to Martha. But you can't say he had a lot of girlfriends or that he was the richest man in the country, unless you can offer an authority to back you up. Whether you actually cite the authority depends on the tone of the piece.

Writing is superior to speaking in one important respect. It allows the writer time to check the facts. This makes for work, and the writer may have to find many more facts than she will actually use, as she explores the terrain around her subject. She wouldn't want to write that bees die after they sting, if bumblebees don't, or write that black slaves were materially better off than poor white farmers, if they weren't. Of course, she could go ahead and say these things. It's a free country. She can blow herself up skipping and hopping thru a minefield of facts.

One way of making sure you have the facts is to apply the standard questions that reporters tack to their desks for reminders: Who What When, Where How and Why. Kipling wrote: I keep six honest serving men, They taught me all I know; Their names are What and Why and When and How and Where and Who. (It's interesting to see that in Kipling's day *Who* comes last, and in our day—the day of the Owl—*Who* comes first.) These six questions protect you from sins of omission and help you to grasp the scope of your topic. What will you emphasize—the Who, the What, the How?

Though you're now convinced of the preciousness of facts, you still may not know where they are. Chase them down in their hiding places thru legwork and fingerwork. Legwork in a library, fingerwork on a telephone dial. Professional writers and researchers stay away from the library as much as they can and do their research over the phone. They know that those they call are surprisingly eager to offer information—everyone likes to be asked. So never be shy about phoning or asking. If you're writing about Japanese beetles, talk to the county agricultural agency—about marijuana, talk to your local police, about gun control, talk to the National Rifle Association, about women priests, talk to a local clergyman.

Of course not all research can be done over the phone; you may have to go to the library. Libraries have many dead ends and detours, so don't dash in and dash around. If your topic is narrow, technical, or of recent origin you had better check with the reference librarian to see where the materials can be found and whether your library has them. There are now a surprising number of guides to reference materials *according to subject.* Whether you ask the librarian for help should not depend on whether you're an extrovert, but on the nature of your topic.

Some people go straight to the card catalog. But since this catalog lists books, it's not much help. For almost any assignment, facts you require are to be found in reference works or periodicals, or they are hidden deep within books. Don't think of calling for a pile of books; get the right book or two and read just the right parts.

Orient yourself to your topic by reading about it in a general or special encyclopedia. Articles in the encyclopedia include bibliographies, or lists of relevant books and articles. The smaller the bibliography, the more useful it is. Encyclopedias are lovable since the information is so compressed and since the articles are often written by experts. What the encyclopedia knows, you don't have to.

In taking notes on what you read keep these tips in mind.

1. Do no serious or deep research until you have a plan for the writing. Your plan may change as research proceeds, but if you don't start with a plan you'll waste time. 2. Write your notes on small cards. Make sure that each card somehow indicates the name of the book or the article you're using and the page you're on. By putting single ideas and single facts on separate cards you'll be able to move the cards around later on to help arrange your own argument. 3. Jot down facts, and put arguments in your own words. Paraphrase only good arguments you might use. 4. *Copy* only those statements that are *quotable*. A statement is quotable when it is extraordinary or wrong, when it comes from an authority, or when it expresses an idea so well you could not say it better.

Copy very little. You're taking notes; a note is only a note. When you run across something useful, decide right off whether to compress it into a few words or copy it out exactly and fully. Do paraphrases any way you want, and use lots of abbreviations. *Copying* has to be perfect, because if you ever quote what you've copied, fairness requires that the quote be full and exact. Don't forget to mark what you copy as being copied, since you don't want to plagiarize, accidentally or on purpose, for that's a choice between being a boob or a crook.

Writing

It's easy to talk about the steps that lead to writing, but the writing itself, that's a mystery. You just do it. When you learned to talk, you had to learn it all by yourself, and you must do the same with writing. In learning to talk you prepared for it by listening to others for a year or two before you could do it, and in learning to write you have to prepare for it by many years of reading. If you haven't read much, or haven't read closely, you will find writing a torture—not because you have nothing to say, but because you're not used to the mere mechanics of writing. All the composition courses, drillbooks, and cute teachers in the world cannot turn non readers into writers. If you can't write without frequent mistakes, you have to catch up on reading.

Then learn writing by doing. Write anything—tirades, nonsense, letters, reviews, harangues, prayers, abuse, stories, poems, bawdy pieces—anything that comes easy. The hand has to get used to writing, has to take over the mechanics—spelling, punctuating, paragraphing. Anyone can make sounds on a piano and anyone who can talk can write something, but with practice anyone can make agreeable sounds on a piano or learn to write agreeably. To make beautiful music or write beautifully, that of course requires a gift. Some writers lack the necessary feeling for sentences, and are said to have a tin ear, like unmusical people. But many unmusical people learn to listen better, and many poor writers learn to listen to what they write.

Like a pianist, a writer will lose her place from time to time. When this happens to you, talk to yourself, focus on what you've just put down, try to make the idea clearer by saying what it is. That you have a subject means you felt a predicate nearby. If no respectable predicate steps forward, move on and work on something else. If an idea refuses to come clear, it may very well turn out to be an unclear idea.

Famous writers are always being asked how they write, and they can only say such things as: I crank myself up at dawn, I write on a portable down in the basement, I scribble on cards and then on pads, I turn purple. Obviously, they don't quite know what goes on. Their hands seem to know what to do. There's no best time or best way or even good way to write. Dr Johnson said: A man may write at any time, if he will set himself doggedly to it. You may have to dog it. If you sit there long enough glaring at your notes or outline, you'll get bored and then start to write. Glare at the outline then, and start to fill in what's missing. Writing is only a matter of turning scratch notes and outline into a hasty draft. In this draft use abbreviations and initials to maintain speed. Don't expect the draft to be good. And don't write with a pencil; the smell of cedar is intoxicating.

If you can't think how to begin, for goodness sake, don't begin at the beginning. The importance of the beginning is overrated. Some teachers of writing make students throw away their first paragraph or first page or first chapter. In writing it's the middle that counts. Begin to write the part most interesting to you, for that will be the easiest. Just as the choice of the title is the final touch, the writing of the beginning and the ending should be the next to final touches. Besides, you have to know what's in the middle before you can do a proper beginning and ending. A redeeming feature of writing is that you can do any part of it at any time (before your deadline). As Dr Johnson said: Sir, it is no matter what you teach them first any more than what leg you shall put into your breeches first. Sir, you may stand disputing which is best to put in first, but in the meantime your breech is bare.

The fact that writing can be done anytime is not always a blessing. If the writer postpones the work, she'll feel guilty. Or she may work too long and hard, striving for the unattainable goals of accuracy and eloquence. In either case she'll learn to hate to write. The best way to write is to do it, get it over with, turn it in. Many of my students write better under time pressure in class than when they work on assignments at home.

The idea is to write urgently but not frantically. Writing that comes fast is never as good as it seems and needs a lot of revising. Writing that comes slow lacks natural flow and spoken tone. If the writing doesn't come, stay where you are and keep struggling with it. Something will get done. It won't be easier tomorrow. You needn't be in a receptive mood to write, though you have to be in a receptive or creative mood to find new ideas or make breakthroughs in problems. The writing is not so much a matter of finding ideas as of revealing ideas already found. A writer's mind is like an udder: it fills up and is then milked. Milking is a relief. It only hurts on a dry udder.

Creative Writing

Whatever kind of writing you do—letters reports briefs memos sonnets—the *basic* problems of expressing yourself are the same—finding the point of view and the tone, planning the whole, choosing the right language, hammering out decent sentences. With the basics mastered, you're ready to write anything.

Those who turn to creative writing (narrative, dialog, and verse) suffer from a vivid imagination and a strong need to make something of their own. Everyone has some imagination and the desire to create. Everyone wants to talk, everyone wants to write. The writer is one who keeps on writing until people listen. You probably can tell you're a writer if you like to write despite being aware of how hard it is (Thomas Mann said the writer is one who finds writing more difficult than others), if you get excited when you read certain passages and think them beautiful, and if you find yourself frequently composing—framing consecutive sentences and hearing people talk inside your head. While ordinary people hear notes and words, musicians listen to music, and writers, to sentences.

Though writers are born and not made, there's no problem in teaching anyone who knows the rudiments of writing how to be competent in a particular kind of writing. Nearly all that is written is done within a strict form—short story, three act play, textbook, editorial. The requirements of form can be taught by a master and learned by an apprentice. Tuition is needed, not intuition. If creative means original, creative writing has to be the hardest kind. When there are no models to follow, writing is excruciating. But there are models for whatever you want to write, and you should read aloud and copy these models.

You shouldn't think that because you are *creative* you have to avoid the established forms. When a form is strict, it's because the product is in demand. Chase after a Great American Novel and you may never be heard from again. Of course, when a writer is really good, she can be overwhelmingly good, creating new forms. Works of art are judged—at least by the wiser judges—according to their merits rather than their formal shortcomings.

Writers will go on writing, but those who want to write particular things and maybe sell them should take courses from professionals. But not many of us should be encouraged to sign up. Pickings are slim. If *Redbook* receives 30,000 unsolicited short story manuscripts a year, why put yours on the pile? And instead of writing verse that no one wants because it's free, work in a bank and write me a good letter for a change.

Revising

The word *revision* originally meant *taking a second look*. Now it means *changing* or *improving*. Evidently there's no difference between taking another look and wanting to fix up what you see. What if you like what you see? You may like parts, but no writer ever likes the whole thing. All writers revise, and are constantly being drawn back to the scene of their crimes. A few lucky writers are experienced enough to make revisions as they go along, after each sentence. Inexperienced writers have to make painful revisions and sometimes re revisions.

All writing is rewriting. Revision only extends the criticism brought to bear during the writing into the period after the writing. Each sentence as it is put down represents a triumph over its competition. The triumph is always temporary, the number of competitors is infinite, and a bigger faster meaner sentence can come along at any time.

That figure of speech was intended to remind you that revision is a nasty business. You are not supposed to like what you see; you're supposed to attack it. If you create on Monday, on Tuesday you're still fond of your accomplishments. If you look at the stuff the next Monday, you'll see it more clearly. The longer the time between first and second draft, the better the second draft will be. This draft, with polishing, you may be able to tolerate. If the second draft fails to come clear or provide satisfaction, there's something wrong with the plan: a new plan should be devised and the whole piece rewritten. Though you will always feel that more revision is needed, if you revise too much you get far away from the original flow. Certain writers, like Conrad, revised too much, and made their prose stiff and careful.

Instead of subtracting when they revise, writers are tempted to add, jamming up the flow, or polish, making the surface too shiny. Let's say you've written: *I always like to say that golf is a good way to ruin a good walk.* In revising you cut lazy modifiers, so you cut *good* from *good walk.* The reader is not Mom, so you cut *I always like to say* and just say it: *Golf is a good way to ruin a walk.* You hope to jazz this up, so you write *Golf is a great way,* and then change that to *Golf is the best way to ruin a walk.* Maybe you want to drop a name and attribute the saying to a wit, so you write: *Golf, as Schlomo Pinkus says, is the best way to ruin a walk.* Where does this get you? You seldom improve the writing by adding and polishing. You improve it by stripping it. *Golf is a good way to ruin a walk.* That's the way to say it. In revising Kipling used a brush to block out words, and never touched the pen.

You can pick away at your writing like a slave in a jute mill, but the idea is to get it down quick and leave it pretty much alone. The temptation to add and polish leads to what's called overwriting. Overwriting is a poor term, because writing is a good thing and we need lots more of it. Overwriting can only refer to sentences that are overstuffed or distracting.

When you revise you apply what you know about good diction and good sentences and paragraphs. In final proofreading you work on little details, in revising you look at the parts in relation to the whole. Big revisions are made first, since that can relieve many smaller problems. If you feel that parts are not in the best place, drop your pencil and pick up the scissors. Cut the composition into paragraphs or sentence groups and shuffle these around until you come up with a better arrangement. Or draw arrows showing what goes better where. If you don't need the scissors, keep working with the pencil, repairing mistakes, cutting out and changing words, and recasting bad constructions. Anything that causes a lot of trouble has to go, has to be completely redone, or has to go away and stay away. The writer's best friend is the wastebasket.

Sometimes you'll run across a bit you can't bear to let go. When that happens ask yourself why you're defending *this* part. The more you fight, the more suspicious it is. You want to keep it because it's unusual, it's personal, it's you. That's just why the audience won't like it. We seek praise for what we're *not* good at. Murder your darlings, a Cambridge professor told his students. The runts in the litter have to go. I could have written several books with the adorable sentences I couldn't fit into this one.

When you revise ask yourself these questions. Was the main idea clear, or does it need more emphasis here and there?

(Often the main idea is not just clear, but belabored.) Have I used enough examples and illustrations to be persuasive? Have I given the audience too much credit or too little? Have I gone too fast or too slow? Is this paragraph necessary? Is this sentence necessary? And ask the most telling question of all: How would I like somebody to tell me what I just said?

Be sure to look for your kind of fault. Everyone has faults in personal style, since no one—hardly anyone—is a perfect person. Timid writers are wordy, write unemphatic sentences, resort to the passive voice. Those for whom things are simple write too simply, without qualifying and without persuading. Fourflushers send up clouds of smoke. Professors spend a lot of time clearing their throat. Whatever faults are in you will be discovered in your writing (which is a good reason to write).

Writers should face but often ignore the question of seeking and heeding editorial assistance. They are a proud lot and don't like to be helped. But a writer should seek whatever help she can get. She's not required to accept it, but she'd be foolish not to listen. Collaboration and editing often result in improvements. Shakespeare probably accepted assistance with his plays, since plays are subjected to a lot of revision. Writing done by committees is supposed to be terrible, but committees have produced the Bible, the King James translation, the Constitution of the United States, and the Communist Manifesto. Homer's work is the final version of the efforts of many poets.

To be interesting, writing must be personal. But revising and editing, oddly enough, usually makes writing less personal yet better. An editor is said to be someone who separates the wheat from the chaff and publishes the chaff. Only a writer could say something so nasty, so untrue, so enjoyable.

Condensing

Condensing or tightening the writing is only cosmetic surgery, but can make the difference between beauty and ugliness. Let's have more of it. Writers don't cut enough because they love the words they worked so hard to find. If they cut too much, they have to make up the losses. But cutting is so easy it makes editorial work more fun than writing: growing things takes sweat and patience, cutting things down is a kick.

When you condense you may be shocked at how much you can get rid of. Paragraphs can be reduced to sentences, sentences to clauses, clauses to phrases, phrases to words, and words can be thrown away. What's left? Only what's alive. Prose should be lean and muscular, though not be so compact it's unnatural, so musclebound it can't move. Boiling the writing down can be carried too far, and what's left can lose its flavor like the prose in condensed books. But doing too much cutting is seldom a danger. Skinny sentences are hardly so common as fat.

Sentences should breathe, have a certain ardency or glow. Occasionally a writer wants a fat, sleepy sentence to make a weak statement. Here's a hippo of a sentence from the Republican Party Platform of 1976: *The Republican Party favors a continuance of the public dialogue on abortion and supports the efforts of those who seek enactment of a constitutional amendment to restore protection of the right to life for unborn children.* This sentence might have been expressed: *The party favors the discussion of abortion and supports the efforts of those who support an amendment to restore protection of the right to life for unborn children.* The original sentence is unclearly vague, the revised sentence is clearly vague. The trick in being vague is to be vaguely vague, that is, don't get caught. Being obscure and evasive is more frequently called for in writing than teachers like to think. An awful lot of writers constitutionally take the fifth. But if you write this way, don't do it inadvertently, because you might start to believe in it. Too often, flabby, snivelling sentences are not written intentionally but because the words poured out too fast. Pascal once wrote to a friend that he would have written a shorter letter but didn't have time. Serious revision takes lots of time. Condensing takes little time, and becomes second nature with a bit of practice. Let's practice.

Combining sentences may spare a few words and always spares the reader the period pauses. It's easy to combine sentences that have the same subject. *Carol is strong. She can throw the ball as hard as a man. She's the best pitcher in the league.* Revised. *Carol throws the ball as hard as a man and is the best pitcher in the league.*

Another. *First the car was serviced. Then it was washed and waxed.* Revised. *The car was serviced, washed, and waxed.* You can put a number of verbs in one sentence. You can turn sentences into clauses. *We hope that you will come on the sixth. It's Bob's birthday. He will be twenty three years old.* Revised. *We hope you'll come on the sixth, which is Bob's twenty third birthday.*

After hearing me praise the subordinate clause, you may be surprised to hear me recommend that you change many subordinate clauses to phrases. Change the ones in which the verb isn't forceful. Most clauses that start *who is, which is,* and *that is* should be changed to phrases.

> Bob, who is presently a salesman, dreams of being a rock star.
> Bob, a salesman, dreams of being a rock star.

> Napoleon, who had just become Emperor, married Josephine.
> On becoming Emperor, Napoleon married Josephine.

> He told me a story that was scarcely believable.
> He told me a scarcely believable story.

When the subordinate clause has the same subject as the main clause, try to shorten it.

> After Bob bathed the dog, he got ready for the guests.
> After bathing the dog, Bob got ready for the guests.

> When I was a young girl, I did countless foolish things.
> When young I did countless foolish things.

> Carol took the train because she wanted to be there early.
> Carol took the train to be there early.

Many clauses and phrases can be reduced to single words.

> Because the tires were overinflated, the ride was bumpy.
> Overinflated tires made the ride bumpy.

> We sat out under a sky that was filled with stars.
> We sat out under the stars.

> In order to write better you will have to write more.
> To write better write more.

The dress was too hot for her to wear in the summertime.
The dress was too hot for summer.

Certain words should ring *alarms* in your mind, alerting you to flab. Slow roundabout phrases (*there is, that is, it is, it's a fact that, for your information*) should be reduced or left out. *It is easy to lose, Losing is easy. There is a bright future for us, Our future is bright.* Try not to use *thing.* It's often accompanied by some description of what the thing is. *You silly thing, You're silly.* Sentences with the phrase *and that's why* or *the reason is that* should be turned around. *He loves her and that's why he gave up hotdogs, He gave up hotdogs because he loves her.*

The *alarm* words *kind of* and *sort of* can usually be omitted. *This kind of lesson is easy, This lesson is easy.* You don't need to say *in the world* because that's where things are. *This is the best lesson in the world, This is the best lesson.* You seldom need to say *today*—just use the present tense. *Some* and *any* should always sound alarms. *There are some risks involved, Risks are involved. Yes, we don't have any bananas, Yes, we have no bananas. It was done without any fuss, It was done without fuss.* The articles *the, a,* and *an* can often be omitted. *The segregation of the men and the women, Segregation of men and women. The waiting time has been cut, Waiting time has been cut. Bring a lunch, Bring lunch.* If you say *one of,* readers wonder about the others. *Nietzsche was one of those crackpots. . . .* And the others?

Take out lazy adjectives and adverbs. *True facts,* strike *true. Serious problem,* strike *serious. Deeply moved,* strike *deeply.* You'll recall from Lesson Two how common wordiness is, and how much the writing is improved when it's cut.

Now you have your turn. I know you're dying to, it's fun to be mean. Hack away at this sentence. *On the table there were a great number of dolls that had been made by hand.* Did you cut that to *On the table were many handmade dolls?* Another. *The farmers here grow the apples which are used mainly for the juice.* Did you get rid of the farmers and say *Apples are grown here mainly for juice?* Do the rest of these yourself.

I like the kind of a cat that has curly whiskers.
He spoke to his audience in a boring manner and went on

without any conscious awareness as to how his audience was responding.

Even though there is a lack of water, I'll water my grass which is dry anyway.

It is the most serious drought in twenty years that is affecting farming in Iowa.

Perhaps the main cause to be deduced for the rebellion was that the people were beginning to not get enough to eat.

When you write a sentence like this last one—it happens—don't tinker with it, scrap it and try to express the idea simply. If you don't like the idea when it's expressed simply, scrap it. Somewhere, somehow, there's much more to say. If the words fall short of the number you have to produce, go back, get more ideas by thinking widely or deeply, and plenty of words come with them.

Proofreading

Sooner or later you will have to submit. Proofreading is the last desperate scrutiny of your manuscript before you hand it over for your reward or punishment. The circumstances of proofreading are scary, the work to be done is minute and at times upsetting. No wonder it's done poorly. Few people proofread their letters, and few students proofread their exams. But proofreading catches mistakes, and nothing should leave your hands with even one mistake. Reading maketh the full man, conference the ready man, and writing the *exact* man.

The majority of mistakes—these are in diction, spelling, grammar, and punctuation—result from carelessness and not ignorance. This carelessness is redoubled when the mistakes are not caught by proofreading. So what is worse—being ignorant of the correct form or forgetting on two occasions to use it? Those who are offended by mistakes don't care whether the mistakes result from stupidity or from laziness. In either case you lose, they win.

Once you're used to proofreading it's not so scary, but

routine and maybe even enjoyable. A copy editor or composition teacher catches mistakes the way an anteater catches ants. Here's how to find the ants in your writing.

First check the form. Do you have the right margins and spacings? Check the title and opening. Do they set the tone? Is the title accurate?

Now comes the trick of proofreading, a trick requiring you to do two things at once, like rubbing your belly and patting your head. You have to coordinate looking and listening. Beginning readers listen too much and look too little, mature readers look too much and listen too little. Unless you have been proofreading all your life, you *must* do it out loud. Reading aloud catches ugly constructions and faulty spelling and punctuation. Reading *slowly aloud* is the only *fast* way to check spelling and the word division at the end of lines. You can't look up all the words in the dictionary. You can't analyze the grammar in every sentence to check the punctuation. Misplaced words can only be caught by reading aloud, since the ear is the test for these.

This is how to proofread. Read the MS twice, read it aloud and with feeling. If you're some place where you can't read aloud, read softly while moving your tongue and lips. Pause at the end of each sentence to listen to what you heard. If everything sounds OK, move to the next sentence. Stumbling while reading shows where repairs are needed.

After rereading the MS reflect on it and decide whether to do it over. You've already revised once or twice, but maybe you've thought of improvements that justify rewriting the whole piece. In deciding, recall that planning was the hard part, not the actual writing. Writing goes fast. Planning goes slow, proofreading goes slow.

Finally, hand the paper in, send the memo up, sign the letter, sigh with relief. Maybe pray for mercy. People will be merciful if you haven't made mistakes. Generally, writing just has to look all right. Lying, misleading, and plagiarizing often pass, but mistakes don't.

No one much likes to submit writing. They feel it does not do them justice or it does. In either case they must step to the bar. Who ever heard of a proud writer? Writers seem to miss the satisfactions that other artists enjoy. Shakespeare never published. If he was disappointed imagine how I feel. Don't expect too much.

Lesson Seven

Persuading

Writing Is Persuasive

We speak for the same reasons a baby cries: I am! I want! It's surprising, in view of the basic purpose of language, that we so often use it without having the foggiest notion of what we're after, and so often lapse into talking to ourselves—badly. Chances of getting what we want must improve when we know what it is. The writer should know what she's after. If it's money, attention, respect, or mastery of a certain form, then that should be her aim. Instead of thinking What can *I* say? she should first think What do I *want*?

The general aim of expression is the general aim of life: to be praised. Casanova wrote: I expect the friendship, the esteem, and the gratitude of my readers. All writers long for such praise, and the fear of not getting it makes them clam up. Even when they're misleading or manipulating an audience they're still looking for praise in some form for doing a bad job well. Writing can have any number of special aims: inform, analyze, amuse, enrage, flatter, brag, unite, warn, sell, deceive, seduce, convert. The writer does not have to let anyone know what she's aiming at, but to do a good job she ought to know herself. Writing has a moral benefit if it prompts one to think about her motives.

The art of doing a praiseworthy job and getting what you want is the art of persuasion, called rhetoric. Expression always includes this element of persuasion. When you calm a child, you're persuading her to stop crying. When newspaper editors arrange the front page they're persuading others that this is the important news and that it can be arranged in order of importance. When you send a letter without erasures you're persuading others of your efficiency.

Whether the persuasive aim is overt or hidden, standard

devices of persuasion are used. These devices work because they please, enabling you to get what you want from the audience by giving them what they want. Persuasion involves a contract with the audience; something is expected from each party. Writers do not become good persuaders if they resent having to adjust themselves to the audience. The writer needn't try to please everyone like a whore, but should try to please someone besides herself. Grabbing the mike is not enough: if you don't coo or yell or drone the way you're supposed to, the audience may not listen.

The audience expects to be persuaded, they know the writer wants something, and thus they resent being confused about her intentions. They want her to show she needs them. Her job is to know what she needs and go after it. She doesn't announce her purpose, but indicates it through tone.

She needs something to argue. This may seem odd, because when people are at home they don't like argument—You should take an umbrella, You should have another piece of pie. But they accept it from strangers, for they know that the persuasion will be well mannered and can be ignored. They don't just want exposition, don't just want to be told, they want to be asked. No matter how much straightforward exposition a writer has to present, it will be presented better if it has an argumentative edge. An encyclopedia article on, say, horseshoe crabs, will be more readable if the writer conveys her impression that these creatures are extraordinary. In Formal, the writer is usually expected to pull a disappearing act, so the audience can concentrate on the subject, but this disappearance should only be an illusion.

Publishers are often mistaken in thinking that audiences want news and facts and other forms of pap. By not offering ideas, issues, and values they lose readers, as Hollywood lost its adult audience in the Forties. A personal attitude toward the subject gets the audience to listen. Turn to the editorial page of your newspaper and compare the editorials with the letters to the editor. The letters are readable because they are written by real people with axes to grind. So when you express yourself, sound like a person who wants to say what she's saying.

Readers may look at stuff, but if it has no voice they won't listen to it. No voice, no style, no reader, just print, and lots of trees cut down for nothing. Writing for the masses loses its voice as it's homogenized, deodorized, and flavorized by a gang of market experts, and the product is like a salty sugary imitation barbecue flavored imitation potato chip. Never think you're feeding your audience, assume you're talking to them and they can talk back. Don't tell them anything you wouldn't like to hear. Holden Caulfield always knew a book was good when it made him want to call the writer up.

What's Wrong with Rhetoric?

Persuasion is used for bad ends as well as good. Lawyers lie and win cases, politicians lie and win elections, advertisers lie and make bags of money, parents lie to children, boys lie to girls. Many thinkers have observed that we have language to protect ourselves from the truth and to permit us to lie.

Then what can be said about the role of truth in persuasion? Is a good speech, a good ad, a good argument the one that succeeds or the one that tells the truth? Should those who teach rhetoric tell their students not to lie, or tell them the truth about lying? That's a good question because I don't know. One may get to Heaven by honoring the truth but fall short of Madison Avenue or Capitol Hill. It seems to me that much can be said in favor of lying and a little can be said against it. But I won't go into the arguments for and against. Who am I to encourage people to lie? Nowadays no one seems to need lessons. If they receive as it is said they do a thousand advertising messages a day they soon learn for themselves how to hit others where they live.

In these lessons I've praised rhetoric of the better sort—language that is simple and direct—so I can't contradict myself now and start praising the other kinds. But my kind of language is not always rewarded, not even in the academy, much less in the society. The language that persuades and is rewarded is often unclear, pretentious, or deceptive. There is so much fraud that the term *rhetoric,* like *propaganda* before it, has become a term of abuse. But one should not distrust rhetoric, one should master it, since it's not about to go away. To say that a certain speech is only *a lot of rhetoric* is itself the use of an unsubtle rhetorical device, name calling. Rhetorical devices are plentiful, and they're all good, as devices, if they work. Some are crude, some ingenious. Rhetoric has as many levels as language does.

Rhetoric at the highest moral level, where the speaker respects herself, the audience, and the truth, is far above rhetoric at the lowest level, where audiences are pandered to and manipulated thru their fears and desires. But whatever the level, rhetoric is always rhetoric, always impure, never completely truthful. There cannot be a perfect speaker or perfect audience. Any speaker who claims she's levelling with you is one to distrust. Any statement making a special claim to be true has to be dubious. No one says *Truly two and two are four,* they say *Truly, women are far more interesting than men.* One of the most effective and time honored devices of rhetoric is a lie, saying what you're not going to do and then going on to do it: *I come to bury Caesar, not to praise him.*

Despite its shortcomings, rhetoric should be treated with respect and should be learned because the alternative to it is force. Those who refuse to persuade or to listen to persuasion fall back on power, and power, as we know, comes out of the end of a gun. Rhetoric takes the place of guns among the weak and gentle, and that includes a lot of people.

Another reason rhetoric is good to have around is that having to persuade others helps to make persuaders less self centered and more aware of other minds. Expression always requires some subjecting of one's own personality to what is common and impersonal. Though persuasion may have selfish ends, it cannot be done in a selfish way. In ancient times it was claimed that only a good person could be good at rhetoric because she would have to forget about herself in speaking for the audience and in swaying them thru reasoning. This view that the good speaker represents the audience is agreeable, though few people nowadays put much faith in the supposed reasonableness of the audience. Cardinal de Retz said that Everyone is open to insinuation but scarcely anyone is open to persuasion. A cardinal would say something like that.

Mastering the tricks and strategies of rhetoric is not necessarily corrupting, and it's usually improving. You don't need to know much about rhetoric to sell mouthwash or militarism. Subtle rhetoricians are hardly so dangerous a threat as the ignorant and the innocent. To become skilled in rhetoric one must learn to think like others, and this takes sympathy and imagination. From time to time persuasion calls for speaker and audience to forget personal interest and pursue an argument wherever it may lead. An audience is a blessing in that it prevents the speaker from being herself. One's thoughts are free, of course, which means they are worth nothing. Only an audience gives them value. Dr Johnson said No sir, a man has not a right to think as he pleases; he should inform himself and think justly. The only way to find out if you're thinking justly is to see how others respond to what you say.

What Is Arguable

In presenting a topic, the writer begins her argument that the topic is worth discussing. The experienced writer knows that the audience really wants an argument. She also knows that they do not want controversy or contention, and suppresses whatever urge she may have to sock it to them. Arguments are to be slipped across. The audience thinks they already have the arguments. They have so many they can give you some.

For practice in preparing arguments I'll now offer you some propositions you might want to work with. Decide whether to argue for or against, and see if you can find at least three or four points to support your views. (In thinking of arguments, gather wild and free thoughts, ask the reporter's questions, and crossexamine yourself.) Try a few of these easy propositions.

> Dogs are better than cats.
> If one is old enough to fight, he's old enough to drink and vote.
> No one should make over two hundred thousand a year.

If everyone is equal, everyone should be allowed to have a
   machine gun.
The hand that rocks the cradle rules the world.
Every girl should have a pony.

That exercise was hard to do in your head, and I wonder if
you were clever enough to jot your ideas down and try to sort
them out. Ideas come and go fast, and you want to catch them on
paper. But the point of the exercise was not to remind you to
make notes. This was the point. Think about which side of the
proposition you chose to support. You probably chose to argue
that dogs are better than cats if you have a dog. If you make a lot
of money or intend to, you probably chose to argue that high
incomes can be justified. I suspect you did not argue any proposition you did not *immediately* like. Our minds are quick: when
they are not already made up on a question, we quickly make
them up. We can always change our minds, of course.

Resume the exercise. Now try to find arguments on the
other or unsympathetic side of the case. Once you've done this,
ask yourself which had the better arguments—the side you
favored or the other side. You probably still came up with better
arguments for your side. Did you have trouble finding arguments on the other side?

Now consider whether knowing some arguments on the
other side will not help you argue your own case better. In
thinking of arguments against your case you'll be prompted to
find answers to them. An argument is effective only insofar as it
answers a counter argument. What goes without saying does not
have to be said. Good arguments only appear when the counter
arguments are strong. Only a dubious proposition is arguable.

For thousands of years writers have been trained in persuasion by having to argue both sides of a case, and this is still the
best training. In the Middle Ages philosophers had to draw up
thorough arguments in *Sic et non* (yes and no) form. Debaters
today do not always know what side of a case they will have to
present. When a lawyer prepares a case, he prepares not only his
but his opponent's as well, for he can't risk being surprised by a
good argument from the other side.

This willingness to grapple with both sides of a question strikes many who aren't used to it as artificial and hypocritical. They see it as unprincipled sophistry, as ignoring right and wrong. They fear that the habit of weighing both sides leads to liberalism and skepticism, undermining value, doctrine, and authority. They're right. That's what happens when people habitually consider both sides of a question. The open mind is messy, mixed up, and quite often useless. In an open mind so many ideas are welcomed that pretty soon the place looks and sounds like the famous Marx Brothers' stateroom.

What happens when you draw up arguments for the other side and find them convincing? Should you change your mind? You don't have to. Anyone can persist in thinking and acting the way she wants even when she knows she's wrong. You can make two hundred thousand a year and think it's wrong, cheat on your spouse and think it's wrong, take the Hippocratic oath and perform radical cashectomies. But doing this may hurt your self respect, which may hurt your confidence. Good arguments haunt you.

Fortunately, no one can always tell good arguments from bad. Many more questions are arguable than we like to think. Most propositions, and *all* propositions involving the idea *should,* are reasonable enough to argue, however unreasonable they may be under the All Seeing Eye. How about these common assertions? *Capital punishment is necessary. Marriage is finished. The German people are guilty. God is dead. Intermarriage is the only answer.* Those who can instantaneously tell a reasonable proposition from an unreasonable one outnumber those who can't, but they're probably overconfident.

Preparing an Argument

In writing, you judge sentences and decide which ones deserve to be put down. If you are tenderhearted, the writing will be worthless. In arguing you have to judge opinions and values, which is harder to do, since they belong to other people. The struggle between ideas can be so fierce it makes people shut their eyes and ears. But to argue well you must look and listen. One is either afraid of the struggle or not. The First Amendment protects Americans from those who are afraid to watch ideas mix it up.

When writing you talk to yourself and crossexamine yourself, and when preparing an argument you do the same, but more fiercely. A good way is to pretend you are your opponent—it takes two to tango. Let's say you strongly believe the following is correct, but someone is going to make you argue it: *Since rich women can afford abortions, the government should provide abortions for poor women.* What you want to do is get a piece of paper and sketch a dialogue, such as this.

Con. Well, rich women afford many things poor women can't afford.
Pro. Well yourself, abortions are special. They're not like other purchases. They're health care, which is provided for the poor.
Con. They're special all right, they're murder.
Pro. We're not arguing about abortion, we're arguing about whether poor women can get them.
Con. Let them save their money for it like me. I save money.
Pro. They can't. They can't save twenty dollars much less two hundred.
Con. How do *you* know?
Pro. I guess I don't. I imagine a few of them might be able to save enough, but not many. But why should rich women get abortions and only a few of the poor?
Con. Life is unfair. Why should government pay for abortions?
Pro. Who else?
Con. Get the private sector to pay.
Pro. How?
Con. Persuade them.
Pro. If they don't?
Con. Ask local government.
Pro. They won't, they're afraid of the voters.
Con. Then ask federal government to do it. They have ways of bypassing the voters. But you won't get Congress to vote to pay for abortions.
Pro. We women will make it hot for them.
Con. You good at making things hot?
Pro. They say women are. I'm learning.

Once you get a dialogue of this sort going, you'll soon

collect enough material to work into an argument. Dialogues like this are easier than you think and require little imagination. People do not think them out and they argue badly because they prefer to simply state what they believe, repeat it, yell it, try to force it down someone's throat. Argument is much more often self assertive and self defeating than a genuine attempt to reach agreement.

In preparing an argument remember that there may be many views of an issue, not just yours and your opponent's. During the Cuban missile crisis, John Kennedy asked his brother Bobby to play *devil's advocate* and present the argument against bombing Cuba. His argument won: it would not look right for big US to surprise bomb little Cuba. In the deliberations no one pointed out that the Cubans might not like being bombed, no one presented the Cuban point of view. So remember in arguments to include the simpleton's point of view as well as God's and the devil's.

In preparing an argument try to think of as many ideas and points as are relevant, even though only a few will appear in the argument itself. And it's good strategy to make several points, even when only one of them is crucial. A repetitious argument is suspected to be weak. If an argument, like a chain, is no stronger than its weakest part, no point you make should be weak. One fat generalization can ruin an argument: *All animals are sad after sex.* Several unsupported assertions in a row turn an audience off. Protesting too much is common: *And thus I have proved that my client does not own a dog, that if she did own a dog it did not bite Mrs Jones, and lastly, that Mrs Jones was never bitten by a dog.*

In selecting your arguments, pretend that your clever and cruel opponent will put everything you say under a microscope. You must find the flaws before he does. In logic as in grammar, *pinpoint* the mistakes even if you don't know what to call them. *Exactly* where do the following arguments go wrong?

> My parents believed in Quetzalcoatl, which is why I do.
> If people believe that it's possible for a person to be right, then there is such a thing as being right.
> Stale potato chips are better than nothing, nothing is better than ice cream, stale potato chips are a lot better than ice cream.

The wish is psychologically equivalent to the act.

Abortion is a form of killing engaged in to evade the consequences of sex.

The decision to go into Viet Nam was morally right but prudentially wrong.

How to Win an Argument

Anything a persuader says that turns out to be untrue wrecks her case. Let's say you're ready to buy an old desk at a garage sale. The seller claims it's maple, but you see that it's cheap pine. You refuse to buy from someone who's even under suspicion of lying. Audiences are like that, they get huffy when offered terminological inexactitudes subsequently proven inoperative. For her own protection the persuader should be honest with herself and try to discover if she's telling the truth, not because the truth is sacred—maybe it is—but because it has a way of coming thru in the bottom of the ninth.

Though the audience deep down inside wants the truth, it never wants to be hit over the head with it. The persuader should be modest about revealing a naked truth, and if it's not pretty, dress it up. A naked truth. *Scientific studies show that Americans are thieves.* Half dressed. *Some studies indicate that most Americans will steal.* Dressed. *A few studies by psychologists suggest that most Americans, given the right circumstances, are prepared to steal something small.* Another example. *Workers do more work in a four day than in a five day week.* More acceptable. *Certain test cases have shown that workers can do more work in a four day than in a five day week.* Another example. *Blacks do not make good swimmers.* More acceptable. *So far, blacks have not had real success in winning championships in swimming.* Even better. *Black athletes have not yet shown much interest in swimming titles.* You see in these examples what you already know: you can get away with saying anything, even the truth, by saying it diplomatically. A diplomat is one who says *Unless I'm mistaken, your soil here in the Sahara is rather thin,* or *I didn't succeed in gaining victory in the first set, and in the second set my more experienced opponent prevailed, while in the third set I proposed a draw and regrettably it was declined.* Diplomacy may not always work in international politics, but in the real world it works fine. Gentle, diplomatic statements have a way of sounding more accurate than forceful statements, probably because they are. Of course, being too careful makes the writing dull.

Facts do not have to be blown up. One way you can tell you probably have a fact is that you feel no need to garnish it. Trying to improve it may ruin it. Fact. *Some people maintain that pigs are smarter than dogs.* Non fact. *Scientists prove that pigs are smarter than dogs.* Fact. *A two ounce hotdog generally has a gram or two more protein than a four ounce slice of pizza.* Non fact. *Hotdogs are more nutritious than pizza.* When you have a fact, just say it accurately, and that way it won't burst.

Now let's have a little practice in putting the truth forward in a proper light. Here are ten assertions; assume they are true, and try to express them in such a way that an audience will accept them. (Don't tone them down so much they're wishy washy.)

> Taking the train to Florida is better than flying.
> No woman should wear a girdle.
> Not eating eggs prevents you from having strokes.
> Kansas City boys are the cutest in the country.
> When a Democrat is president we have a war, and when a
>   Republican is president we have a recession.
> Your grass needs fertilizer.
> Using Blizzard toothpaste prevents cavities.
> The Church interferes in politics.
> That pizza last night made me sick.
> Women are much more sensitive and complex than men.

In working with these sentences you probably noticed that some were worse than others; some were matters of personal opinion, some dealt with facts, and some were disgusting mixtures of fact and opinion. These are the three different kinds of statement, and each kind has to be handled in a different way to be persuasive. *Kansas City boys are the cutest* and *No woman should wear a girdle* are clearly statements of opinion. The writer shows she's offering an opinion by obvious exaggeration. What is clearly opinion need not be qualified. You don't have to say *I feel,*

I think, I believe, because no one wants to listen to a mouse. An audience rejects opinions offered timidly. Don't say *I believe Diet Rite is better than Tab* or *Croquet may be the finest sport,* just say *Diet Rite is better* and *Croquet is the finest.*

Certain sentences were presented as matters of fact: *Blizzard toothpast prevents cavities, Not eating eggs prevents strokes.* These are the dangerous statements. Facts can be verified. If the supposed fact is not so, the writer has insulted the audience. That's why she should not present opinions as facts. All of us confuse facts and opinions, and pretend to have many more facts than we have. No one goes around asking herself every time she wants to say something: Is this fact or opinion? But a writer should try to be careful. Facts are rare, elusive; courtroom trials are laborious attempts to find the simple facts. But despite the scarcity of facts and the dullness of most of them, they are often worth looking for, and last longer than diamonds.

Two more of the assertions pretended to be facts since they brought up the business of cause and effect: *When a Democrat is president we have a war,* etc, and *That pizza last night made me sick.* The first assertion was acceptable as it is in Informal where exaggeration is permitted for the sake of a forceful or funny statement. In Formal the assertion would have to be weakened (or abandoned): *In this century wars have tended to begin when a Democrat was president and recessions when a Republican was president.* The assertion *That pizza last night made me sick* would have to be explained in Formal: *That pizza last night made me sick because I get sick every time I eat a whole pizza.*

Now we come to the awful mixtures of fact and opinion: *Taking the train to Florida is better than flying, Your grass needs fertilizer, The Church interferes in politics.* Most of our assertions are like these: they sound a little plausible, but can't be verified like facts or dismissed like opinions. These assertions need to be defended, qualified, or explained. *Taking the train to Florida is better than flying because it's not too slow, it's cheaper, and stays on the ground. Your grass probably needs fertilizer since it's not a deep green like mine. The Church interferes in politics in areas that have nothing to do with doctrine.*

Just as you should have some sense, while writing, of when

you start foaming at the mouth or falling asleep, you should have some sense while arguing of what kind of assertions you're making. If you're offering opinions offer them forcefully, because audiences admire force and may thus come to share the opinions. (Of course, if you don't want your opinions shared, that's a different story. Then why offer them?) When you have a fact, present it modestly and accurately.

Whether your assertions are accepted depends on how they're presented. A badly presented truth ceases to be true, a well presented untruth becomes true. Language is an imprecise medium for the truth, since words mean so many things and suggest so many things. The categories of true and false seldom apply to assertions, despite the popularity of those True False tests one finds in magazines and social sciences. So if an assertion of yours is in any way doubtful, soften it or add to it some defense, explanation, or example. The more unusual or doubtful the assertion the more help it needs. How would you handle that last sentence—*Women are much more sensitive and complex than men?*

How to Lose an Argument

The best way to lose an argument is to believe there is no argument, that the other side knows you're right and is just acting ornery. Overconfidence and self righteousness prevent anyone from seeing the arguments on the other side and guarding against them. An arguer should really be grateful to her opponents, for without them she would have no argument to present. They should be treated respectfully for reasons of strategy as well as courtesy. Part of the audience may share their views. Also, vicious attacks are generally disliked. Do just enough to win. Refuting others can be harsh and combative, so it must be done politely. Sarcasm, ridicule, and mockery are out of style today, except in the home.

The arguer should guard against showing her feelings, especially anger. This may be hard to do, since our familiar route to articulateness is outrage: a newborn is symbolically whacked to begin his career in self expression. We all complain so much we confuse complaints and arguments. An argument taken personally becomes a complaint. But heated words are only hot air. Effective writers, like effective lawyers, try to accentuate the positive and avoid the sound of the whine.

There are certain rhetorical devices to be used gingerly because they backfire. You should not impute motives to others or in any way caricature the opposition or their arguments. If you have to talk about the opposing view as you answer it, try to be fair. The cleverest ploy is to act kind and understanding to your opponents. With so much folly in the world there's no need to set up *straw men* to knock down. Real men do fine, and can be knocked down with a breath—with one good question.

A tempting device is the *reductio*, or pushing the opposing argument to the point where it becomes silly. *If guns are outlawed only outlaws will have guns. If pornography is censored, that will lead to censorship of other writing. You only think of me as a sex object. Washington will soon be telling us businessmen how to blow our nose. If you shake it more than once, you're playing with it.* The *reductio* is usually a clumsy, undignified blurring of distinctions. If you want to be annoying, it's good for that.

Danger is involved in the use of rhetorical questions, or questions whose answer is supposed to be understood. These questions can be effective, used sparingly, but are a bit old fashioned, and if you try them on smart alecks you will get a smart answer instead of the right one. *You want me to risk having a baby? What about the Joint Chiefs—you think all of them are crazy? What if every woman had an abortion? What has violence ever accomplished? Is it a sin to pay $180 for a man's cologne?*

How to Destroy an Argument

First, the bad news. Almost everything you assert can be subjected to destructive questioning. Now the good news. Almost everything that anyone asserts can be subjected to destructive questioning. Assertions are so vulnerable that people have a silent understanding to do little questioning of each other. Questioning is not the mode of conversation among gentlemen, as Dr Johnson says. It is the mode among arguers. Just a little practice in analyzing statements for their logical defects gives you very sharp teeth.

The first thing to do in analyzing an argument is to find its premises. Arguments are often based on faulty evidence. *People on welfare should not be given so much money; they're lazy.* Is it true they're lazy? *Criminals are sick people and require medical attention, not punishment.* Are there no differences between criminals and sick people? Are the crimes of no significance? Instead of attacking the conclusion, find the shaky premise of the argument. An unacceptable conclusion is seldom caused by an error in the process of reasoning, but almost always by an unacceptable premise.

Since the general method used in argument is to refer particular subjects to general principles, the way to break up the argument is to destroy this link—by pointing out distinctions, by insisting that different things are really different. Simply by asking for clarifications of the ideas, you destroy the argument, as in the following examples.

Argument	Pornography is wicked because it arouses lust.
Analysis	What is lust and why is it wicked?
Argument	She's against abortion because the Church has indoctrinated her.
Analysis	What does it mean to be against abortion? Is a view wrong because it's held by the wrong people—in this case, the Church? What does indoctrinated mean?
Argument	Property is theft. America was stolen from the Indians. I get to steal too.
Analysis	Isn't there any property to which people are entitled? Do you have any? When the white man stole America, he had the army. Do you have an army?
Argument	Italians act like children.
Analysis	Do other people act like children? What do Italians do that others don't?
Argument	The universe is good because God is good, and the universe is proof of his goodness.

Analysis	Is the universe good? Does good outweigh evil? How do you know?
Argument	Death can't be so bad, because people who have been resuscitated no longer fear dying.
Analysis	Do they fear death less now than before? Did they die?

These examples give you the idea. Don't refute or contradict an argument. Don't answer with your own arguments; if you don't propose an argument, you can't lose it. All you need do is ask one or two polite questions. Why deny an argument when you can question it? The arguer is obligated to deal with questions about what she's proposed. The most effective way to attack any argument is also the easiest—by asking to have the ideas a little clearer. For asking deadly questions like these, Socrates' fellow citizens executed him. Maybe you don't want to become that good at it, but you want to be good at it, if only to examine your own arguments and be ready in case someone tries it on you. It's humiliating to have an argument sink under you. We need to take our ideas and beliefs seriously, and will even die for them. Losing an argument is not like losing a ping pong game.

When you think about it, it's amazing that so little of this simple questioning is done. When a person says *We Germans are a nation of poets and philosophers,* the answer is heard *We Italians are just as good as you Germans.* The proper response should be a question: *What, you mean most Germans are not slobs like everyone else?* When one says *There's too much competition in school* another answers *Life is competitive* instead of saying *How much competition is too much?* People fight unclear ideas with their own unclear ideas, rather than with clear questions. They get so used to dealing in unclear ideas they forget to ask others, as they forget to ask themselves, to make the ideas clear. Unclear or general ideas cause great mischief in the world. Of course they help people to live active lives based on beliefs, but there's a lot of action we could do without.

Don't shy away from questions because you think they don't really say anything or that they're impolite. One good question is worth several doubtful assertions. As a wit once said,

For your information I have a question. Insinuations *(He went to Moscow, I will go to Korea, You're soft on street crime, You have ring around the collar)* these can only be countered by questions. When you are questioned, fight back. *Why does a Jew always answer a question with another question?* Answer: *What do you mean by why does a Jew always answer a question with another question? Does he? Do all of them do this? Shouldn't they?* and so on forever.

A final tip before we have a drill. Just as you look at a person's eyes to see whether he's shifting them and lying to you, you look for certain words that tip off your opponent's embarrassment: *means, seems, appears, perhaps, may be, almost, consists of, results in, in effect.* Example. *To go easy on the criminal* means *going hard on his victims.* When your opponent has to begin a statement with *The truth is, The fact is,* you've got him. *The truth is, criminals are born, not made. The fact is, criminals are made, not born. It's true your mother wears army shoes. The Amityville Horror: A True Story.*

Since I had fun pricking arguments maybe you'd like a turn. It's great fun, except when the arguments are your own. Here are some unclear propositions. See if you can't zero in on their vulnerable spot with a clear question.

> Drunken drivers must not be allowed to drive.
> Private organizations should be allowed to choose their own membership.
> If a person doesn't work, he shouldn't eat.
> Students should have a voice in hiring and firing their teachers.
> No state is worse than that in which the richest people are considered the best.
> By remaining in a society you are promising to obey its laws.
> Anyone who does not protest the war is an accomplice.
> Those who have suffered from discrimination deserve special assistance to catch up to those who have had advantages.

Personal Appeal

In making a personal appeal the speaker or writer relies on the audience's liking or admiring her. She should therefore be likeable or show she's trying to be. In speaking she will command the basic skills of a speaker. She will not be afraid, but will look her audience in the eye and speak loudly, slowly, and clearly. She will show she wants to be liked by being well groomed and dressed. If she's writing, she can't rely upon appearance and voice, but has to please the audience with words alone. It's easier to charm with looks than with words.

If one's looks are known, it's even easier. A famous comedian can say anything and people laugh. A football star holds up a can of beer on television, and people buy the beer. A pretty girl in an expensive dress gets in and out of an automobile, and both men and women flock to buy it. Patriarchal males and girlish females have strong appeal. The ideal male is the president, the ideal female is the Bunny, and it's hard to say which ideal is the more difficult to achieve.

Do these remarks imply that personal appeal is low and undignified? I can't say that, for I've been guilty of admiring the masculine and feminine. There's no question that personal appeal is a basic and powerful persuader, and one would be foolish not to exploit it. As our society comes to rely more and more on television, personal appeal becomes ever more important. Writers will feel increasing pressure to be friendly, assured, confiding, as if selling something in one's living room.

If you seek to increase your personal appeal, remember that whatever is an asset or a liability in your personality shows up as an asset or a liability when you express yourself. One usually knows if she's gushy, surly, timid, etc. It's easy enough to advise removing the liabilities, but that will take work. T S Eliot said: At the moment one writes, one is what one is, and the damage of a lifetime . . . cannot be repaired at the moment of composition. If you have many moments of composition, though, some repairs can be made.

When you approach an audience you don't want to be guilty of the personality faults that suggest deficiencies—being apologetic, hesitant, confused, bashful, squeamish. These faults are disabling because the audience thinks you're not eager and ready to address them and that you're wasting their time. They're right. You shouldn't try to say anything unless you want to and are ready to. Timidity has to be conquered, whether in speaking or writing. It's conquered by getting experience. If you think you can't speak, you must, or think you can't write, you must. Do it. Human beings get used to anything. Timidity is often cured by getting angry. Even the lowliest worm turns and bites the foot that steps on it. Anger is a road to eloquence, though a rocky one. Be brave or get mad.

Excesses are not as bad as deficiencies. Famous writers dither and babble, and get away with it because their energy and boldness are loved as virtues in themselves. Speakers behave deliriously, like quiz show emcees, and the audience loves it. No spark of life—that's what audiences do not forgive. It's hardly possible to be too animated, though one can have the wrong kind of animation and be too chummy, cute, excited, nasty. Audiences are disappointed by expression that's cold and rational, and assume that the speaker or writer is more interested in what she's saying than in them.

My advice to work at being charming may fall on some deaf ears, for some people aren't interested in pleasing and persuading. Because of their own troubles they would rather stay silent or would even rather antagonize others. I'd like to think that those who want to sulk or lash out are not among those taking these lessons.

That was flattery. Did you recognize it? People seldom do; that's why you needn't be shy about using it. Flattery is so common in ads it goes unnoticed elsewhere. President Carter was elected after asking for a government as good and as decent and as honest and as loving as the American people. *Cosmopolitan* shamelessly says We believe in marriage if *you* do. You really have to exaggerate before an audience discovers it's being flattered, and when they do they'll forgive you.

The question sometimes arises whether the speaker or writer should be sincere. The answer is no. Being sincere suggests an uncritical attitude toward one's material. Acting sincere runs the risk of appearing sanctimonious. Forget about sincerity. Sincerity is a virtue only because its opposite, hypocrisy, is a vice. The young overrate sincerity because it's one of their virtues.

Hitler was sincere. Be honest rather than sincere. Sincerity is respect for what's going on in one's own mind, honesty is respect for what goes on in the minds of others.

These remarks lead back to the old question of whether the speaker or writer should lie. From the moral point of view liars should be encouraged so they will be discovered sooner. From the nonmoral point of view they should be discouraged because lying is too hard to do well. The poor liar is not allowed to say what he wants but is always satisfying some demand. Thinking that people are victims of liars is like thinking that johns are victims of prostitutes. And lies are much too hard to remember. The pleasure in telling the truth, as Mark Twain observed, is that you don't have to remember what you said.

Emotional Appeals

Effective writing appeals to the emotions and not just to the reason. If you want something from people you must move them. The emotions are not dirty—only about half of them are—and appealing to them is not dishonest. The danger in relying on emotional appeals is that emotions change. When Spiro Agnew said that McGovern was soft on communism, everyone laughed at Spiro. Also, when emotional appeals are too coarse, too transparent, the audience sees thru them and feels ashamed.

Like everything else, emotional appeals have been named and classified. When they work they're called *emotional appeals* and when they don't they're called *logical fallacies.* The most common way of appealing to the emotions (emotions are basically *for* or *against*) is to call things by good or bad names. This is the favorite rhetorical device of children and adults. *Name calling* ranges from out and out denunciation and abuse to subtle and imperceptible *slanting* of the languag. Some bad names being heard are *racist, sexist, populist, establishment, old boys' network, regulation, welfarism.* There are so many bad names one wonders whether humans are not more aggressive and nasty than kind and loving. Do you know?

Slanting of language is more subtle. Many words have

favorable or unfavorable connotations—some have no denotation at all—and skillful use of the connotations brings about the desired effects in the audience. *Fight* is good, but *violence* is bad. L B Johnson: *We will fight in Viet Nam until the violence stops.* Do you think *cults* should be taxed but not *religions*? Are you *neutral* or *indifferent*? A good old man can be called *senior, elderly, dignified, silverhaired, experienced, vigorous, wise in years, fatherly;* a bad old man can be called *jowly, balding, rumpled, stooped.* Just as language can be slanted, so can evidence: favorable or unfavorable facts are emphasized or obscured, half truths are offered, quotations edited and twisted, motives attributed to others, and *straw men* set up in order to be knocked down.

Another emotional appeal is the *bandwagon* appeal. The audience is called on to feel or act a certain way because their associates seem to be doing the same. All racial, ethnic, patriotic, and party appeals rely on this need to belong to a group, a need so deep and powerful that appealing to it is often the main thing a speaker does. Bandwagon appeals can be base or noble, depending on where the band is going. *Let us extend a helping hand*—a noble appeal. *Love it or leave it*—a base appeal. People don't seem to mind bad music from a band, just so it's loud.

Another type of appeal is the appeal to *authority. Doctors report, History shows, Pismeyer of Yale says.* In our time respect for any authority that is not scientific has weakened, and the appeal to authority works better with older and more hypocritical audiences. In arguing logically, authority can only be used to *support* other arguments.

Another appeal is the direct *attack* on the person holding the wrong views. The personal attack is a good one, though sometimes its appeal is to prejudices. *You're only saying that because you're a man. A draft dodger is a coward. This witness is a convicted criminal and cannot possibly be believed.* The personal attack is not illegitimate. Lawyers use it on hostile witnesses. If one is a criminal it may well be true he's a liar too, or a draft dodger may be a coward. A fault in our politics is that the personal attack on politicians is avoided even when appropriate. People should say Do not vote for so and so: he took campaign money from the oil companies, he paid no income tax for three years, he's a millionaire, he has twelve children, he wears too much makeup. Such information can not only be relevant but can win for you.

Another appeal is the *blush,* or appeal to shame. *Everybody on the block gave; won't you? This is the holiest day of the year.* Another appeal is to the *purse. Our tax dollars are being poured down the welfare rathole. This new million dollar tank can be destroyed by a twenty dollar shell.* Another appeal is known as the *stick,* or threat. *If you don't eat your spinach, you get no dessert. In a year or two the Teamsters will have an atomic bomb.* Threats are forceful persuaders, but are seldom considered in discussions of rhetoric because their effectiveness lies in the threat rather than in how it's expressed. But threats are everywhere, and are the basis of social and political control.

In short, there is nothing wrong or undignified in using any type of emotional appeal. They are not offenses against truth or logic; they become offensive only when used clumsily, insulting the audience. But audiences are seldom insulted by appeals to their emotions, for that's where they live. They have real interests and needs that are in themselves a truth to be understood and respected by the writer. Success in persuasion depends less on devotion to the truth than on knowing what the audience wants to hear. So important is knowledge of the audience that trial lawyers exercise most of their cunning in the selection of the jury. As Mencken said: The average man does not get pleasure out of an idea because he thinks it is true; he thinks it is true because he gets pleasure out of it.

In most arguments no distinction can be made between logical and emotional appeals. If I say Women should not perform the sacraments of the Church because they have never done so before—is that a logical appeal? If I say Policemen and ministers who commit adultery should get the sack because we hold them to a higher standard of behavior than we do others—is that a logical appeal? Arguments emulsify logic and emotion. It's not easy to separate the two, especially when we feel the emotion and believe it to be true. Emotional appeals should not be thought of as logical errors, for respectable arguments are riddled with them. Is it an error to think that your spouse is beautiful or that Heaven exists or that fast food hamburgers are delicious?

Logical Proofs

Logic plays only a minor role in persuasion. What is logical need not be argued. The discipline of logical thinking helps to destroy arguments rather than find them. In Formal one is only expected to *act* as if she were being logical and not emotional. Appearing to be logical, acting calm, cool, fair, reasonable, that is more important than being logical. And the more sophisticated the audience, the more reasonable the persuader should be in her manner.

In arguing logically, whatever is a matter of personal belief or opinion is supposed to be laid aside. Facts should be put forward and supported when necessary by evidence. The tone must be calm and reasonable, no matter how outrageous the facts. The tone is not only cool but impersonal. Try not to refer to yourself or what you *think* or what the audience *thinks*. Refer to yourself only if introducing evidence from personal experience.

Your basic method is to show that the particular subject you're talking about is a member of a larger class, and that general principles, which people agree on, can be applied to the particular case. If you're arguing that the power of police to search should be restricted, you would convince your audience that they would not like to be frisked. If you're arguing that police should be free to make searches, you point out how many sacrifices of privacy people already make in the interest of public safety. If you're arguing against having to wear a helmet when riding a motorcycle, you point out how this infringes on privacy, particularly on one's right to dress as he pleases. If you're arguing for having to wear a helmet you point out that the rider is a member of society, and society has rights in protecting one of its members from hurting himself.

After the particular example is referred to the general class or principle, then supporting examples, facts, or illustrations should be added. Logical arguments are not hard to develop since they move from the particular to the general. They move outward, like ripples on a pond, and lead quickly into large issues. The easy development of an argument is one of the reasons people love to argue. Take the argument about wearing a helmet and see how it opens up. Society does restrain someone trying to hurt himself. Does society have this right? If society has this right, does it outweigh the individual's right to do what he wants? How can we tell which has the stronger right? What does society lose if it gives up its rights in this case? What does the individual lose? After working thru the argument one might conclude that society has the right to restrain suicides, but interfering in suicides is not the same as interfering with a motorcyclist who loves to have his hair in the wind and sun. Or one could conclude the argument thru *compromising*, deciding that society can make riders who are under twenty one wear helmets.

Though it's easy to argue, by making this move from the particular to the general, one can take the argument only so far. Everything that is is a member of a class, but is also different from other things. Comparisons, analogies, and extensions of principles can only be pursued so far until they break down and no longer apply. Every comparison becomes at some point untrue, since everything is what it is and not another thing. Nothing in the world is exactly identical. And nothing is entirely unique. Aquinas well described thinking as *combining* and *separating*.

All of us have been treated to many overextended comparisons, such as these: *If white ethnics can make it so can black people. Handguns are no different from other lethal weapons like knives. Nations grow old and weak. A zygote is a human being.* Test yourself now on this argument by analogy, and figure out what's right and what's wrong with it: *The law should crack down on obscenity, though it can't be precisely defined, as it cracks down on cruelty to children, which can't be precisely defined.*

In arguing you have to use comparisons, but guard against extending them beyond the point where their falseness becomes apparent. Therefore, to argue well keep comparisons brief and simple and use several comparisons instead of pushing a single one.

When one is arguing logically and referring to general truths and principles, she may neglect to examine the general truth or principle itself, and fall into the error of relying on a *generalization*. Generalizations have a bad name, even though our knowledge consists entirely of generalizations from experience. Two and two are four. A generalization. Tomorrow, or somewhere else, two and two may be one, five, or a temporary or new number. Night follows day. A generalization. The earth might stop rotating, like the moon. A good generalization is one that a particular audience will accept. A poor generalization is one they won't accept. If the audience believes that one swallow makes a summer, you may tell them that. But sometimes the audience just looks gullible. There's a smart person born every minute.

If the writer believes she may say nothing but what is logical or truthful, she might as well hang up her gloves. She should waste little time thinking about whether her propositions are right or wrong, true or false. She should think about whether her audience will accept the propositions, and her defense of them if there is any. Look at the following typical propositions and you will appreciate the folly of thinking in terms of true or false. *America's young people (will, will not) fight for their country. Cats (do, do not) like ham. Actors (are, are not) selfish. Students today (can, cannot) read or write. Love means (always, never) having to say you're sorry. Washington is (the enemy of, controlled by) private enterprise. He loves me, he loves me not.* In this puzzling world where very few assertions can be verified (some say *none*), you have an easier time of it if you present and work with the ones that entertain your audience.

When you're arguing you sometimes have to talk about cause and effect relationships. My advice is to talk about these as little as possible. They are difficult to discuss and often have no bearing on the argument. The purpose of your argument is a certain practical result that is to come. To talk about causes makes you talk about the past. Forward looking people are admired. The analysis of cause is chancy, and most events are too complicated to be analyzed for their cause. Whatever occurs does so as the result of much that has happened before, not as the result of some cause or a few causes or an immediate cause. No person ever acted from a single pure unmixed motive, and groups of people do not do so either. Just as you should not go around assigning causes to events you should not say this or that was a person's motive. The imputing of motives is not only unfair but a waste of time. People do not know why they do what they do and they're not pleased when you tell them. So stay away from causes of events and motives of actions. What about these? *He beat his wife because he got drunk. I use drugs because my parents didn't love me. Our army lost in Viet Nam because Washington wouldn't let them win. The students are rioting because they are the Spock generation. Lt Calley was convicted because they needed a scapegoat.*

Sometimes the causal relationship is expressed indirectly, without using *because* or *since*. *I have strong oral needs and can't stop smoking. If you forgive others God will forgive you. One fourth of the hiway accidents are caused by beer drinkers. She got diabetes from eating too much sugar. Tight underwear gives you migraines.* You get the picture. If you want to appear to be logical, and who doesn't? avoid assigning causes. It can be done less offensively if you proceed to talk about a number of causes and weigh them for their relative importance. But this way of talking is boring except to a select audience.

Because may be the most treacherous word in the language, leading many honest people into error. *Because God made you mine, I'll cherish thee. Why do you want to be president, Billy? Because. Because why? Just because.* Nowadays, students are encouraged to be simpleminded in thinking about cause, because they've taken so many multiple choice exams in which they're expected to pick the right or best answer. Did you notice how I used *because* in that sentence and got away with it? Do you agree that's why students are simpleminded?

Reasoning

Reasoning means talking in a calm or reasonable manner, and it also means ideal reasoning, or thinking in a cold, logical, analytical way that is not affected by personal attitudes, prejudices, or beliefs. This second kind of reasoning, true reasoning rather than the show of it, is extremely difficult and rare. It seems impossible for any human being to be perfectly reasonable. When Martin Luther cried out Reason is the devil's whore, he was pointing out that the human mind cannot work correctly. But he was also blurring a real distinction between reasoning that is a show and reasoning that is close to the ideal. I've talked often in our lessons about the need to speak and write in a cool and reasonable manner. Let us now consider ideal reasoning. I hope to show you not just how difficult but how useful it is.

In order to reason, one must lay aside beliefs. Whatever is thought to be right or wrong can only be a matter of belief. Few people will agree with that statement since most people have fervent beliefs that certain things *are* right or wrong. They believe in an abstract or absolute right and wrong, and associate these with good and evil, or God and the devil. Particular rights and wrongs lead them to believe in a general good and evil, and belief in a general good and evil reinforces their belief that certain things are right or wrong. The mind interpreting reality, moving as it does from the particular to the general and back again, invents the categories of right and wrong (and applies these categories to nearly everything).

Though people may nod in agreement at Hamlet's truism, There is nothing either good or bad but thinking makes it so, very few of them are willing to question their beliefs in good and bad. In reasoning these beliefs must be put aside if one hopes to analyze what a certain thing is in itself. Maybe because our emotions are basically love and hate and because we have a right hand and a left hand, our minds are far too easily inclined to think in terms of pairs, opposites, dualities, as if there were only two great boxes to put everything into. When the mind goes blithely along sorting everything out as right or wrong, popping it into a box where it's hidden from view, the mind is hardly working at its best. Shark = bad. Fighter pilot = good. Weed = bad. Flower = good. Suicide = bad. Money = good. When the snake told Eve she would *know* good and evil, he told a whopper.

Let's look at some examples of how belief in the right and the good interferes with analytical reasoning. When the nation's leaders decided to go to war in Viet Nam, they thought along these lines. We have to do it. Viet Nam is our ally. Our credibility as defenders of freedom is at stake. It's right to draw the line here against communism, which is a wrong system. Thoughts such as these shoved out of the picture other important questions: what happens if we fight *there,* what happens to *them,* what happens to *us,* what happens if we *win,* what happens if we *lose?* No one thought we could lose. How could we lose, if we were right? Instead of thinking in a practical way of consequences, the leaders thought overconfidently about the cause of the situation and emotionally about the rights and wrongs of it. The Confederacy knew they had a *right* to leave the Union, and look what happened to them.

Another example. In 1970, New York City opened up its own colleges, in a program called Open Admissions, to any student who had been in high school for four years. Those who decided to open the colleges thought they had to do it to prevent rioting in the colleges and on the city streets. The students had to be allowed to escape the draft; it was *not right* that the urban poor were being sent to Viet Nam. Also, offering a college education to students who wanted it was the *right* thing to do. Education is a *good* thing. The city's leaders did not think practically along these lines: What happens to the colleges when the doors are opened? What happens to standards in the colleges and the high schools? What happens if the city can't pay for Open Admissions? No one asked this last question, and the city did run out of money. Thinking about the future should range widely and assess many probabilities, not plod along wearing right and wrong blinders.

When a question causes serious disagreement, it generally has a crux, or single point over which the disagreement arises. When people argue they avoid the crux because they want to keep on arguing or they dislike the solutions. But a reasonable arguer locates the crux right away and refuses to move off of it to talk about other things. The crux of the abortion question is not sexual behavior or male oppression, but whether one should be allowed to kill a fetus. The crux, killing, should be discussed. What can be killed—soldiers, animals, the feeble, the dying, no one?

Another emotional issue is capital punishment. People think along these lines: Is it right to kill? What made the criminals go wrong? Are they bad? Are we good? Once again, the thinking proceeds along lines of right and wrong instead of practical lines.

The reasoning should be: What happens if we execute criminals? What happens if we don't? These two questions would give us enough to work on without our having to indulge in emotions of hatred of the criminals or compassion for them. Is this being too rational? What could be a better subject for reason than killing people? Reason requires that no thought be embraced because it's pleasant or avoided because it's unpleasant. Reason does not deny that emotions exist, it requires that they not be brought into play during the analysis of a question. One can be tenderhearted and still be tough minded. So when you reason, see that right and wrong are left outside the door, as prayers are left outside the classroom. People don't agree about praying and don't agree about right and wrong. It's upsetting that they don't, but if you want them to agree with you, you have to reason with them and never get mad.

Thinking freely, without reference to good and evil, is called free thinking, or rationalism. It's extremely rare, so rare that one wonders why people get so upset at the very idea of it. Free thought can be upsetting, since it undermines certain kinds of authority and punctures beliefs and dreams that help people get thru the day. But what authority or belief is secure, if it can't stand inspection? In the Age of Reason, the eighteenth century, a number of famous rationalists believed that common people could not reason and should not try, that they should not be required to look into their beliefs. In our country today, this view will strike most of us as condescending. Our democracy is based on the belief—unfortunately it's only a belief—that people are reasonable and can be reasoned with.

If you want practice in reasoning, here are some propositions to analyze. See if you can work on them in a purely *practical* way. Brace yourself.

> It's part of a teacher's job to make sure the Pledge of Allegiance is recited.
> A confessed homosexual minister or priest should not be given a parish.
> The one million illegal aliens in New York City should be deported.
> Equal pay for equal work.

Starving peoples should not be fed, because they will continue to overbreed.

Women should not be allowed to have more than a certain number of children.

I hope you could reason on these burning questions without getting smoke in your eyes. If you can't come up with a *long* argument on each of these questions, you're not used to reasoning. If you're confused by tough questions like these, that's good, you should be confused, you won't think unless you're confused. A teacher's job is to confuse students—no wonder there's no money in it—and a student's job is to be confused—no wonder they act so strange.

But don't give up in confusion. If you reason long and hard enough you're bound to come up with a few arguments you can live with and a lot you can use. Remember that in the arena where ideas are the weapons, the fighter who keeps a cool head may win. Everyone loses sometimes. But don't quit. As Freud said: The voice of the intellect is soft, but is not quiet until it has gained a hearing.

Lesson Eight

Pleasing

Personal Style

In this our final lesson, which ends with your easy final exam, we'll look at the means of pleasing an audience. These are usually discussed under the heading of *style*. An interesting word, *style*, for its contradictory meanings: it means distinctive or personal style—it once meant *handwriting*—and it also means stylishness, or fashionable style, which is not personal at all. You can succeed in writing by having a good personal style or by mastering any of the current fashions in writing. The one is like music and the other like Muzak.

It may be hard to see that personal style is valuable, because when we learn to write there is so much Form to master. For over twenty years people tried to teach me to write, and did it by telling me what not to do. Parents, teachers, and bosses peer over our shoulder, give us lots of erasers, and stand ready to wash out our mouths with soap or stab us with red pencils and blue pencils. We get the idea we will never be allowed to express ourselves in any natural way. Each move we want to make seems to be against the Rules. Though teachers tell us Just Be Yourself, when we try it we are told You Can't Do That! We feel we're being jived, and don't realize that this feeling is a stage everyone must pass thru in learning to write.

Like playing an instrument, writing must be tediously learned. One in a hundred takes to it easy. Once it's learned, then you can express yourself, then you can sing. It's not a torture intended to break your spirit, though it may feel that way. It's our only way of communicating with many people. In learning the piano we start in a faulty, wooden way, but once we can play, we're not supposed to sound like the teacher or like someone's recording.

Writing is thinking, thinking is talking to yourself, and only you can talk to yourself. If you're out to lunch, you'll have nothing to say, and will have to mimic and plagiarize. Too many young writers fear that if they do not come on in the accepted way and sound slick or humble or whatever, their teachers won't let them into medical school or advertising. They put down stuff they would never say, forgetting that the point of writing is to solo, not blend with the chorus, and forgetting their Emerson: But do your thing and I shall know you.

Trying to sound like others is of course easier than trying to sound like yourself. Even easier than that is trying to sound like the place where you work. Since no one knows what an industry, company, or office sounds like, it's safe for a while to sound like one, and make pompous, shifty, and inane noises. But sooner or later, if there's real work to be done, someone in the outfit will have to start sounding like a person. In the long run *business* English is the worst way to do business. A business cannot talk. Would you want to be a spokesman for an industry? Or a mouthpiece? When all the communications are coming from houses, offices, boards, chairs, and desks, the human voice cuts thru loud and clear.

Here is a chair talking.

Even now we are in the process of formulating new service concepts to deal with changing health care needs of subscriber groups. And, of course, we plan to adhere to GHI's longtime guiding principle of innovative service at controlled cost for families who participate in our programs in both private industry and government service.

Here is a person.

We're doing our best to keep up with changing demands for services, while we try to keep the costs down for our members.

Here is an airplane talking.

If by chance your choice is not available due to previous passenger selection, please accept our apology.

Here is a person.

I'm sorry but we're out of that.

Printed apologies and thank yous are only *litter*ature.
Here is a house talking.

We have examined *The Truth About English* and have concluded
that there is no specific market for it. Unfortunately it does not
fit into our (perhaps artificial) categories.

Here is a person.

I and three other editors have read your book and we all liked it.
But it's a little odd, and if we took a chance on it and it didn't sell,
the oil company that owns us would give us the sack. Try those
brave, reputable publishers, Prentice-Hall.

Today many people feel they are not being addressed as
persons by persons. To reach them you should talk to them, not
talk down to them like an officer or expert and not suck up to
them like an ad. When you're writing a business letter pretend
the addressee is sitting right across from you, and just tell him
what you want to say. A good letter is written to someone, not just
about something. Whether speaking to a crowd, writing a
scientific paper, or scribbling a note for the milkman, sound like
a person, and members of your species will hear your cry.

If you have no voice, no one listens, but if you fall in love
with your voice and talk too much, no one listens very long.
Beautiful voices only disguise for a time the lack of substance. It's
better to say something or try to than just seem to. During the '79
fuel crisis President Carter was warned by his political expert,
Patrick Caddell: Too many good people have been beaten
because they tried to substitute substance for style. Being good
and not wanting to be beaten, Carter substituted style for
substance, and was beaten anyway. Slamdunkers and skywalkers
may make the All Star Team but not the Hall of Fame.

To develop your personal style it's best to do a lot of
writing on simple enjoyable topics until your own voice gets
strong enough to hear. Once you're more experienced, studying
and imitating other styles helps make your own more flexible. As
composers use certain formulas so do writers come up with

sentences that fall into patterns. The more patterns you master, the easier the writing goes, and that's where the exercise of imitating comes in handy. Writers used to train by imitating famous stylists, but today this is seldom done for fear it will constrict one's originality. But it's still a good way to train the ear. You might have fun doing parodies—all good writers can be parodied, their voices are so clear and peculiar. But no matter how much you work on your style, your basic style will stay the same. If you're cheerful, decisive, meticulous, that shows up in your writing as it shows up on a smaller scale in your handwriting.

All valuable papers are signed.

Readability

Readability is hard to analyze. It does not depend on short words, short sentences, and lots of names, though these help nowadays. It depends on who's talking to whom about what. Writing can be clear and simple, and be totally unreadable. If it's beautifully clear and simple, though, it's readable. Writing needs beauty of some kind, and there are many kinds. A professor can find a piece unreadable because it's *not* difficult, an editor can find it unreadable because it's not marketable, a sociologist, because it's not couched in the jargon that's his bread and butter. Audiences do not always look for easy reading even when they're just flipping thru magazines at the hairdresser's. If the reader thinks the material important, he'll read despite the difficulty.

Simple writing gets boring. Complicated writing is wearing. Writers can succeed by writing simple stuff for simple audiences or special stuff for special audiences, but the most esteemed writers are those who address a wide audience without aiming at the lowest common denominator (also known as The Bottom Line). It may be right to say that the *best* writing addresses as many people as possible and tries to be simple and direct. But of course there are many styles of writing that pay, many uses of language besides declaring—suggesting, deceiving, puzzling, arousing, pontificating.

Writing for special audiences runs the risk of being impersonal, dull, and jargony. Writing for mass audiences runs the risk of being impersonal and dull. Much writing today is so dull it's embarrassing, and that's why publishers love fewer and shorter sentences, pictures, white space, and one sentence paragraphs. The *Reader's Digest* not only has ads but cartoons: the reader has finally been digested and is ready to be eliminated. Many people now believe that readability means something that needn't be read, that a non book is a book and a library is a media center. What happened to the readers? They're still out there, waiting for you to say something. Instead of thinking of writing as an industrial product with a shrinking market, remember what it used to be—a person talking.

Though readability is a relative virtue, we can still talk about what helps or hurts it among *most* audiences. Writing that lacks energy, writing where the sentences go nowhere and nothing is asserted—can anyone like that? No one likes wordiness or the piling up of qualifiers and modifiers. In writing as in any art, whatever is excessive results from weakness in the concept or idea.

To get the reader under way, the tone of the piece should be sounded early and clear. The audience approves the tone, and it's not sounded too loud or long. It's not too breezy (cute), too pompous (solemn), too solemn (lugubrious), too funny (facetious), too technical (unintelligible), or too ironic (confusing). The writer can modulate the tone—writing without surprises is dull—but the surprises are in the material, not the point of view. The audience assumes the writer has settled on a point of view before lifting her pen—though this is often not the case.

Tricks of style are used—sound effects, questions, appeals, figures of speech—but used without drawing attention to themselves. The greater the variety of tricks, the less conspicuous a particular trick will be. The artistic principle of nothing too much applies especially to these flowers of rhetoric. One rhetorical question on a page—fine. Two questions—disaster. A writer can sneak two metaphors into a sentence, add a third, and collapse the whole sentence. Tricks of style are like high notes and trills for singers: they embellish the performance but also jeopardize it.

Readable style avoids the use of synonyms. It avoids lists and items in a series. Terms are not defined, since they are being used the way the audience uses them. Readable style does not include retractions or corrections. *He was the handsomest lifeguard I ever saw, I suppose. The two parties will not agree; but maybe they will. Everyone is religious, or else they know someone who is.*

Readable style uses a variety of sentences. The anticlimactic or loose sentence, the characteristic sentence of modern style, is avoided as much as possible. This is the timid sentence that starts off all right, and then has a lot of items tacked on to it, like this sentence now, and it just goes on and on, until it finally peters out, with a trailing with phrase or a trailing participle bringing up the rear, plus any other bits and pieces the writer has lying around.

Readable style does not mumble *more or less, part and parcel, by the by, as it were, by and large, what I would like to say is, in my view, in the final analysis, as such, it seems to be the case that,* etc. Certain expressions only prove that silence is golden.

The writer should choose words that are predicted or anticipated by the reader. If he's given too many unusual words, his anticipations have to be corrected, slowing him down. If he slows down too much he'll stop. Words should be normal like pencils should be yellow. You can use some big words, but if they're all big, then none of them is. Idioms and natural turns of expression speed the reader along. Sometimes you'll even want to risk being trite to make the reading smooth as silk and easy as rolling off a log.

Occasionally the writer hits a homer with an adjective or an adverb, but this is a fluke, and steady singles with the verbs are what's wanted. Don't say *Upward, downward, pulsatingly, throbbingly, the giant piston moved.* Say *Up and down the giant piston slid.* Instead of writing *This great statesman grew up in a tiny village* and then sweating to fix up *great* and *tiny*, just write *This statesman grew up in a village.* Don't say *He has a small black nervous curly haired poodle dog.* Say *He has a small black poodle.* Have you met small poodles that weren't nervous and curly? Many adjectives tell us what we know—*warm sun, given subject, visible scar, bad cold, shining stars, personal friend.*

Try to write sentences that end with a verb or a direct

object rather than an adjective. Long sentences are never justified if all they deliver is a measly adjective. Sentences that end with an adjective have their focus on the subject rather than on subject and predicate. Writing doesn't just name, it asserts something about what it's naming; it doesn't just describe, it comments. Don't say *The rose is red, I am negative, This problem is difficult.* Say *The red rose blooms, I worry, This problem would make anyone pick his nose.*

Another fault in modern prose is the triumph of nouns over verbs. This has been called noun plague, nounitis, nominalization, reification—each term being an example of the problem. Thomas Carlyle said Things are in the saddle and ride mankind. Things are also in the saddle in modern sentences. Don't lose a verb inside a noun.

Bad	Good
We had recreation.	We played.
Give me a welcome home.	Welcome me home.
It gives me pleasure.	I'm pleased.
It's an additive.	It's added.
The college expansion was rapid.	The college rapidly expanded.
There should be an outreach to these people.	We should reach out to these people.
There is a necessary choice between the punishment and forgiveness of criminals.	Criminals must be punished or forgiven.

Abstract nouns often end in *-tion,* so when you have a . . . *tion* see if you can't change it back into a verb. *We made an examination, We examined. An observation of mine, I observed. The separation of church and state is desirable, Church and state should be separated.* When an abstract noun is the subject, try to find an active verb to use with it. *Punishment is a problem, Punishment eludes, puzzles, worries. Clarity is desirable, Be clear.*

Don't try to make new verbs from nouns—to *critique, concertize, distance, waitress, structure.* Don't turn adjectives into nouns—*I'm a black, a pink, a crazy, a rapee, a retrenchee, the most.* Don't encourage nouns by using them as adjectives and stringing them together—*county tax assessment record keeper, State of Alabama law, anti missile missile missile, Singer Sewing Machine Sales Representatives' Fourth of July Picnic Dance Contest Winner Award.* Nouns have weighted writing down so much, particularly those thousands of nouns that are mere concepts, it's no wonder people watch the Tube. If you're lucky, that can be a Family Strength Acknowledgment Experience.

Brevity

Everyone knows that brevity is the soul of wit—even Polonius, who said it, and who was so tedious Hamlet had to kill him. Brevity is a rare and thrilling quality in writing, and marks the distinguished mind. We admire those mental powers that see things clearly and express what they see simply and clearly. Mathematicians and scientists talk of elegant proofs and demonstrations; elegance is another way of talking about brevity. Here is brevity.

Dr Johnson: Marriage has many pains, but celibacy has few pleasures.
Julia Child: When you are alone in the kitchen no one can see you.
Abraham Lincoln: As I would not be a slave so I would not be a master.
Martin Luther King, Jr: A riot is the language of the unheard.
Garibaldi: Only a slave has a right to go to war, against a tyrant.

And here is the first sentence of Bertrand Russell's *Autobiography:* Three passions, simple but overwhelmingly strong, have governed my life: the longing for love, the search for knowledge, and unbearable pity for the suffering of mankind.

Only clear thinking finds such clear expression. In each quotation the diction is simple; the words do not have punch, the ideas have power. That kind of force, the force of the idea, is hard to achieve, but should be aimed at all the same. Wordiness tries to cover up weakness, brevity reveals strength.

Being brief is not to be confused with being quiet or taciturn. If someone is a man of few words, those words are probably poor ones. To talk well you must talk a lot, like Hamlet or Don Quixote. Today the style in speaking is to be cool and say little, while the style in writing is so verbose that many people who once read have turned to stamp collecting and houseplants for excitement. Here is a significant passage of modern prose from the science pages of the *Times*.

> Most people can prevent flatus for a time. But it can build up and cause pain and eventually must be released. Sometimes flatulence that is normally well controlled passes at embarrassing moments. This results from a relaxation of the rectal muscles.

Do we learn something new every day?

Both the modern speaking and modern writing styles are mistaken. In talking you should try to be loquacious and in writing you should try to be brief. If you succeed in either you will stand out.

You have to decide whether you want to stand out or sort of merge in. In a world where everyone shuffles papers you may not get paid to be brief. Journalists bureaucrats and professors get paid for words. Upsetting this applecart will not butter your parsnip. You may have to drivel and bloviate like your elders in the information industry, report, review, refer, research, comment, confer, criticize, analyze, and plagiarize till kingdom come. If you enter law politics or business you will discover that brevity and clarity can be disadvantageous, in addition to being hard work. But however Goethe felt about it, I'm glad he spent sixty years working on *Faust.* Of course, with a Wang word processor he could have done much, much more.

Using Force

Writing has to speak with a certain force if it is to command attention. Much of what is written today lacks force or has the mere show of it. People get so used to the false assertions of ads they begin to suspect all assertions. They think that writing must either be dishonest, hyped like advertising, or honest, with the poor writer chirping away like a cricket and nobody listening. Young people are right to balk at learning to write if they have to choose between crooks or crickets.

Here's a typically modern, overassertive sentence from *The Whole Earth Catalog:* [This is] *not only the best how-to book on drawing, it is the best how-to book we've seen on any subject.* No one would say that. *We* don't talk. One person talks. A non person talks blurbese.

Here's half a sentence (the whole sentence would be unhealthy) from a letter to the *Times Literary Supplement: It is imperative that the ahistorical tendencies of the Lacanian model of the constitution of the subject be articulated upon a historically specific account of the evolution of the bourgeois consciousness.* Would you say that again?

Here's a sentence from *Esquire: For the first time our educated liberals no longer believe instinctively in majority rule.* That's a mouthful. But I don't think it would be said to another person. Sentences like that can only be written by someone unaware of an audience: they're announcements over the PA.

Here's a sentence from *Time: Most people find great works of art oppressive, since such works invariably center on the nature of human destiny, and that destiny is tragic. Oppressive* and *invariably* are off the mark. What is *tragic?* What is *destiny?*

Here's a sentence by a feminist, Ellen Willis: *A woman cannot hope to find a man who is free of sexist attitudes, nor can she make a man give up his privileges by arguing.* Willis apparently thinks that half the human race is *sexist.*

Here's a history professor at Princeton in *The New York Review: It now seems probable that the population bomb will not explode after all, and that the number of human beings in the world will stabilize at about double the current figure of four billion.* Why this seems probable is not explained.

Here's Jimmy Carter in his 1980 State of the Union address: *I know the limits of moral suasion.* That should be *Moral suasion has limits.* Why did he say it as he did?

In these samples of pushy assertion, who is being fooled—the writer or the audience? Luther said *Pecca fortiter,* sin big, but he didn't mean sin *that* big. The writer as well as the audience should be alerted to the big bad statement by its impersonal, official tone.

Advertising has had such a corrupting influence on language that people forget what they sound like. But a careful writer insists on sounding like herself instead of an ad, and avoids overassertion, so that what she wants to say has a chance of being heard. She will speak modestly, avoiding overkill adverbs like *phenomenally, absurdly, definitely, undoubtedly, demonstrably, truly, infinitely, endlessly, absolutely, positively, significantly, importantly, meaningfully.* She will try to avoid superlatives—*most best finest worst.* She won't exaggerate—*run to the nearest, it's a must, it's imperative.* She'll try to be reasonable after she says *The reason is, This is because.*

Then what can a poor girl do? She can look for assertions that don't require stimulation. She can simplify without over-simplifying. She can figure out what *she* would say and hear herself saying it. Berryman's advice is always apt: Write as short as you can, in order, of what matters. But if it is true as Lord Acton said, Few things matter and nothing matters very much, it would then be true that there's not much to write about, and if one must write short, there's very little to write. The writer's job, though, is to make things matter. Nothing matters in itself, it can only be said to matter. Either the subject has to matter to the writer or the writing does, if they're going to matter to others. You need an attitude, a tone. You matter, not the subject. Subjects don't have predicates, you do. Cicero maintained that the easiest letter to write was the one that dealt with nothing.

There's no need ever to get *involved* in the subject or to be serious or sincere. Belief limits your thinking. In his opening sonnet Sir Philip Sidney writes, Fool, said my Muse to me, look in thy heart and write! He went on to write 107 more sonnets. Surgeons have opened millions of hearts and have never found a sonnet. Those sonnets must have been in Sir Philip's tongue. White man speak with forked tongue and so do black yellow and red.

The overassertive sentences I showed you a while back were more typical of professional writing than amateur. But in my teaching experience I've found many male students being assertive like that while the women remained unassertive and quiet. The following advice is for the ladies. Don't try to be too careful, too precise. To express yourself forcefully you must commit some offense against the truth, which is deep and silent. Man is an abyss, but you talk about him, don't you? You can't tell the truth in a sentence, no sentence can say it all. You need a period for a sentence and there are no periods in the universal flux. You have to make them up.

Dr Johnson said, In all pointed sentences some degree of accuracy must be sacrificed to conciseness. When Lord Acton said Few things matter he meant that few things matter to him. When Lincoln said As I would not be a slave so I would not be a master, he was not telling what he would do if he had to be one or the other. Bertrand Russell spoke of his *unbearable* pity for mankind, and bore it for ninety seven years. Learning to write is learning to cut. If you're a woman or a big gentle guy you have a disadvantage. To write swiftly and clearly requires a *touch* of arrogance.

For the sake of discourse, people allow each other to make the most surprising assertions. If you're a student or some other nobody, naturally you're not allowed to say anything, but you should look forward to graduation when things will be better. The unforgivable sin in a writer is timidity. Blustering is unacceptable only because it's timidity turned inside out.

If you are too careful you'll find it hard to assert anything, for your tentative assertions will be smothered by misgivings and afterthoughts. Don't let these silence you. What you put down isn't the final word, it's only a report on your thinking. Whatever is proposed implies its contradiction. If you say Pigs is pigs you imply pigs is not pigs, or you wouldn't have had to say they were. You say things because there is so much more to say. Try to get your thoughts down as they come, and don't worry about conclusions, answers, and solutions.

If you say two and two are four, who listens? If you say two and two are five for these reasons, everyone listens. When you write you paint. If you liked things the way they are you wouldn't be writing about them. So assert away. You can assert anything if you explain or defend it a little or say it in a *pleasing* way. The trick is to be personal and assertive without sounding like a bully. In short, no mumbling, no mumbo jumbo either.

Pleasing Sound

Good sentences are like musical phrases, each has a form or logic of its own. No one knows what makes a melody shapely and pleasing, and no one knows what makes a sentence shapely and pleasing. The musical phrase may appeal because it's like a good sentence, or the sentence may appeal because it sounds like music. Music has melody, harmony, and rhythm, and so does speech. Of the three melody is the most elusive. Writers who have no feeling for melody are said to have no ear. Having no ear is not so great a handicap for the writer as for the musician, but is a handicap. A study of good models, that is, reading aloud and imitating good writers, helps train the ear.

Harmony in writing refers to similarity of sounds, and *rhythm,* to repetition. Rhythm in music is strong and clear; in writing, more subtle and complicated. The rhythm of good prose can't be taught; it's never been analyzed, though it is the most significant element in the writing of good stylists. Rhythm comes mainly from the writer's preference for certain kinds of sentences. All of us write sentences in patterns we like, but don't use such distinct and forceful patterns as the heavyweights.

Today we find too many sentences that are rhythmless accumulations of words. They are written quickly and are never tested by the ear. Here are factory made sentences.

> An important if not critical consideration is whether it is possible to replace one group of men by another within the existing political organization.
> In England the critical reception is invariably hostile to American confessional poetry.
> There are many aspects of this large problem all of which are to a certain extent interrelated.
> He followed the river through the forest around the great bend into the southern part of the country.

Where were the verbs? If the writer doesn't listen for them, the audience won't either.

Since prose rhythm is ordinarily subtle, when it becomes pronounced it wakes the audience up. You need a reason to wake them up, so you better have something special to say, like: *It is a far far better thing I do than I have ever done; it is a far far better place I go than I have ever been. We shall fight on the landing grounds, we shall fight in the fields, and in the streets, we shall fight in the hills, we shall never surrender.* Prose that sounds like verse is only to be used when you're swinging for the bleachers. Repetition is so powerful and so easy a device it is overused, especially in speeches.

Repetition is a rhythmic device, the *balancing* of phrases and clauses is a subtle harmonic device. Many sentences contain complementary or antithetical ideas: This blah blah *and* that blah blah, or This blah blah, *but* that blah blah. Like me, you can be addicted to these sentences, but no one will notice since they are so common and natural—so natural they help to excuse repetition: *Brown eyes say Kiss me or I'll kill you, blue eyes say Kiss me or I'll die.*

You can repeat once. Do it twice and the audience wonders what you're up to. The adage Two's company, three's a crowd also applies to repetition. An occasional *doublet* will pass, defying the risk of wordiness: *reasonable and acceptable, happy and joyous, disturbed and dismayed, share and participate, hide and conceal, awe and majesty.* Triads are riskier: *neither flesh nor fowl nor good red herring, the energy the faith the devotion which we bring to this endeavor, fat fortyish and foolish.* Lincoln brought it off when he dared to say *of the people, by the people, and for the people.* But notice how he switched from -*ate*, -*ate* to *hallow*: *We cannot consecrate, we cannot dedicate, we cannot hallow this ground.*

When you repeat, the audience assumes either that you're doing it for emphasis or else that the writing has not been properly tightened. That's why you search for needless repetition, drop the unnecessary words, rework the sentences, and use pronouns. You never use a circumlocution to avoid repetition. You don't say *Nation . . . nation . . . nation* and then switch to *state.* We do shift from the pronoun *one* to *he* after using it once because continuing to use it, as Thurber said, sounds like someone practicing the trombone: *One should not take one's pencil and chew it in one's teeth if one cannot find words to express oneself the way one likes.*

The question arises whether to start a string of sentences

with the same word. Sure. A half dozen sentences could begin with *He*, for example. But you'd want variety within the sentences. A string of sentences should not start with an unusual construction, like an adverb, adverb clause, or participial phrase. *After arriving, he unpacked. After shaving, he came down for breakfast. After breakfast, he had his facial.*

Let us now consider some harmonies to be heard in prose. (Did you hear those *s, r,* and *h* sounds? I hope you heard them without noticing.) Harmonies are near rhyme, assonance, alliteration, and echo words. You can't use rhyme in prose since people believe it's reserved for poetry. You have to guard against jingles: *creation of this nation, refuse to choose, knew it grew.* Would you accept *usual use, makes one wonder,* and *cool pool?* You probably would, unless you were editing.

Assonance, the repetition of vowel sounds, can be clever and subtle. *This is an insipid drink. Change of pace. Even before the green appeared in the leaves.* Alliteration is the repetition of the initial sounds in words. *Patty's Pancake Palace.* The alliteration of vowels is usually unnoticed, but the alliteration of consonants is distracting and objectionable in Formal. *The car can carry the cases. His hotel was hardly a half block away.* Alliteration can be fun, but it's too easy for serious people to get much kick from it. English is thick with consonant sounds (hear those?) and alliteration is sometimes hard to avoid, but you should avoid it.

Echo words imitate noises in the real worlds: *bang, shriek, splash, murmur, hush, tinkle.* These are among the most powerful words in the language, and the more you use them the livelier your writing will be. Almost as lively are those words that *suggest* the actions in their sound—*rush, pull, open, grip, drop, kick, call, look.* Any word referring to movement—*lift, drag, up, over, back*—and any word referring to sound—sound is caused by movement—animates the writing. Language is dull that makes no reference to what lives and moves. Good writing like all good art produces effects in the body, and produces them more easily thru the ear than the eye.

To prove to yourself that hearing is a more important sense than sight, try to say the alphabet backwards by *visualizing* the letters. You can't do it. You can do it by remembering how the letters *sound* when *spoken* forwards. In writing sound is much more important than images. But neither sounds nor images should call attention to themselves, because when they do they lose their effect. The Duchess was quite right to remind Alice: Take care of the sense, and the sounds will take care of themselves.

Vividness: Figures of Speech

Figures of speech are daring, imaginative expressions not meant to be taken literally. If on examination your writing seems dull, it's probably lacking the vividness and energy that come from figurative language. Figures are expressions one step further from reality than ordinary language. *Her tears rained down, That's baloney, She laughed like a hyena.* There's no clear distinction between figurative and ordinary language, since all words were originally figurative and were not meant to be taken literally. *Literally* itself is a figure: it means *according to the letter. Taken* is a figure: here it means *mentally conceived. Conceived* is a figure meaning *giving birth to* and so on. Emerson said Every word was once a poem. In talking about figures of speech, then, one is not referring to regular figurative uses of language but to specially vivid and conspicuous uses.

Figures of speech have been classified as similes, metaphors, exaggerations, personifications, addresses to the absent, name changes, etc. You're familiar with these devices and have used them all your life, though you may not be able to classify them and call them by their Greek names. Similes, or brief comparisons, are the best known figures. When we want to speak vividly we turn to similes: *beer flowing like wine, American as apple pie, face like the front of a truck, enough to make a cat laugh, tougher than a two bit steak, soft as the voice of the adulterer.*

Avoid similes. Almost every simile that is usable is old and tired. And if it's not old it's too odd to use in Formal. A simile that has never been heard before attracts attention to itself away from the subject, and the audience thinks the writer is showing off. Here are examples of what I mean. A trite simile. *The lights on the bridge looked like a diamond necklace.* A forced simile. *The diamond necklace looked like the lights on a bridge.* Trite. *She looked like a million dollars. She looked like a movie star.* Forced. *She looked like Aphrodite. She looked like a tigress.* Trite. *Grinning like the cat that swallowed the canary.* Forced. *Grinning like a boll weevil in deep cotton.* I bet you can't invent similes that you could use in Formal that are neither too hot nor too cold. Try it.

Metaphors, on the other hand, are not only usable but invaluable. They can be vivid and daring, the giving of new names to things and thus a renewing of language, which is the giving of names to things. *He pulled his oar. My hands are clean. She dropped her voice. The words flew.* Effective predicates often depend on strong metaphorical verbs. *The wind stirred. The barometer fell. The skies threatened. The moon climbed.* Such language is packed with metaphor. *Packed* is a metaphor. The wind did not stir, the barometer did not fall, the skies did not threaten—they only do so metaphorically.

Metaphors are not an unmixed blessing. In similes one thing is compared to another, in metaphors the two are confused. *Battlefield = field of honor. Sickness = punishment. Woman = rose. Shadow = monster. God = daddy.* Every metaphor misrepresents both the thing being compared and what it's being compared to. *There's a cancer on the presidency. Religion is the opium of the people.* Metaphors allow the mind to invent what never existed: *in a provocative light* (what's a provocative light?), *from the dramatic point of view* (what's that?), *I am a white American male* (am I white? am I American? am I male?). Everything is what it is and not another thing, but humans are poets.

When metaphors are used so often that their original meanings are forgotten, they may be *mixed. That rat's a snake in the grass. These jeans go with where fashion is at.* When dead metaphors are laid beside each other they all pop up like zombies. *The fly in the ointment of the American Dream. We were caught with our pants down and have been playing catch up ball ever since. The other side of the coin is the tip of the iceberg.*

Metaphors must be used to make writing vivid, but used carefully, so that they are neither dead clichés nor farfetched and strained. In Formal the writer guards against over vivid writing.

All metaphors must stand inspection. When language becomes unusually forceful, metaphors are being used, and each must be checked to see if it can stand the test of being visualized. Can these? *leaned over backwards, wet blanket, wipes his feet on, take the bull by the horns, close the door on, take off my hat to.* Whether the audience would visualize these metaphors depends entirely on the tone of the piece where they appear. Metaphors pose a big problem in Formal, because if you don't use them the writing is dull, and if you do, it may be too vivid. Good metaphors never attract attention; they are not visualized, but are felt. Safe metaphors are generally the ones that come to the writer without her looking for them.

Exaggeration is a particular kind of metaphor. *I'm starved. You're a better man than I am. My check is in the mail.* These exaggerations (hyperboles) are permitted in Formal when the exaggeration is very common or when it is so gross it's clearly a relaxation from the need to speak precisely, rather than a failure to do so. So if you exaggerate, risk a cliché or do it on a grand scale: *big as a house, missed by a mile, golden tongued, filthy rich.*

Personifications, another figure, are commoner than you think. *Your country needs you. It's a sad day. The plant stood on the table.* Another figure is the address to the absent. *Elvis, what happened?* These addresses are not much used now, since they're thought rather fancy, but they are the basis of prayers. Calling things by new names (metonymy) is a kind of metaphor used all the time in slang and obscenity: *shrinks, suds, bread, soup, stew, broads, blood, jungle.* These figures are too exciting for Formal.

Questions directed at the reader, whether rhetorical, phony, or real questions, are also figures of speech. Real questions are good questions that don't have answers. These are avoided by writers who have the answers. Rhetorical questions have answers everyone is supposed to know. Phony questions, such as teachers and journalists are always asking, have answers you're about to be given. *What can you do with leftover spinach? How long should a girl wait? How can we tell a noun from a verb?* I've asked a few phony questions, but I'm not Formal.

In short, the best figures are those that seem natural and unforced. But just as you sometimes have to tell a joke, you sometimes have to use a certain figure despite the risks. Figures of speech are seasoning, you have to use them, but lightly. Formal people are literal minded, and hate what's literary.

Specificity: Names, Quotes, and Anecdotes

Good style is not grand, abstract, big words, big thoughts, but clear and specific. Details do the job. Never trust the teller, trust the tale. Shakespeare is tops because he said nothing and let his characters do the talking. The philosopher Sartre even goes so far as to say Evil is the substitution of the abstract for the concrete. (An evil thing to say.) Goethe kept rocks on his desk to remind himself to stay away from abstractions. He also said Thinking is more interesting than knowing, but less interesting than looking. Make your readers look. Focus right away on the small, the particular, the visible, to get the reader looking and listening. Flaubert told Maupassant to learn to write by describing a horse in such a way as to distinguish it from all other horses. If you're writing a movie review don't start by telling the plot or delivering your verdict, start with a scene or some lines of dialogue. If you don't see and hear what you're writing about and present it clearly and sharply, your audience will wave goodby as you rise up into the clouds.

An easy trick of style is dropping names. When you use a name you flatter the audience, as if saying to them You know about him or You know about this. Even if they don't know they're flattered because you assumed they did. But if you mention many names they haven't heard of, they will feel accused of ignorance and resent your showing off. Professional writers drop names automatically, and figure that if they don't have two or three names per paragraph the writing will be dull. Names are often put in bold print. Audiences want to know about what they know about, and will continue to follow with interest whatever Jacqueline Onassis and Elizabeth Taylor are doing. Those names wake you up? If not, newer can be found.

An allusion is an even more pleasant flattery, implying that the audience is sharp enough to catch an indirect or remote reference. To mention *Watergate* is to refer, to mention it twenty years from now will be to allude. Allusions are private language like slang and jargon, and stroke the audience. Much of the appeal of soap operas, formula novels, and literary criticism, is allusive.

Quotations please by being references or allusions and by saying something useful. *The Koran says. Bob Dylan says.* When you have a good quotation, squeeze it in. To quote you have to have one. You get it not from a dictionary of quotations—these will seem artificial—but from your own notebooks, in which you enter sayings you love. Such notebooks, called commonplace books, are seldom kept nowadays, but not keeping one shows little foresight in anyone interested in writing. Commonplaces should especially be collected in the areas of one's interests; they're not just a stockpile of quotations but a fountain of ideas. A writer uses quotes to refer to authority, to flatter the audience, and to help the argument. In view of these strong reasons to quote, one wonders why more is not done. If you don't fall in love with writing that begs to be quoted, you're not likely to become quotable. Isaac Disraeli said Those who never quote, in return are seldom quoted. Never heard of Isaac Disraeli? Nine words have made him immortal. Let's see you in nine words or less become immortal.

Akin to the quotation is the *anecdote* that illustrates your point. Anecdotes can be about the famous or about you. They needn't be funny, and if they aren't, guard against introducing them as if they were. Don't be shy about telling personal stories. Every speaker knows that the moment she says *I* the audience wakes up. If she keeps saying *I I I* the audience falls asleep. If you're discussing hotdogs you can talk about your worst, your best, your ideal hotdog. You can talk forever about you and the hotdog, but you can't change the subject to you.

The audience is temporarily interested in you, perhaps more than in what you're saying. That's why personal style, revealing you, is so important. The audience wants your number in order to interpret what you're saying. But skillful writers, like skillful teachers, mystify their audience about themselves. Audiences love to label you—gonzo, dipso, psycho, homo, pinko. Tantalize them with your target, but if they hit you, you deserve it.

Those who write for a living know how important it is to make the writing lively. The quick way to do this is to jazz up the diction, making everything sound more glamorous than it is. The better way is to dramatize the material. Drama is struggle, people struggle, so introduce people. Make ideas important by giving them to people, real or fictitious. Say what they think. Make up quotations. A writer is someone for whom the first, second, and third persons are the same.

Wit and Irony

Few enterprises are riskier than a serious discussion of wit, but I have to do it, I have to warn you not to be witty. Whenever you're tempted to try something clever or funny, remember how serious the world is, think of those long faces out there—you're going to amuse them? They will think you're trying to be funny. Only funny men and homely women get to be funny. Is the Pope funny? Is Walter Cronkite?

Also, writing wittily is too hard, because every witty remark you make brings things to a halt. You can't write a paragraph with remarks, you can only write a paragraph with a paragraph. If you say Power over men is what men and women want, what comes next? If you say A hen is an egg's way of making another egg, where do you go from there? In wit you compress thought, in writing you expand it.

To be witty is to be familiar, and Formal is not familiar. You're not even allowed to be witty in the footnotes. One spark of wit in almost everything that's written—market analyses, research papers, political speeches, psychological studies, editorials, dissertations—one spark sends the whole thing up.

Humor smiles, wit grins, shows its teeth. Humorists exaggerate: *My kids made sixty pounds of dirty laundry over the weekend and the washing machine went berserk and attacked the dog.* Wit hits the nail on the head: *The trouble with living at home is they treat you like one of the family.* Both wit and humor are based on the truth, humor on truths that are worth being given an artistic treatment, and wit on truths that cut and stab.

To attack is the motive of wit. As Bacon says, Anger makes dull men witty, but it keeps them poor. Only you can decide whether to be witty and poor or stupid and rich. Maybe it's best to have just enough wit to hide it. You write to persuade, not to be shot down in flames. The truth hurts. People laugh it off. Groucho said he was genuinely surprised that he made people laugh, because all he did was tell the truth. Writers quickly discover that when they tell the truth people laugh and when they tell jokes people frown, and that's why truths and jokes are so seldom written. So restrain your attempts to be witty until you are a big shot, when it will be too late.

If in spite of my warnings you still want to be witty, go, and my blessings go with you. Wit is after all our only defense against seriousness, and far too many things of this world are taken seriously—war, money, seduction, Formal English. As Gertrude Stein wisely said, We are not serious because we are serious. As you go off on your hopeless mission, I will whisper to you the secret of being witty.

Where there's good writing wit is nearby. A good writer is one who says the unexpected. A successful writer pretends to say the unexpected. A witty writer says what is very unexpected. You become witty by first becoming an expert on what is expected. Wit depends on the *paradox,* or saying *outside* the normal way of saying things. *Nothing succeeds like excess. I am a victim of an intact home. Did you take a bath? No, is one missing? I'm not afraid of work, I can lie down next to it and fall asleep. Take away the miniskirt and what have you got? I now bid you a welcome adieu.* To be a wit you find a *dox,* an old thought or saying, some cliché, and make it your doxy by suddenly taking it in a new way.

To do this you have to love words and love to play with them, which is natural among good writers. The *pun* is a miniature paradox, a discovery of a new way to use a word. *The teenagers are revolting. That conductor knows the score: he goes for baroque. Stop beating around the Freudian bush and get down to sexual morays.*

Puns are inexcusable in Formal because they are distracting and unserious. Puns are inexcusable in Informal because the others didn't think of them first. Puns are at their best and therefore their worst (our wurst is the best) when both meanings that are jumbled in the word fit the context, when the pun is quickly flashed, and when the words are not strained as in a *tur de force.*

In paradoxes and puns, new meanings are revealed. In irony, another form of wit, new and often rich meanings are suggested. *He said he was not a crook. Is it hot enough for you? He's a team player.* Writers are tempted to use irony because it allows them to say things without being held accountable, and because it compliments the audience's cleverness. Rilke: *What will you do, God, when I die?*

In speaking, the audience is easily tipped off to irony by the speaker's voice and expression, but in writing irony is much harder to convey. The danger in irony is not that it is devious and evasive but that it isn't perceived. Also, too much irony, too many secret meanings, are mere self indulgence on the writer's part, if not downright wackiness. Only expert writers find the ironic tone, and even then many of their ironies are missed. Readers have gone thru the many volumes of Gibbon's *Decline and Fall* without noticing its irony. After five hundred years people still cannot decide if Machiavelli is ironic. They argue about whether Jesus was ever ironic. Are these verses by Kingsley Amis ironic? *Women are really much nicer than men: No wonder we like them.*

The reason irony is missed when it is there and found when it isn't is that life itself is ironic, full of hidden meanings and contradictions. The perfectly ironic tone is therefore no tone at all, or the tone of the truth. Writers have an easier time of it if they take a point of view and sound a particular tone, rather than try to honestly reflect life's ironies. You will always be under pressure to take a basically tragic or comic point of view, though your position may be that life is neither tragic nor comic.

Life is said to be a tragedy for those who feel and a comedy for those who think. You will find almost everyone requiring you to be tragic. God loves a joke, it's said, but apparently everyone else is afraid to laugh. Maybe God's joke, like a German joke, is not a laughing matter. Thou art too damn jolly, says Captain Ahab. But Measure the size of a man's understanding by his mirth, says Dr Johnson.

Heavy irony has a tone easily discerned. When it's harsh and biting, it's called *sarcasm*. *This is good tom tom music for glue sniffers*. Twain: *Our Heavenly Father invented man because He was disappointed in the monkey*. Wilde: *Prayer must never be answered; if it is it ceases to be prayer and becomes a correspondence*. Sarcasm can be clever and dignified, but audiences find it too potent for Formal, and they get plenty of it at home.

Elegance

In writing, showy elegance is using big words, true elegance is leaving words out. Showy elegance is a thousand dollar wristwatch, true elegance is a nurse's Timex or no watch at all. The elegant writer does not show off much. She would rather die than use jargon, and is embarrassed to have to explain a word. She never feels she has to instruct her audience, but addresses them as if they already knew as much or about as much as she. She says as little as she can as well as she can. If a writer has only one way to write, let it be elegant. A classy person can talk to anyone.

Of course many audiences are impressed by special language. But large audiences are not. And using it corrupts the writer's thought. Precious style says precious little to precious few. There are telltale signs that a writer is coming on—using *shall*, using *which* in place of *that*, leaving *that* and *who* in where they could be omitted, saying *we we we* like the little pig, and using lots of qualifications, subjunctives, absolutes, and passives. Let's run thru a few of these usages that mark showy elegance.

Shall versus will. *Shall* is now used only in first person questions. *Shall we have lunch? Shall we dance?* Any other use of *shall* is only a literary quotation. *They shall not pass. We shall overcome.* *Shall* is thought by some to be emphatic—*collection shall be made*— but it isn't. It isn't elegant either, though the English still use it.

Which versus that. In American usage there is a distinction between *which* and *that*. *That* is used to start off clauses that *define* what they refer to. I just used it for the clause *that define what they refer to*. *Which* is used to start off clauses that do not define what they refer to. *That* is not preceded by a comma, *which* is preceded by a comma, since *which* introduces a *new* idea. A comma *pins* on new ideas. *Here is the dog that bit me.* No comma. *Here is the dog, comma, which seems to want to bite me. Look at this dress that I've never worn. Look at* this *dress, which I've never worn.* In speech, *that* usually replaces *which*. In writing, *which* is called on to reinforce the comma sounds. Since *which* seldom appears in speech, it's overused by people who associate it with writing and mistakenly think it's elegant. I've used *which* only a few times in these lessons, which you can check. Some people think that if you use *that* a couple of times in a sentence that you should switch over to *which*, but that's not necessary. I used *that* four times in the previous sentence and nothing terrible happened to me that I know of. Elegant people, by the way, are not embarrassed by their words and therefore do not resort to synonyms.

Dropping the relative pronoun. When should you leave the relative pronoun *that* or *who* in? Do you say *Here's the chair that I bought* or *Here's the chair I bought? Ask the girl whom you prefer* or *Ask the girl you prefer?* Omitting the relative pronoun used to be a mark of Informal, but it is omitted so often now in Formal you only have to write it in the places where you'd have to say it. Do not use it to be elegant: use it or omit it as your ear decides, according to the rhythm of the sentence. Here's a test: which of the following do you like best? *I hope that I have proved that he did it. I hope that I have proved he did it. I hope I have proved he did it. I hope I have proved that he did it.* The best of these versions seems to me the last. By using the *that* you can sometimes emphasize the clause it starts.

The relative pronoun *that* refers to persons as well as things. *He's the man that I met. Who* can only be used for persons. You can't say *I think it was the bank who sent it back.* But you can use *whose* to refer to things. *This is the book whose cover is loose.* Wherever you can substitute *whose* for *of which*, an ugly phrase, do so. Similarly, don't say *that which*, say *what*. By all means drop the pronoun when you have a *preposition plus which*. Say *Here's the glass I drank from*, not *Here's the glass from which I drank.* Fix this one yourself: *You need to have something about which to write.*

We versus I. A writer should not say *we* when she means *I,* if she wants to say what she means. If she clearly means *we women* or *we Republicans* she can say *we.* If she vaguely means *I and all the wonderful people like me,* she should not say *we.* Sloppy use of *we* is sloppy thinking. It's never elegant to say *we* instead of *I,* or to avoid talking about yourself when you are relevant to the argument.

Using the subjunctive. I had better remind you what the subjunctive is. It's a special way of using the *being* verbs and the dropping of the *s* from third person singular verbs. *I ask that the report* be *distributed. I wish Christmas* were *here. The contract provides that each party* pay *half. God* damn *it.* This special subjunctive is not much used now, but it's not dead, and still very lively in proverbial expressions like *So* be *it* and Come *hell or high water,* and in resolutions and commands. *She demanded that he* offer *an apology.* In Formal, the subjunctive is used more often than in Informal: *I insist that you* be *on time, I insist that you* are *on time. If I* were *president, I'd talk straight, If I* was *president, I'd talk straight.* I recommend that the subjunctive be used. Of course, you'd avoid oldfashioned and showy uses, such as *I hope that he* be *punished,* and *Would he* were *behind bars, lest he* do *more harm.*

Similar to the subjunctive, as an oldfashioned, literary form, is the *absolute.* An absolute is a noun linked with a participle and has no grammatical connection to the rest of the sentence, which is why it's an absolute. *The bus having come, we got on board. The case was lost, the lawyer being to blame.* Since the absolute construction is disappearing but not yet gone, it's effective to use.

The *present perfect tense* is being wiped out by overuse of the simple past, so you should use the present perfect every chance you get. *I ate, I have eaten. They wanted it, They have wanted it. Carol said no, Carol has said no.* Important nuances are conveyed by the present perfect. But you don't want to use it after a past tense question, as in *Did you do it?* Say *Yes, I did it,* not *Yes, I have done it.* When someone asks you a question, reply in his language. *When do you leave?* Say *I leave tomorrow,* not *I will leave* or *I am leaving.*

Elegant people avoid using *if* to start off noun clauses. Instead of *He asked me if I'd come* they say *He asked me whether I'd come.* A little note of elegance they try to keep secret is the use of *so* instead of *as* after negatives. *This piece is not* so *large as that.*

As elegant people always seem attentive, listening, so does elegant writing have an openminded, alert tone, a tone of conversing rather than lecturing. Elegance depends as much on what you refrain from saying as on what you say. Instead of wondering whether an adverb or transitional expression goes better at the start or the middle of a sentence, be really elegant and leave it out. The word *elegant* means *choice,* and the writer's work lies in choosing rather than finding. Though some people like to have fingers wagged in their face or like a complete massage, most people prefer the light touch.

Five Finger Exercise

The poet Brecht said: We must write for the people in the language of kings. To make your language a little more kingly or queenly, and to make sure you're not circumscribed as you write by the few *kinds* of sentences you're used to hearing on TV, you might want to do this drill. Write ten or twenty sentences each using

1. introductory subordinate clauses (*Because I love her,* I'll stop smoking.)
2. introductory participial phrases (*Succumbing to her pleas,* I promised to stop.)
3. trailing participial phrases (I cheated, *realizing that a woman is only a woman but a good cigar is a smoke.*)
4. long appositives (She still married me, *the only one of her suitors who dared to smoke.*)
5. passive voice (My cigarettes *are* mysteriously *being spirited away.*)
6. subjunctives (If I *were* single again I could light up.)
7. absolutes (*The long torture over,* I'm no longer addicted.)

Pleasing Listeners

What is written just to be read seldom works when used as a speech; speeches have to be specially written. Even on Formal occasions, a speech can include informalities in wordiness, repetition, and vividness that you could not get by with in writing. Many smart people have neglected the differences between speeches and other kinds of writing and have failed as speakers. In writing style, less is usually more; in speeches less is usually a loss. The Gettysburg Address is a great poem, but not a good speech. The tighter, more closely argued a speech is, the less chance it has of succeeding. Lawyers know this and go on for hours making their so called summations. Speakers are supposed to be expansive, allowing the audience to enjoy the honor and treat of being addressed.

In writing, it's the middle that's important, in speaking the beginning and the end are important. The opening of a speech requires the greatest care, for it sets the tone and fixes the relationship between speaker and audience. A speech should end strongly, with a daring thought or conclusion, question, joke, warning, prophecy, or call to action.

Since more freedom is allowed to speakers and fewer demands made on them for instruction, one might conclude that it's easier to write good speeches than pieces meant for the printer. It is. Lesser skills are required in composing speeches, but they are hardly negligible. Special skills are needed not just in composing but in delivering speeches, and everyone should acquire these skills. Everyone should have lessons in speaking as well as in writing. The two subjects are one.

I'll not try to substitute for a course in speaking, but will remind you of how to deliver a speech, for that is part of rhetoric. The traits admired in writers are those admired in speakers. Tact and consideration work with listeners as with readers. In writing, the problem of tone has to be solved, and finding the tone proves to the audience you're interested in them and in the subject. The speaker must also strike the right tone. But her job is easier since her voice can sound the tone more effectively than words can ever do. It's said of dogs, horses, and children, that they learn much more from your tone than from your words. A speaker would be foolish not to exploit the resources of the voice. The tone of candor and sincerity, so difficult to convey thru the artificiality of print, is easily imitated by any speaker. The most powerful trick in all of rhetoric, the sudden change in voice volume, is unavailable to the poor writer who has to make do with punctuation marks.

As the writer must avoid words that bluster or squeak, so must the speaker avoid shouting or mumbling. As the writer has to face up to the possibility that another human being might actually read her stuff, so the speaker must look her audience in the eye. She does not look at her feet or Heaven or the back of the room. She's talking to people, not to a room. Like the writer, she has to remember she's a person talking to other people. Of course this makes her vulnerable. But she's used to it, she's done it all her life.

Most inexperienced speakers go like machines, and deliver the speech too fast and at the same rate. The sound of one person's voice, however beautiful it may be, grows tiresome. The excitement, rhythm, give and take of conversation are lost. The speaker should compensate for the loss by changing pace and emphasis. She controls pace, volume, and pitch, and creates excitement by these devices alone, no matter what is being said. She guards against ending each sentence on the same tone. A speech given in a foreign language can be better, that is, more closely listened to, than a speech given drearily in one's own language.

The tricks of Formal speaking are easy to learn. Tricks like speaking very slowly. Like gesturing with the hands, chopping with one hand, pointing with the index finger, and opening or raising the arms. It's hard to do too much gesturing, though it's easy to repeat the same gesture too often. Another important device is the significant pause before important words. Another is speaking the important words after the pause—*softly*. Jimmy Carter is a virtuoso of the pause. In speaking, pauses are important, they help slow the pace, and must not be filled up with *ers, ahs,* and *uhs.*

These audible pauses are no problem if one reads a speech or recites it from memory. But neither of these ways of delivering a speech is as effective as speaking from notes or an outline. If a speech is memorized there's always the danger of forgetting the lines or leaving hunks of it out. Energy spent remembering the lines would be better spent in delivering them with under-standing. Often with memorized speeches, the speaker forgets what the words say, and sounds like an actor doing Shakespeare without understanding a word. If the speech is obviously being read, the audience feels cheated. When big shots read a speech, everyone knows it's someone else's. Nowadays, with high lec-terns and teleprompters, speakers get away with a lot of reading. You can read your speech if you've rehearsed it well and don't have to look at it too often. The better way is to use an outline that shows the beginning of each sentence or key phrases in the speech. Move your finger down the outline to keep your place as you go. Every speech should be thoroughly practiced before a mirror and before a friend. (If you listen to yourself on tape you're liable to become discouraged.)

Let your posture be natural, let your gestures and voice be fairly natural. You needn't worry about pronunciation, since no one cares about that anymore. Loudspeakers are so common that whenever they're missing, the speaker takes pains to make sure she can be heard. The ideal of fine elocution is dead, and precise pronunciation and beautiful voices are resented by audiences, who think the speaker is putting on airs.

The audience listens to the start of the speech because they want to find out about you, and listens for the end because they get tired of being spoken to. Skimping or botching either is ruinous. It's good to open with extemporaneous remarks, or ones that seem to be so. Before starting, wait for quiet, count to five, and begin. The ending should be built up so that even the sleepiest member of the audience knows you're on the home-stretch. Don't tell a joke unless you're a joker, or unless everyone is, or unless the joke has to be told. Jokes are fiction; anecdotes are true. You can always tell an anecdote.

You should be nervous, for that helps you do a better job. Only a little experience is needed to remove stage fright. If you're terrified, seek practice in speaking, because such insecurity will hurt you in many aspects of your life. Just as the inability to write is overcome by thinking of your audience and what you want to tell them, so the inability to speak is overcome by thinking of your audience and what you want to tell them. If you think only about you, sooner or later you'll have to pay somebody to listen.

Your Final Exam

For your final exam, I'm going to give you thirty sentences you would not want to use in Formal. I'd like you to find the fault (or faults) in each sentence and then revise the sentence so that it will be acceptable. My revisions will be given right after the exam.

1. Sis wrote she was sick on her last postcard.
2. Before we get into all that, let me tell you a little story.
3. I walked and the bus never showed up.
4. He wrote me letters repeatedly, or rather, continually.
5. I hesitate to contemplate the termination of our association.
6. I jogged from Missouri City, Texas, to Texas City, Missouri, during National Radish Week.
7. Neither he nor her are going steady with anybody.
8. Why do we intellectuals always marry homely women?
9. Do not bend, fold, spindle, or mutilate this card.
10. He drinks because he's a Macaroon.
11. At the present time I have not received the widget which I had ordered to be sent.
12. I shall always believe that if I was married, I should be happy.
13. She tore off her feathered boa, whirled around, shook her chestnut tresses, and hissed, Take back your emeralds, Count Rupert!
14. By examination of the x rays, the best treatment can be decided on by your doctor.
15. Wearing a designer dress, she utilized the telephone to make an advance reservation for an old fashion barbecue beef dinner at the pint size air condition patio restaurant.
16. Rationalization of company procedures entails the releasing of selected redundant personnel.
17. It is with great relief that I announce that there is no reason in the world to suppose that Chef Wang has actually started a fire out in the kitchen.

18. He is going to be shot because of his courage in speaking up against the government.
19. I hope that I have shown that this committee's responsibility is clear in this matter of failure to repay the loan.
20. Nixon was always very ambitious; he was a very close student of politics; he was greatly stirred by his boyish dream of living in the White House.
21. The long and the short of it is, to defeat Russia in the Olympics can only be done in the following way.
22. Oranges are more or less round, apples are more or less round, but bananas are different.
23. We are presently sending you our shipment with the remainder of the order to be sent later on.
24. Ten people were present in the parlor when Inspector Pudel began his interrogation of the domestic staff in regard to cook Peggy's knives.
25. My whole family eats weeds and we have no trouble with bleeding gums.
26. When fear comes in the window, love flies out the door.
27. In a criminal society criminal lawyers have an easy time getting criminal defendants acquitted.
28. They are a pusillanimous corps of effete snobs and pointyheads.
29. With a good conscience our only sure reward, with history the final judge of our deeds, let us go forth to lead the land we love, asking His blessing and His help, but knowing that here on earth God's work must truly be our own.
30. Many a crown of wisdom is but the golden chamberpot of Success.

Exam Results

1. *Sis wrote she was sick on her last postcard.*
   Formally, you can't say Sis. The phrase *on her last postcard* is misplaced.
   Revised: *My sister wrote on her last postcard that she was sick.*
2. *Before we get into all that, let me tell you a little story.*
   The tone is not just chatty but apologetic. What's the matter with *all that* and why is the story *little*?

Revised: *Before I talk about that, I'd like to tell this story.*

3. *I walked and the bus never showed up.*

    The relationship of the two ideas is unclear. *Showed up* is Informal.

    Revised: *I'm glad I walked since the bus never came.*

4. *He wrote me letters repeatedly, or rather, continually.*

    The writer should decide which word is best and not offer alternatives.

    Revised: *He wrote me letters continually.*

5. *I hesitate to contemplate the termination of our association.*

    Stuffy diction, and two jingles.

    Revised: *I do not like to think of your leaving us.*

6. *I jogged from Missouri City, Texas, to Texas City, Missouri, during National Radish Week.*

    Anticlimax.

    Revised: *During National Radish Week I jogged, etc.*

7. *Neither he nor her are going steady with anybody.*

    Three mistakes. *He nor her* should be *he nor she*. *Neither he nor she* should be followed by a singular verb. *Anybody* should be *anyone*. *Going steady* is Informal, but precise and brief enough to graduate to Formal.

    Revised: *Neither he nor she is going steady with anyone.*

8. *Why do we intellectuals always marry homely women?*

    Rhetorical questions like this one backfire. And who is *we*?

    Revised: *Many intellectuals marry homely women, and I've asked myself why.*

9. *Do not bend, fold, spindle, or mutilate this card.*

    Lists are tedious. No one knows *spindle,* so cut it. *Mutilate* has inappropriate connotations of sacrilege.

    Revised: *Please do not fold or damage this card.*

10. *He drinks because he's a Macaroon.*

    Faulty reasoning about cause. If you feel you have to talk about why he drinks, say something like *He's a Macaroon, and Macaroons are notorious for their drinking.*

    or more suggestively

    He's a Macaroon who loves to drink.

11. *At the present time I have not received the widget which I had ordered to be sent.*

    Wordiness and a jingle—*widget which.*

Revised: *I have not received the widget I ordered.*

12. *I shall always believe that if I was married, I should be happy.*

> Three verbs, three mistakes. *Shall* and *should* are affected. *Was* is not Formal enough, and should be the subjunctive *were*.

Revised: *I will always believe that if I were married I would be happy.*

13. *She tore off her feathered boa, whirled around, shook her chestnut tresses, and hissed, Take back your emeralds, Count Rupert!*

> Too rich. The words are acceptable, considered separately, with the possible exception of *tresses*, but together they distract from the excitement of the events.

Revised: *Pulling off her boa, she whirled around and hissed, Take back your emeralds!*

14. *By examination of the x rays, the best treatment can be decided on by your doctor.*

> *By examination of* should be *By examining,* since the gerund is more forceful than the noun. The passive voice is used unnecessarily.

Revised: *By examining the x rays, your doctor can decide on the best treatment.*

15. *Wearing a designer dress, she utilized the telephone to make an advance reservation for an old fashion barbecue beef dinner at the pint size air condition patio restaurant.*

> Here we have nouns masquerading as adjectives. *Utilized the telephone* is fancy and nouny for *called.* What does her dress have to do with anything? Get rid of it.

Revised: *She called to reserve an oldfashioned barbecued beef dinner at the small, air conditioned patio restaurant.*

16. *Rationalization of company procedures entails the releasing of selected redundant personnel.*

> The diction is *too* euphemistic, and doesn't do the job it wants to do. It also suffers from nounitis.

Revised: *The company has to let some people go.*

17. *It is with great relief that I announce that there is no reason in the world to suppose that Chef Wang has actually started a fire out in the kitchen.*

> Wordiness here. *It is, there is, in the world, actually, that that that.* General pomposity.

Revised: *You will be relieved to know that the kitchen is not on fire.*

18. *He is going to be shot because of his courage in speaking up against the government.*

   This loose sentence fizzles. Change to emphatic.

   Revised: *Because he courageously spoke against the government, he will be shot.*

19. *I hope that I have shown that this committee's responsibility is clear in this matter of failure to repay the loan.*

   Ugly sound in *I hope that I have shown that this.* Also, the nouns smother the verb.

   Revised: *The loan has not been repaid, and the committee is responsible.*

20. *Nixon was always very ambitious; he was a very close student of politics; he was greatly stirred by his boyish dream of living in the White House.*

   Needless qualifiers, *very, greatly.* Clichés, *close student, boyish dream.* Circumlocution, *living in the White House.* Try to combine clauses starting with the same subject.

   Revised: *A student of politics and ambitious even as a boy, Nixon dreamed of being President.*

21. *The long and the short of it is, to defeat Russia in the Olympics can only be done in the following way.*

   The long and the short of it is an Informal stall. The infinitive phrase *to defeat Russia* can't be the subject of a passive verb. You probably didn't know that rule, but you don't have to, since it's a logical one.

   Revised: *Russia can only be defeated in the Olympics in this way.*

22. *Oranges are more or less round, apples are more or less round, but bananas are different.*

   Nothing wrong with this except it's boring. Comparisons are tedious and should be justified.

   Revised: *Thank goodness bananas are not round like apples oranges and all those other fruits.*

23. *We are presently sending you our shipment with the remainder of the order to be sent later on.*

   Wordiness. Vagueness. Dangling trailing *with* phrase.

   Revised: *We are sending you half your order now and will send you the rest as soon as we can.*

24. *Ten people were present in the parlor when Inspector Pudel began his interrogation of the domestic staff in regard to cook Peggy's knives.*

   Alliteration of *p*s. Wordiness. Extra details.

Revised: *Ten persons were seated in the parlor when Inspector Pudel began to question the servants about the cook's knives.*

25. *My whole family eats weeds and we have no trouble with bleeding gums.*

> Logic. The *and* merely *suggests* a causal connection between two events.

Revised: *After my family started to eat weeds, all of our trouble with bleeding gums stopped.*

26. *When fear comes in the window, love flies out the door.*

> Not a bad sentence, not a bad idea either. But too vivid for Formal.

Revised: *When love begins to fear, love dies.*

27. *In a criminal society criminal lawyers have an easy time getting criminal defendants acquitted.*

> Too assertive. The audience might doubt that society is criminal.

Revised: *In a criminal society criminal lawyers would have an easy time getting criminal defendants acquitted.*

28. *They are a pusillanimous corps of effete snobs and pointyheads.*

> Probable faults in diction. *Pusillanimous* (cowardly) and *effete* (worn out) are not known to an audience that uses the hateful term *pointyheads,* but that audience might like the sound of them anyway. *Corps* is vague. The stylistic objection to the sentence is that it's mere description

Revised: *These intellectuals can no longer rise to the occasion.*

29. *With a good conscience our only sure reward, with history the final judge of our deeds, let us go forth to lead the land we love, asking His blessing and His help, but knowing that here on earth God's work must truly be our own.*

> Two dangling *with* phrases. *Let us go forth* a literary cliché. *To lead the land we love*—alliteration. *Truly* is meaningless. These words of John F Kennedy, preceding assassination attempts on Castro and the secret war in Viet Nam, are sanctimonious.

Revised: *I can't.*

30. *Many a crown of wisdom is but the golden chamberpot of Success.*

> This sentence by Mark Twain cannot be improved. But you couldn't use this sentence in Formal because *you* can't talk about chamberpots. That make you mad? Good, it's a way to get smart.

Commencement Address

I have one last question for you, one which sums up the entire course. What is the best way to say it:

perform coitus   engage in sexual congress   practice venery have carnal knowledge   have intimate relations   have intercourse   have sex   have an affair   have a go   have   copulate couple   know   go in unto her   do   use   plow   swive   undertake   occupy   cover   mount   service   serve   tup   jig   poke jape   plug   jump   hump   screw   bang   ream   roger   plumb scaff   ball   score   get in   get over   get laid   get some   get any get it on   make   make love   make out   make time with   take take on   lie with   sleep with   put out   let loose   he and she slap and tickle   rub and tumble   roll in the hay   go all the way take a full step   get your cookie   ring the bell   do the dirty deed sink the social sausage   put the devil back in hell   or f——?

That was a trick question. Everything depends, there is no best way to say anything (though much could be said for *f—k*). In Formal, in a matter this sensitive, you'd probably prefer a neutered term like *have intercourse.* But you can always defy the Formalities if you know what they are and are prepared to stand by what you say. What you say doesn't only depend on *it* and *them*, but on *you* too.

I'm sure you did well on the final exam. It's not hard to find the faults in someone else's sentences. Revising the sentences is hard. I made it look easy, but it takes a while to learn. Some of my sentences could stand improvement, but I've had it with this book. Getting something down that's halfway decent is the most tiring work—though never tiresome. Writing beautifully? Forget it.

Somerset Maugham said, To write simply is as difficult as to be good. This Game of English is wickedly hard. But if it was easy, it wouldn't be worth playing. And it is worth playing, for its real and its symbolic stakes. The symbolic stakes are worldly success. The real stakes are improvements in one's understanding.

Keats said that Fine writing is next to fine doing. He didn't say it was right behind, he said it was next to fine doing. People sense that the two are somehow associated, and that's why they admire and want to imitate those who express themselves well. Since ancient times teachers have asserted that talking and writing well is essentially a moral matter, rather than a matter of being clever. Good expression does seem to require courtesy, patience, self knowledge, and courage.

Can people be taught to express themselves well? That's a good question. I don't know. If you could teach them to be good, you could teach them to talk and write well. But then, if they were good, would they have much to say? Walter Bagehot said The reason so few good books are written is that so few people that can write know anything.

Unless you're good, in the old sense of the word, you're not likely to win satisfying victories in the Game. The Game is fairly honest, and in the long run cheaters never prosper. If you speak with the tongues of angels, advertisers, politicians, professors, louts, and harpies, when do *you* get to talk?

So speak up—let the others take their turn at listening.